An Anthology of Concrete Poetry

An Anthology of

concrete

1967

Something Else Press, Inc.

New York Villefranche Frankfurt

poetry

Edited by Emmett Williams

L. C. Catalog Card No: 67-24980

Manufactured in the United States of America

Foreword and Acknowledgments

And what is Concrete poetry?

For those who make it, a modified version of the handy definition "poetry is what poets make" would be sufficient: Concrete poetry, then, is what the poets in this anthology make. But anthologies are not made for poets. They are made for the general reader. And the general reader, unfamiliar with the practices of the poets in this anthology, will not be put off so lightly. For him there must be at least the materials to help him formulate his own definition. To this end, there are comments by the poets on their poems, and biographies and bibliographies intended to lead him to the fuller body of material to which the present collection serves as an introduction. The editor's own definition—were he to attempt one—would place the emphasis on *poetry* rather than on *Concrete*. Concrete as opposed to what? Abstract? Analogies with the visual arts de-emphasize the poetic element in favor of the visual, which is but a single (though consequential) aspect of the new poetry. Yet it has been labeled (and the general reader will probably come to the book with some such preconception) a return to the poem as picture: to the *Calligrammes* of Apollinaire, the mouse's tail in *Alice*, the permutational poems of the cabalists, the anagrams of the early Christian monks, the *carmina figurata* of the Greek Bucolic poets, the pattern poems of the Babylonians, picture-writing itself. Indeed, the poem as picture is as old as the hills, or the men who once lived in them, scratching their histories and fantasies in preliterate strokes on the walls of caves.

But the makers of the new poetry in the early fifties were not antiquarians, nor were they specifically seeking the intermedium between poetry and painting, the apparent goal of so many of their followers. The visual element in their poetry tended to be structural, a consequence of the poem, a "picture" of the lines of force of the work itself, and not merely textural. It was a poetry far beyond paraphrase, a poetry that often asked to be completed or activated by the reader, a poetry of direct presentation—the *word,* not *words, words, words* or expressionistic squiggles—using the semantic, visual and phonetic elements of language as raw materials in a way seldom used by the poets of the past. It was a kind of game, perhaps, but so is life. It was born of the times, as a way of knowing and saying something about the world of *now,* with the techniques and insights of *now.*

The confused geography of its beginnings reflects the universality of its roots. Eugen Gomringer, a Bolivian-born Swiss, was the acknowledged father of Concrete poetry. He called his first poems in the new style, written in 1951, "constellations." The "constellations" were similar to, but uninfluenced by, the semantico-visual poster poems of Carlo Belloli, protégé of F. T. Marinetti, the founder of Futurism, published in 1948. When Gomringer and the Noigandres poets of São Paulo, Brazil, agreed upon the name "Concrete" to describe the new poetry in 1956, they were mutually unaware that Öyvind Fahlström (who spent the first three years of his life in São Paulo!) had published the first manifesto of Concrete poetry—*manifest for konkret poesi*—three years earlier in Stockholm. While Diter Rot, German-born and Swiss-bred, was publishing his "ideograms" in geographically remote Iceland, and Carlfriedrich Claus was experimenting with *Klang-gebilden* and *Phasen* in politically remote East Germany, in Vienna, Concrete poetry was developing out of the collaborative efforts of a composer, Gerhard Rühm, an architect, Friedrich Achleitner, a jazz musician, Oswald Wiener, and the poets H. C. Artmann and Konrad Bayer. In 1957, the year Haroldo de Campos of Brazil introduced Concrete poetry to Kitasono Katue of Japan, a Romanian-born artist, Daniel Spoerri, leader of the "Darmstadt Circle" of Concrete poets (which included a German dramaturgist, Claus Bremer, and an American expatriate, Emmett Williams), published the first international anthology of Concrete poetry.

A decade later, after the Concrete "renaissance" in England, Germany and Sweden during the early sixties, and the growing interest in the new poetry in such diverse social settings as Czechoslovakia, France, Spain and the United States, the poet Jonathan Williams could write, with apparent justification: "If there is such a thing as a worldwide movement in the art of poetry, Concrete is it."

The "international movement," however, is blessed with a disunity that unshackles it from the aims and aesthetic principles of the many manifestos it has engendered; a mixed blessing, to be sure. Poets of a feather flock together, perhaps (at least during the exhibitions of "Concrete" and "visual" poetry that yoke them together with increasing frequency throughout the world); fortunately, however, they do not all sing the same song. Side by side are militant social reformers, religious mystics, lyricists of love, psychedelic visionaries, engaged philosophers, disinterested philologists and poetypographers. Such diversity, reflected in the pages of this anthology, may seem to rob the label "Concrete" of any concrete meaning whatsoever. On the other hand, it shows the extent to which the dynamic concepts of the new poetry have been accepted as a *Poetics* valid for our time.

* * * * *

The editor wishes to thank the poets in general for making the anthology possible. He feels compelled, however, to express particular gratitude to Haroldo de Campos, for bringing Portuguese—and Japanese—poems to life through his translations and notes prepared especially for this anthology; to Dick Higgins, the publisher, whose idea the book was in the first place; to Edwin Morgan, for the use of his English versions of the Noigandres poets; to Ian Hamilton Finlay, for transatlantic friendship and encouragement; and to Eugen Gomringer, The Noigandres poets, Hansjörg Mayer, Pierre Garnier and Henri Chopin for permitting the editor to pick and choose from the works they had the courage, and the wisdom, to publish in their periodicals and anthologies through the years.

Thanks are also due to the following poets and publishers for permission to reprint previously published poems and statements. Page numbers refer to the pages in this anthology.—

FRIEDRICH ACHLEITNER—*Eugen Gomringer Press,* Frauenfeld, Switzerland, for the poem on page 4, from ***ideogramme*** (n.d.); *Wilhelm Frick Verlag,* Vienna, for page 6, from **hosn rosn baa**, 1959.

ALAIN ARIAS-MISSON—*Zaj,* Madrid 1966, for page 7.

H. C. ARTMANN—*Werkstatt eV,* Vienna, for pages 9 (from ***erweiterte poetik***) and 10.

RONALDO AZEREDO—*Edições Invenção,* São Paulo, Brazil, for pages 12 and 14, from ***Noigandres 4***, 1962; pages 11, 13 and 15 from ***Noigandres 5***, 1962.

STEPHEN BANN—*Edition Hansjörg Mayer,* Stuttgart, for page 16, from **concrete poetry britain canada united states**, 1966.

CARLO BELLOLI—*futuristi in armi,* Milan, for page 18, from ***parole per la guerra***, 1943; *edizioni erre,* Milan, for pages 19 and 20, from ***testi-poemi murali***, 1944; for page 21, from **panorama**, 1944; *Edizioni Gala,* Rome, for pages 22 and 23, from ***tavole visuali***, 1948; *Mediterranean Publishing Co.,* Rome-New York, for pages 24, 25 and 26, from ***corpi di poesia***, 1951; *Editions Material,* Paris, for page 27, from ***textes audiovisuels***, 1959; *Eugen Gomringer Press,* Frauenfeld, Switzerland, for page 28, from ***texte poème poème texte***, 1961; *Edition Hansjörg Mayer,* Stuttgart, for page 29, from *sole solo* (**futura 14**), 1966.

MAX BENSE—*Max Bense and Elisabeth Walter,* Stuttgart, for pages 30 and 31, from ***vielleicht zunächst wirklich nur*** (**rot** text 11), 1963.

EDGARD BRAGA—*The Wild Hawthorn Press,* Dunsyre, Scotland, for pages 32, 34 and 35, from **Poor.Old.Tired.Horse. 21.**

CLAUS BREMER—*Limes Verlag,* Wiesbaden, for page 38, from **movens**, 1960; *Eugen Gomringer Press,* Frauenfeld, Switzerland, for pages 39–42, from ***ideogramme***, 1964; *Edition Hansjörg Mayer,* Stuttgart, for pages 43–45, from ***engagierende texte*** (**futura 8**), 1966.

AUGUSTO DE CAMPOS—*Edições Invenção,* São Paulo, Brazil, for page 46, from ***Noigandres 2***, 1955; pages 48 and 50, from ***Noigandres 3***, 1956; pages 51 and 52, from ***Noigandres 4***, 1958; pages 49 and 53, from ***Noigandres 5***, 1962; page 54, from ***Invenção 4***, 1964.

HAROLDO DE CAMPOS—*Edições Invenção,* São Paulo, Brazil, for page 55, from ***Noigandres 4***, 1958; pages 56 and 58, from ***Noigandres 3***, 1956; pages 60 and 61, from ***Noigandres 5***, 1962; Edicões Noigandres, São Paulo, for the complete text of ***servidão de passagem***, pages 62–67, and to ***El Corno Emplumado***, Mexico, for the translation by Edwin Morgan.

HENRI CHOPIN—*Cinquième Saison,* Paris, for page 69, from ***Cinquième Siason 16***, 1962; *Institute of Contemporary Art,* London, for page 71, from the catalogue **Between Poetry and Painting**, 1965.

CARL FRIEDRICH CLAUS—Pages 73–77 reproduced from works in private collections.

BOB COBBING—*Edition Hansjörg Mayer,* Stuttgart, for page 78, from **concrete poetry britain canada united states**, 1966; *Coptic Press,* London, for pages 79–81, from **Extra Verse 17**, 1966.

REINHARD DÖHL—*Edition Hansjörg Mayer,* Stuttgart, for page 82, from ***4 texte*** (**futura 4**), 1965, and page 84, from 16/4/66; *Editions André Silvaire,* Paris, for page 83, from ***Approches 2.***

TORSTEN EKBOM—*Bonniers,* Stockholm, for page 85, from a forthcoming novel.

ÖYVIND FAHLSTRÖM—*Bonniers,* Stockholm, for pages 87 and 88, from ***Bord-dikter*** 1952–55, 1966.

CARL FERNBACH-FLARSHEIM—*Cypher Press,* Philadelphia, for page 89, from **readio**, 1967.

IAN HAMILTON FINLAY—*The Wild Hawthorn Press,* Scotland, for pages 90–91, from **Tea-Leaves and Fishes**, 1966; pages 93 and 96, from **Poems From My Windmill**, 1964; page 94, from ***Poor. Old. Tired. Horse. 14***; page 95, from Rapel, 1963; **The London Times Literary Supplement**, No. 3, 258, Aug. 6, 1964, for pages, 92, 97 and 98; ***Vers Univers*** for page 99; **Form 3**, London 1966, for pages 100 and 101; the **Beloit Poetry Journal**, Beloit, Wisconsin, for the photograph by Patric Eagar on page 102.

LARRY FREIFELD—***Hika***, Vol. XXIX, No. 2, 1967, for page 103.

HEINZ GAPPMAYR—*Pinguin Verlag,* Innsbruck, for pages 112 and 113, from ***zeichen II***, 1964.

ILSE & PIERRE GARNIER—*Editions André Silvaire,* Paris, for page 114, from ***Les Lettres 29***; pages 115 and 116, ***Les Lettres 33***; page 117, from ***Poèmes Mecanique***; pages 118 and 119, from **Prototypes**; page 121, from ***Poèmes Spatiaux Picards.***

MATTHIAS GOERITZ—*Edition Hansjörg Mayer,* for page 122, from ***mensajes del oro*** (**futura 1**), 1965; Kati Horner for the photograph on page 123.

EUGEN GOMRINGER—*Eugen Gomringer Press,* Frauenfeld, Switzerland, for pages 124–35, from **the constellations**, 1963.

LUDWIG GOSEWITZ—*Christian Grützmacher Verlag,* Berlin, for page 136; *Jürgen Graaf,* Berlin, for page 137.

BOHUMILA GRÖGEROVA & JOSEF HIRŠAL—*Max Bense and Elisabeth Walter,* Stuttgart, for page 138, from ***konkrete poesie international*** (**rot** text 21); *Edições Invenção,* São Paulo, Brazil, from pages 139 and 140, from ***Invenção 4***, 1964.

JOSÉ LINO GRÜNEWALD—*Edições Invenção,* São Paulo, Brazil, for pages 141–43, reprinted from ***Um e Dois*** in ***Noigandres 5,*** 1962, and pages 145–46; page 147, from ***Invenção 4,*** 1964.

BRION GYSIN—**Fluxus,** New York, for statement on cut-ups and permutational poems on page 148, from **Fluxus 1,** 1965.

AL HANSEN—Page 150 reproduced from work in private collections.

VACLAV HAVEL—***modulo 1,*** Genoa, for page 151.

HELMUT HEISSENBÜTTEL—*Bechtle Verlag,* Esslingen, for page 152; ***spirale*** (n.d.), Bern, for page 153; *Walter Verlag,* Olten, Switzerland, for pages 54 and 55, from ***textbuch 4,*** 1964.

ÅKE HODELL—*Raben & Sjogren,* Stockholm, for page 156, from **General Bussig,** 1964; *Kerberos Forlag,* Stockholm, for page 157, from ***igevär,*** 1963.

DOM SYLVESTER HOUÉDARD—*Openings Press,* Woodchester, Gloucester, England, for page 158, from ***plakat 1; The Insect Trust Gazette,*** No. 2 (Philadelphia), for page 159. Summer 1965.

ERNST JANDL—*Walter Verlag,* Olten, Switzerland, for page 161, from ***Laut und Luise,*** 1966.

BENGT EMIL JOHNSON—*Bonniers,* Stockholm, for pages 164–65, from ***Essäer om Bror Barsk och andra dikter,*** 1964.

RONALD JOHNSON—*The Wild Hawthorn Press,* Dunsyre, Scotland, for pages 166–75, from **Poor.Old.Tired.Horse. 19.**

HIRO KAMIMURA—*Edition Hansjörg Mayer,* Stuttgart, for page 176, from **5 *vokaltexte* (*futura* 16),** 1967.

KITASONO KATUE—***VOU magazine,*** Tokyo, for pages 178–81, from No. 58, Nov. 1957.

JIRI KOLAR—*Artia,* Prague, for pages 182–84, from **Signboard for Gersaint,** 1962.

FERDINAND KRIWET—*M. DuMont Schauberg,* Cologne, for pages 185–87.

FRANZ VAN DER LINDE—*Editions André Silvaire,* Paris, for page 188, from ***Les Lettres 23.***

ARRIGO LORA-TOTINO—Pages 190 and 191, reproduced from posters printed by the poet.

JACKSON MAC LOW—**Fluxus,** New York, for pages 192 and 193; La Monte Young and Jackson Mac Low, New York, for page 194, from **An Anthology, 1963; Workshop in Nonviolence,** New York, for page 200, from **WIN,** Vol. II, Nos. 14 and 15, August 1966.

HANSJÖRG MAYER—*Edition Hansjörg Mayer,* Stuttgart, for page 201, from **alphabet,** 1963; page 202, from ***fortführungen,*** 1964; pages 204–07, from ***alphabetenquadratbuch 1,*** 1965.

CAVAN MCCARTHY—*Bristol Arts Centre,* Bristol, England, for pages 208–09, from the catalogue Cavpo 67.

FRANZ MON—*Neske Verlag,* Pfullingen, for page 210, from ***artikulationen,*** 1959; *Christian Grützmacher Verlag,* Berlin, for page 212, from ***Edition Et 2,*** 1967.

EDWIN MORGAN—*Eugen Gomringer Press,* Frauenfeld, for pages 215–16, from **Starryveldt,** 1965.

HANSJØRGEN NIELSEN—*Borgens Forlag,* Copenhagen, for pages 226 and 227, from ***at det at / laesealbum,*** 1965.

SEIICHI NIIKUNI—*Editions André Silvaire,* Paris, for page 228, from ***Approches 2;*** pages 229 and 231, from ***Poèmes franco-japonais,*** 1966; **Arc/Do,** Milan, for page 229, reproduced from 1967 poster series.

LADISLAV NOVÁK—*Edições Invenção,* São Paulo, Brazil, for pages 232 and 234, from ***Invenção 4,*** 1964; ***modulo 1,*** Genoa 1966, for page 233.

YÜKSEL PAZARKAYA—*Max Bense and Elisabeth Walter,* Stuttgart, for page 235, from ***konkrete poesie international*** (**rot** text 21); pages 236–39, from 16/4/66.

DÉCIO PIGNATARI—*Edições Invenção,* São Paulo, Brazil, for page 240, from ***Noigandres 3,*** 1956; 241–49, from ***Noigandres 4,*** 1958; *Editions André Silvaire,* Paris, for pages 250–51, from ***Approches 2.***

WLADEMIR DIAS PINO—Pages 252 and 253, from ***solida,*** São Paulo 1962.

LUIZ ANGELO PINTO—*Edições Invenção,* São Paulo, Brazil, for page 254, from ***Invenção 4,*** 1964.

CARL-FREDRIK REUTERSWÄRD—*Bonniers,* Stockholm, for page 257, from ***Prix Nobel,*** 1960.

DITER ROT—***material,*** Darmstadt, for page 258, from **kleine antologie konkrete dichtung,** 1957, and for pages 263 and 268, from ***ideograme,*** 1958; *forlag ed,* Reykjavik, for pages 259–62 and 264–67, from ***bok 1956–59.***

GERHARD RÜHM—*Eugen Gomringer Press,* Frauenfeld, Switzerland, for pages 269–72, from ***konstellationen*** (n.d.); *Wilhelm Frick Verlag,* Vienna, for page 275, from ***hosn rosn baa,*** 1959; *Magdalinski Verlag,* Berlin, for pages 276–78, from ***Lehrsätze über das Weltall,*** 1965.

ARAM SAROYAN—*Lines Books,* New York, for pages 281 and 282, from works, 1966.

JOHN J. SHARKEY—*Institute of Contemporary Art,* London, for page 283, from **ICA Bulletin 157,** April 1966; *Edition Hansjörg Mayer,* Stuttgart, for page 284, from **concrete poetry britain canada united states,** 1966.

EDWARD LUCIE SMITH—*Edition Hansjörg Mayer*, Stuttgart, for page 286, from **cloud sun fountain statue (futura 10)**, 1966.

MARY ELLEN SOLT—*Fine Arts Department, University of Indiana*, for pages 287–91, from **Flowers in Concrete**, 1966; *The Wild Hawthorn Press, Dunsyre*, Scotland, for pages 292, from **Poor.Old.Tired.Horse. 14.**

ADRIANO SPATOLA—*Sampietro*, Bologna, for page 294, from **Zeroglifico**, 1966.

DANIEL SPOERRI—*material*, Darmstadt, for pages 295–97, from ***kleine antologie konkrete dichtung***, 1957.

ANDRE THOMKINS—*Galerie der Spiegel*, Cologne, for page 299, from ***DOGMAT-MOT***, 1965; ***nota***, Munich 1960, for page 300.

ENRIQUE URIBE VALDIVIELSO—*Editions André Silvaire*, Paris, for page 304, from ***Les Lettres 33***.

FRANCO VERDI—Pages 304 and 305, reproduced from **tempo**, privately printed by the author.

PAUL DE VREE—*Uitg. Ontwikkeling*, Antwerp, for page 306, from ***pl. acid. amore***, 1963; *Editions André Silvaire*, Paris, for page 308, from **Approches 2**; *de tafelronde—monas* for page 310, from ***explositivien***, 1966.

EMMETT WILLIAMS—*material*, Darmstadt, for pages 312, 313 and 316, from ***konkretionen***, 1958; *Bernard Kirchhoff*, Darmstadt, for photograph on page 317; *Edition Hansjörg Mayer*, Stuttgart, for page 317, from **concrete poetry britain canada united states**, 1966; *La Monte Young and Jackson Mac Low*, New York, for pages 318 and 319, from **An Anthology**, 1963; *Christian Grützmacher Verlag*, Berlin, for page 320, from **Edition Et 1**, 1966; ***Workshop in Nonviolence***, New York, for page 321, from **WIN**, Vol. II, Nos. 14 & 15, August 1966; *Thomas De Baggio*, Arlington, Va., for page 322, from **Underground**, Vol. 1, No. 6, Dec. 14, 1966.

JONATHAN WILLIAMS—*Lerici Editori*, Milan, for pages 324–25, from ***Affilati Attrezzi per i Giardini di Catulli***, 1966.

PEDRO XISTO—*Edições Invenção*, São Paulo, Brazil, for page 326, from ***Invenção 1***, 1960.

YASUO FUJITOMI — *Editions André Silvaire*, Paris, for page 238 from **Approches 1**.

An Anthology of Concrete Poetry

baum
bim

baum
bim

baum
bim

bim

Friedrich Achleitner (195?)

"*baum-bim* is a confrontation of the words *baum* (tree) and *bim*, which is used in German with *bam*: *bim-bam* is for children a synonym for a bell or the ringing of a bell, a sound-painting word. In this constellation the word is used in two ways:

1) *baum* = *baum*
2) *baum* = *bam*

so that we get a tension between the two meanings." (F.A.)

ruh

und

ruh

und

ruh

und

ruh

und ruh und ruh und ruh und

ruh

und

ruh

und

ruh

und

ruh

Friedrich Achleitner (1959)

"In *'ruh und'* there is a contrast between the meaning of *'ruh'* (calm) and the movement of the rhythm, which speeds up in the horizontal part of the constellation." (F.A.)

Friedrich Achleitner (195?)

rot = red

anstatt = instead of

One of the classics of pure concrete. The plot thickens when the poem is printed with each *rot* in a different color.

rot
anstatt
rot
anstatt
rot
anstatt
rot
anstatt
rot
anstatt
rot

ge waida
ge waida
ge waida

ge ge waida
ge ge waida
ge ge waida

ge waida ge
ge waida ge
ge waida ge

ge ge waida ge
ge ge waida ge
ge ge waida ge

kim

Friedrich Achleitner (1959)

ge = *gehe* = walk, go
waida = *weiter* = further, farther
kim = *komme* = come
(Viennese dialect)

yo.

yo? o no!

yo, no, o no.

yo o yo no, o no no!

yo no. o no. o yo no, yo.

yo no o yo yo, o yo no o no.

yo no. o no o yo no, no, o yo no.

yo yo, o no no, o o o no yo o yo no no yo.

o yon o oy no o yon non o yono ooo noyo oyo on

noyo oyo ono, yonoy oy yoy ono yon no non noyo yon

óyonó nóyonó yon noy yoyo noyon onóyon noo oon onon noyon

yonnoy onóyonoy yoyóyno yoyóyono onoyóyonó yonno yonno oyónno yoyn

yoono oyóonoyoo oyonóonoyóyono yonnóyonóono oynnonóonoyo oyonnoyóononoy

oyóyoyóyo onóyonoyono noyónono onnóyonno oyyonnónonoyo yóyonoyónoyonono ono

yoyn nóynoyóyn óynonnóyonoyn oynoyn yóynoyoyóynonono oy yoyyóynonoyóynonoyo yóynyo

nyono oynyónono nyonoyónyo yónynyónyo yónyónyó o yónynyyónno nyónnonyny ynnyónón nyyónyó

oyn. yoo. ono. yoynyo. noy. noyyon. onnoy? o. yoyono. oon. y. o. o. no. nyo. oo! y. o. nn.

Alain Arias-Misson (1966)

"egospeak," a bilingual sound poem.

Alain Arias-Misson (1966)
A "found" poem.

Sur la Beauté et la Variété des Erections

PINUS SYLVESTRIS

PINUS MITIS

PINUS CEMBRA

PINUS PUMILIO

PINUS BRUTIA

PINUS EXCELSA

PINUS SABIANA

PINUS TADEA

PINUS PONDEROSA

PINUS RESINOSA

PINUS HALEPENSIS

PINUS STROBIS

PINUS MONTEZUMAE

PINUS PINEA

PINUS PALUSTRIS

PINUS OCCIDENTALIS

PINUS PINASTER

PINUS MACROCARPA

PINUS LARICIO

PINUS LAMBERTIANA

PINUS STROBUS

PINUS AUSTRIACA

PINUS PYRENAICA

PINUS INSIGNIS

PINUS LONGIFOLIA

PINUS GERARDIANA

PINUS CANARIENSIS

skaglum
hackbraut
griffel
grootpot
potter
squint

kieloog
rjothe
lobb
burr
filburr
muuskarp
pillock

maugster
seekrey
benwahl
kilpo
duunkilp
rip

H. C. Artmann (1954)

"*fische: katwijk an see*" catalogues fish found in the waters off a resort in Holland.

in meinem garten verbluten
die drosseln des wahnsinns
aus geometrischen fontänen
die drosseln des wahnsinns
in meinem garten verbluten
aus geometrischen fontänen
aus geometrischen fontänen
verbluten in meinem garten
die drosseln des wahnsinns
in meinem garten verbluten
die fontänen des wahnsinns
aus geometrischen drosseln
die geometrischen drosseln
in meinem garten verbluten
aus fontänen des wahnsinns
aus geometrischem wahnsinn
verbluten in meinem garten
deine drosseln zu fontänen

H. C. Artmann (1954)

in meinem garten = in my garden
verbluten = bleed to death
die drosseln = thrushes, snowball trees
des wahnsinns = of madness
aus geometrischen fontänen = from geometrical fountains
deine = thy
zu = at
A gradual displacement of modifiers changes and expands the imagery.

a t é
i
c

e s t
a
c a

e s t
i
c a

e t c
a
c

Ronaldo Azeredo, "*tic tac*" (1956)

até = till
estaca = stop
estica = stretch

VVVVVVVVVV
VVVVVVVVVE
VVVVVVVVEL
VVVVVVVELO
VVVVVVELOC
VVVVVELOCI
VVVVELOCID
VVVELOCIDA
VVELOCIDAD
VELOCIDADE

Ronaldo Azeredo (1957)

"The Futurists tried to paint motion. It was an iconic motion, imitative of reality, like, for example, Cesare Simonetti's 'Treno in corsa,' which has the shape of a projectile. Azeredo's poem has a different purpose: its dynamic structure moves—and by itself. We may only think of a kind of abstract iconography. The reiteration of VVV—a vertiginous *decrescendo*—gives on the visual level the same semantic information achieved by the final line of the poem." (Haroldo de Campos)

Ronaldo Azeredo (1957)

como o vento = like the wind
comovido = commoved
com o ouvido = with the ear
como o vivo = like the living
locomovido = locomoted
ou vindo = or coming

como o vento
comovido
com o ouvido
como o vivo
locomovido
ou vindo

r u a r u a r u a s o l

r u a r u a s o l r u a

r u a s o l r u a r u a

s o l r u a r u a r u a

r u a r u a r u a s

Ronaldo Azeredo (1957)

"The sun's rays disclosing themselves along the street. In the last line, the blank conveys the solar information, and the *s*, first letter of *sol*/sun, pluralizes *ruas*/streets. The process becomes endless." (Haroldo de Campos)

corpo a pouco

pouco a corpo

corpo a pouco

pouco a corpo

Ronaldo Azeredo (1960)

corpo = body

a = to

pouco = little

corpo a corpo = body to body

pouco a pouco = little by little

```
i m m e r     m a n n     d o m i n i
m m e r     m a n n     d o m i n i
m e r     m a n n     d o m i n i   k
e r     m a n n     d o m i n i   k u
r     m a n n     d o m i n i   k u s
    m a n n     d o m i n i   k u s
  m a n n     d o m i n i   k u s   z
m a n n     d o m i n i   k u s   z i
a n n     d o m i n i   k u s   z i m
n n     d o m i n i   k u s   z i m m
n     d o m i n i   k u s   z i m m e
    d o m i n i   k u s   z i m m e r
  d o m i n i   k u s   z i m m e r
d o m i n i   k u s   z i m m e r   m
o m i n i   k u s   z i m m e r   m a
m i n i   k u s   z i m m e r   m a n
i n i   k u s   z i m m e r   m a n n
n i   k u s   z i m m e r   m a n n
i   k u s   z i m m e r   m a n n   d
```

Stephen Bann (1964)

"'Dominikus Zimmermann' was inspired by the beautiful 18th century parish church of Steinhausen built by Zimmermann, and the inscription on the organ loft which contained the name followed by the description *architect, plasterer*. The separation of Zimmermann's functions of creating a structure and decorating its interior, which in this church were combined with such harmony, provided Bann with a model of artistic unity. . . . Within the conventions of concrete poetry Bann has explored the graphic and phonetic potentials in the name. The diagonal lines of each letter evolve into a pattern although there is no dominant formal structure. There are two messages divided by a central diagonal—*immer* st. eeples

Stephen Bann, "Landscape of St. Ives, Huntingdonshire" (1966)
Compare this poem with Ian Hamilton Finlay's "Horizon of Holland" and Aram Saroyan's "Ian Hamilton Finlay."

mann, domini and *zimmermann*. The first is a suggestion of the dedication of the architect to a spiritual ideal of the eternal nature of his achievement; the second celebrates the simple human function of his creation—*zimmer mann* (room man). . . ." (Jasia Reichart, introduction to **concrete poetry britain canada united states**, Edition Hansjörg Mayer, Stuttgart 1966)

troppo silenzio
nessuno **spara**
impossibile
attendere
immobili
ordini di postazione
così
a
 n
  c
   o
    r
     a
      per
        o
         r
          e
cantare
è un modo
di piangere
. . . avanti arditi
le fiamme nere
son come il simbolo
delle tue schiere . . .

carlo belloli futurista
fronte centrale, 1943

Carlo Belloli

A poster-poem from the collection ***parole per la guerra***, first published by Edizioni di Futuristi in Armi, Milan 1943. On September 8th of that year, Italy surrendered unconditionally; on October 8th, she declared war on Germany, her former Axis partner.

treni

i treni

i

i i i i i i i i i i i i

umbria 1943

Carlo Belloli

First published in ***testi-poemi murali*** in 1944, with a preface by F. T. Marinetti. In the last of his many manifestos, written shortly before his death, Marinetti, the founder of Futurism, described the new poetry of Belloli as " . . . . *creazione originale di zone-rumori construiti otticamente sulla pagina-spazio totale. . . .* ".

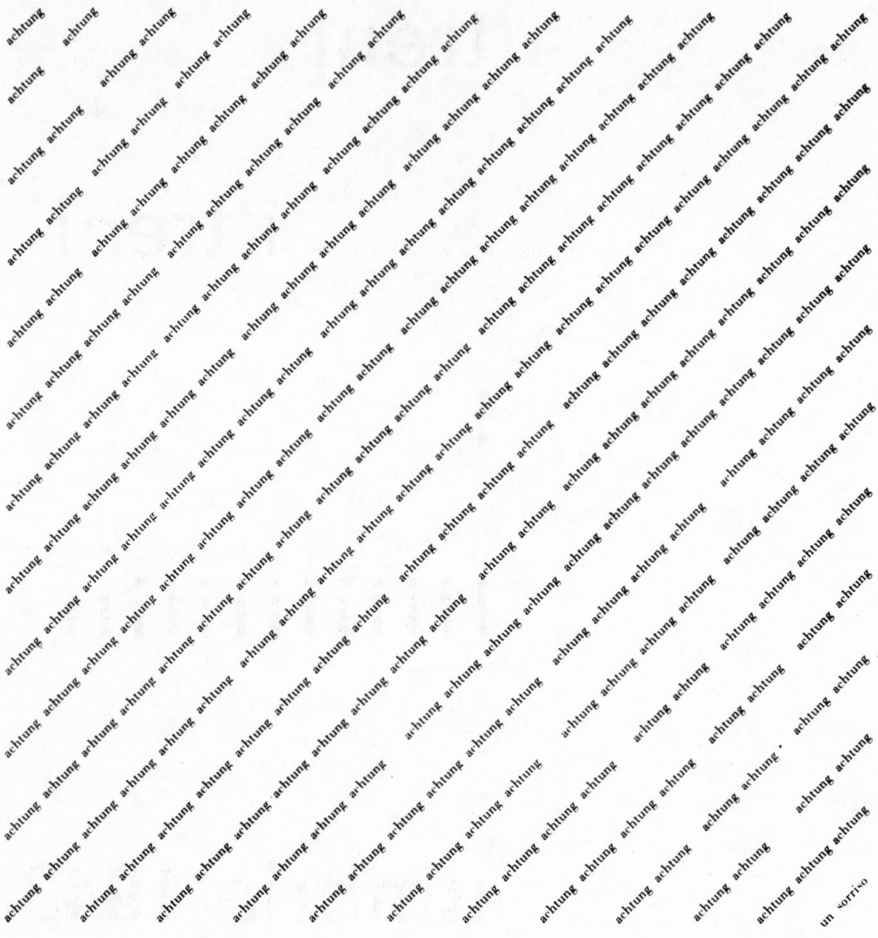
un sorriso

Carlo Belloli (1943)
un sorriso = a smile

Carlo Belloli

Poster-poem 25 in the collection ***parole per la guerra***. In January 1945, when the poem was written, the Allied beachhead forces came ashore at Anzio and began the fierce struggle against the Germans that lasted until the following May.

anzio

s
 b
  a
   r
    c
     a
      n
       o

anzio
lascia
l'italia
aperta
un pube di donna
spalancato
non per amore

carlo belloli futurista
23 gennaio 1944

uomini soli mistici

mistici uomini soli

soli mistici uomini

una donna

•

Carlo Belloli (1948)

The poems in ***tavole visuali*** are the earliest examples of the kind of semantico-visual constructions that were to be called "concrete" in the middle fifties.

T

T

T

T

tempo

primo tempo

secondo tempo

F

F

F

F

fine

Carlo Belloli (1948)

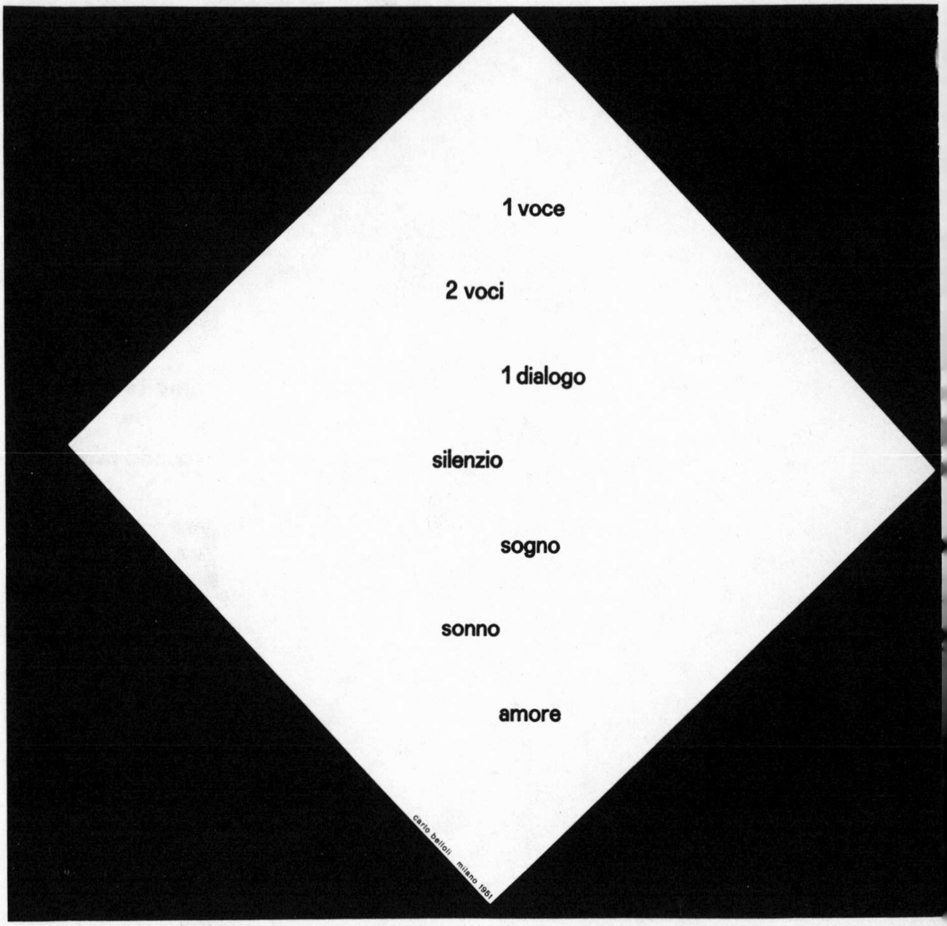
1 voce
2 voci
1 dialogo
silenzio
sogno
sonno
amore
carlo belloli milano 1951

Carlo Belloli (1951)

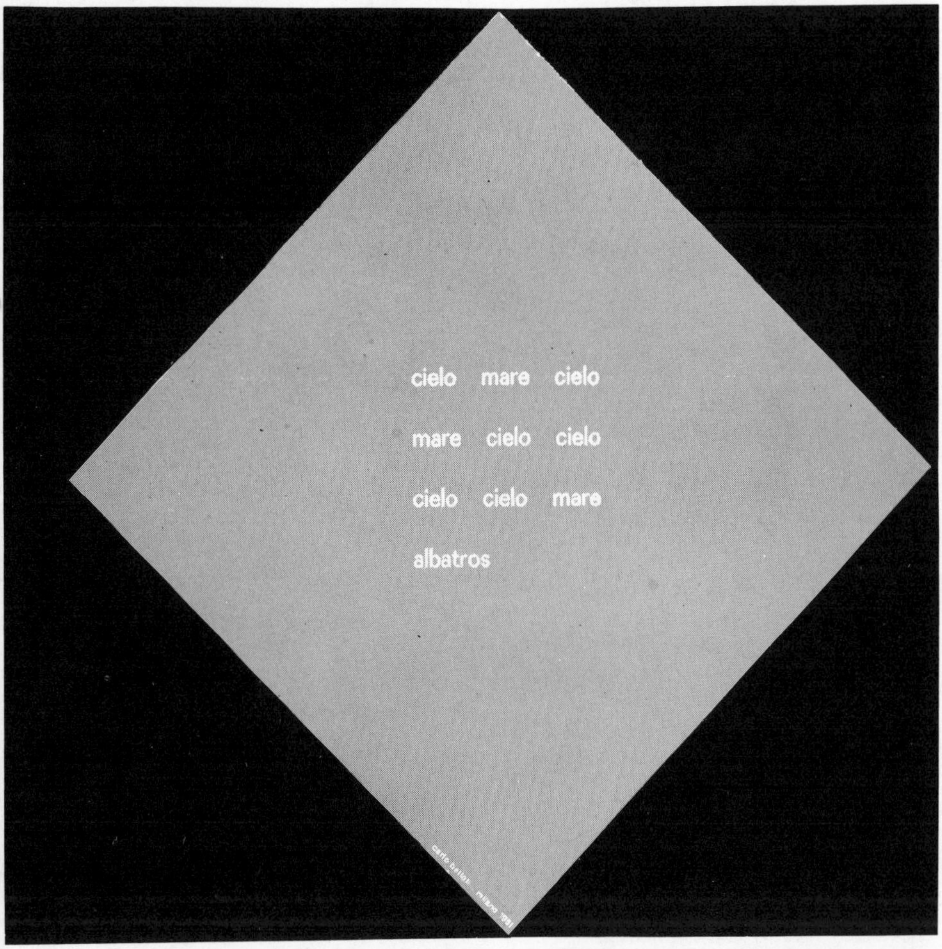
cielo mare cielo
mare cielo cielo
cielo cielo mare
albatros

Carlo Belloli (1951)

Carlo Belloli (1951)

cerchio cerchio cerchio cerchio
cerchio cerchio cerchio cerchio
cerchio cerchio cerchio cerchio
cerchio cer   chio
cerchio cerchio sfera   cerchio
cerchio cerchio cerchio cerchio
cerchio cerchio cerchio cerchio

artico

polare

circolo

o

@

circolo

polare

antartico

o

circolo

o

cerchio

o circo

Carlo Belloli (1959)

An "audiovisual" text.

acqua acqua acqua acqua acqua acqua acqua acqua acqua acqua acqua acqua
acqua acqua acqua acqua acqua acqua acqua acqua acqua acqua acqua acqua
acqua acqua acqua acqua acqua acqua acqua acqua acqua acqua acqua acqua
acqua acqua acqua acqua acqua acqua acqua acqua acqua acqua acqua acqua
acqua acqua acqua acqua acqua acqua acqua acqua acqua acqua acqua acqua
acqua acqua acqua acqua acqua acqua acqua acqua acqua acqua acqua acqua
acqua acqua acqua acqua acqua acqua acqua acqua acqua acqua acqua acqua
acqua acqua acqua acqua acqua acqua acqua acqua acqua acqua acqua acqua
acqua acqua acqua acqua acqua acqua acqua acqua acqua acqua acqua acqua
acqua acqua acqua acqua acqua acqua acqua acqua acqua acqua acqua acqua
acqua acqua acqua acqua acqua acqua acqua acqua acqua acqua acqua acqua
acqua acqua acqua acqua acqua acqua acqua acqua acqua acqua acqua acqua
acqua acqua acqua acqua acqua acqua acqua acqua acqua acqua acqua acqua
acqua acqua acqua acqua acqua acqua acqua acqua acqua acqua acqua acqua
acqua acqua acqua acqua acqua acqua acqua acqua acqua acqua acqua acqua
acqua acqua acqua acqua acqua acqua acqua acqua acqua acqua acqua acqua
acqua acqua acqua acqua acqua acqua acqua acqua acqua acqua acqua acqua
acqua acqua acqua acqua acqua acqua acqua acqua acqua acqua acqua acqua
acqua acqua acqua acqua acqua acqua acqua acqua acqua acqua acqua acqua
acqua acqua acqua acqua acqua acqua acqua acqua acqua acqua acqua acqua
acqua acqua acqua acqua acqua acqua acqua acqua acqua acqua acqua acqua
acqua incolore colore trasparente **acqua** percorso voce e voce **acqua** mare goccia
sfera una mano **acqua** verticale cielo una bocca **acqua** piano fiume una casa **acqua**
filo roccia un fiore **acqua** pioggia volto un bimbo **acqua** nubi atmosfera dèi **acqua**
pozzo eco un villaggio **acqua** ghiaccio cristallo un esquimese **acqua** sole foglie una
donna **acqua** barca silenzio un uomo **acqua** cielo medusa luna **acqua** orizzonte
occhio pesce **acqua** nave acqua uomini **acqua** palma sole voci **voci sole palma**
acqua **uomini acqua nave** acqua **pesce occhio orizzonte** acqua **luna medusa cielo**
acqua **un uomo silenzio barca** acqua **una donna foglie sole** acqua **un esquimese**
cristallo ghiaccio acqua **un villaggio eco pozzo** acqua **dèi atmosfera nubi** acqua **un**
bimbo volto pioggia acqua **un fiore roccia filo** acqua **una casa fiume piano** acqua
una bocca cielo verticale acqua **una mano sfera goccia mare** acqua **voce e voce**
percorso acqua **trasparente colore incolore** acqua acqua acqua acqua acqua acqua
acqua acqua acqua acqua acqua acqua acqua acqua acqua acqua acqua acqua
acqua acqua acqua acqua acqua acqua acqua acqua acqua acqua acqua acqua
acqua acqua acqua acqua acqua acqua acqua acqua acqua acqua acqua acqua
acqua acqua acqua acqua acqua acqua acqua acqua acqua acqua acqua acqua
acqua acqua acqua acqua acqua acqua acqua acqua acqua acqua acqua acqua
acqua acqua acqua acqua acqua acqua acqua acqua acqua acqua acqua acqua
acqua acqua acqua acqua acqua acqua acqua acqua acqua acqua acqua acqua
acqua acqua acqua acqua acqua acqua acqua acqua acqua acqua acqua acqua
acqua acqua acqua acqua acqua acqua acqua acqua acqua acqua acqua acqua
acqua acqua acqua acqua acqua acqua acqua acqua acqua acqua acqua acqua
acqua acqua acqua acqua acqua acqua acqua acqua acqua acqua acqua acqua
acqua acqua acqua acqua acqua acqua acqua acqua acqua acqua acqua acqua
acqua acqua acqua acqua acqua acqua acqua acqua acqua acqua acqua acqua
acqua acqua acqua acqua acqua acqua acqua acqua acqua acqua acqua acqua
acqua acqua acqua acqua acqua acqua acqua acqua acqua acqua acqua acqua
acqua acqua acqua acqua acqua acqua acqua acqua acqua acqua acqua acqua
acqua acqua acqua acqua acqua acqua acqua acqua acqua acqua acqua acqua
acqua acqua acqua acqua acqua acqua acqua acqua acqua acqua acqua acqua
acqua acqua acqua acqua acqua acqua acqua acqua acqua acqua acqua acqua
acqua acqua acqua acqua acqua acqua acqua acqua acqua acqua acqua acqua

Carlo Belloli (1961)

Final page of ***texte poème poème texte,*** one of the great achievements of concrete poetry.

solo
sole
sono
sole
sono
solo
sole
sale
sale
sale
sale

sale
sale

sale
sole
sale
sale
sul sole
solo
sale
sole
ssss
sss
ss
s

solo
solo
solo
solo
solo
solo
solo
solo
solo
solo
solo
solo
solo
solo
solo
solo
solo
solo
solo
solo
nel sole

sole
solo

sono
solo
sole
sono
solo
solo
solo
solo
solo
solo
solo
solo
solo
solo
solo
solo
solo
solo
solo
solo
sole

sole
sole
sole
sole
sole
sole
s
s
s
s
s
solo

sole
scende
solo
sole
scende
scende
scende
scende
scende
scende
scende
scende

solo

Carlo Belloli, *sole solo* (1967)

solo = alone
sole = sun
nel sole = in the sun
sul sole = over the sun
sale = ascends
scende = descends
sono = I am

nicht vergessen

zu vergessen

zu vergessen

dass ich war

Max Bense (1963)

nicht vergessen = not to forget
zu vergessen = to forget
dass ich war = that I was

The texts in ***Vielleicht zunächst wirklich nur*** are determined "aleatorially or topologically, darkly or cautiously, grammatically or visually, as they float in the gray haze of meanings that hovers over each surface, then vanish forever or remain there, as the case may be."

Max Bense (1963)

The text as a "set of words" (homage to mathematics) rather than a set of things, feelings, atmospheres, etc. "Since the words none the less bear meanings," says Bense, "it seems reasonable to say that in this kind of poetry words are not pretexts for objects so much as objects are pretexts for words. . . . It is poetry on a level of metalanguage, poetry in a world of its own."

sog jagd
wand sein
fisch strich tang
nichts
tag stroh
herbst
haus glanz jod
sand
bild jahr
meer
spur rost krebs
schritt laut
tritt last
mohn
flut wind
schiff fall netz
holz rot bar knie
ist strand duft
stein hals salz
kiel
blick gras fuss
halt mund ziel
schlag
rock weg
arm scham
ohr mond see
schlaf glas
strumpf traum
nacht
lid
haut

ich

denke ist

etwas

Max Bense (1966)
"Cartesian concrete." (M.B.)

Edgard Braga (1963)

sim = yes

não = no

um = a

sim	sim	não	não
não	não	sim	sim
um	sim	não	
um	sim	sim	
não	não	sim	
sim	não	não	
	um	sim	não
	um	não	sim
	um	sim	sim
		um	não
		sim	

um
pobre joga
um
jôgo pobre
joga um jôgo
um pobre joga
joga joga joga
um pobre joga
jôgo pobre
um
joga

Edgard Braga, *"a poor play"* (1963)
um = a
pobre = poor
joga = plays (verb)
jôgo = play (noun)

Edgard Braga (1963)

poema = poem

pó = dust

e = and

mó = millstone

poema

poema

poema

poema

poema

poema

pó

e

mó

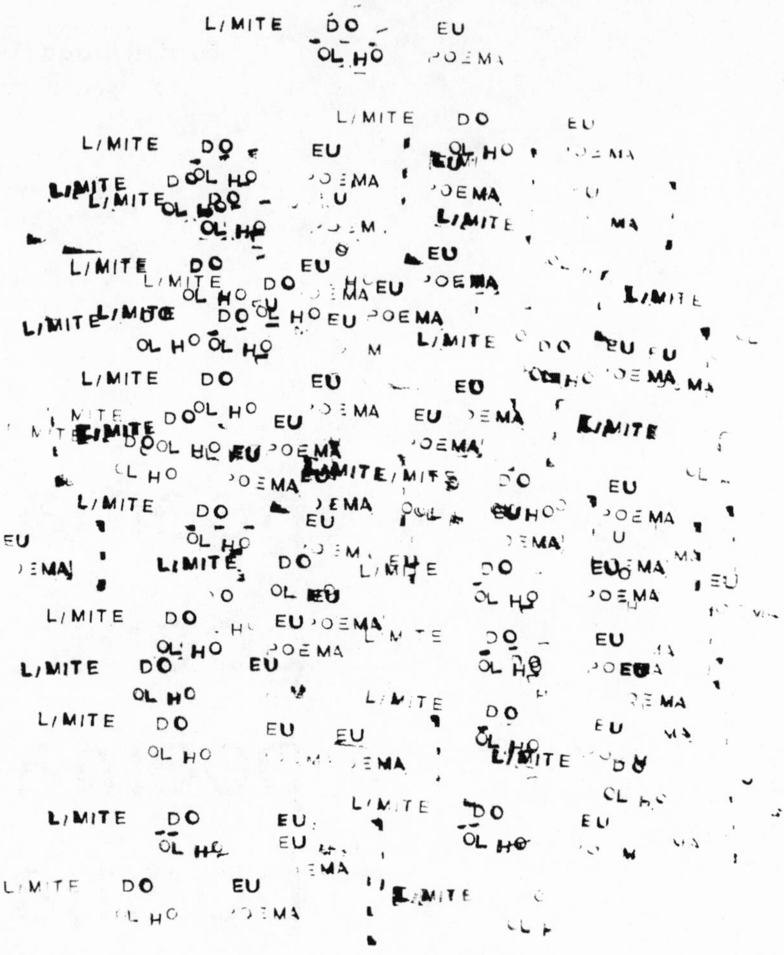
L/MITE DO EU
OL HO POEMA

Edgard Braga (1965)
limite do ôlho = limit of the eye
limite do eu = limit of the I
limite do poema = limit of the poem

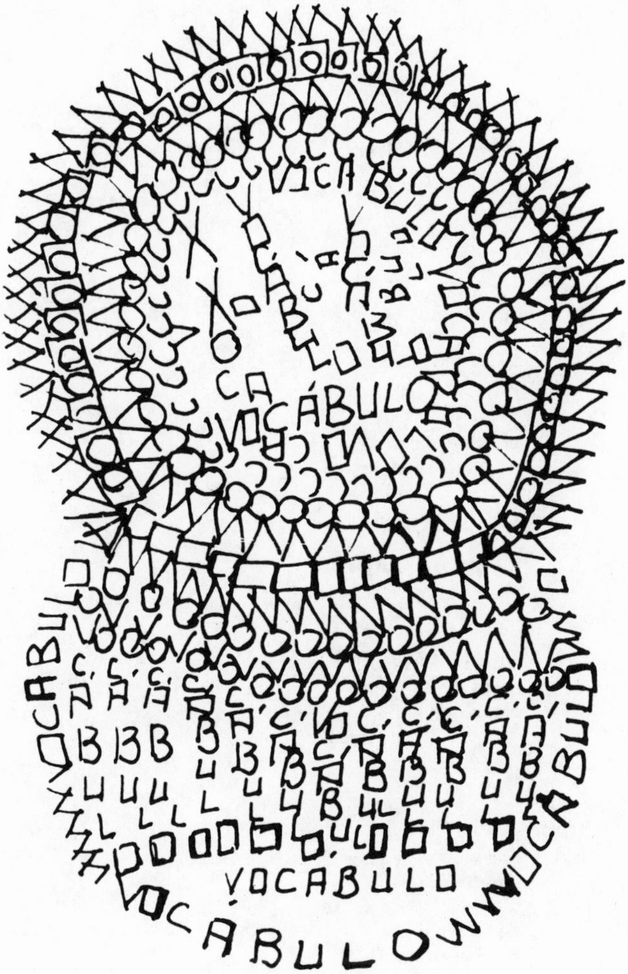
VOCÁBULO
VOCABULO
VOCÁBULO

Edgard Braga (1966)
vocábulo = vocable

eeeee		
		eeeee
	eu i uu	
		i u u iu
drf	d rr	d rr
sschf		
		ft
		w
tt tt		
l		
ch		
drf	ch	df
ss ss ss		
	gf	
	tch	
t t t		
	ch dw	
		drsg
	ru	fi
	rufi	
	sseu	
		rufisseu
der ufi		
sseu		
		glch
	eutti	
	euss	fuudr
	euss	
		gwltisch
der ufi		
sseug		
		wdch
	dru	
	fieu	eussg
	weuttedcht	
		d d dd
	de d de d de	
	ru ru ru ru	
ruieu ruieu		drsg
	eu i eu u	
der ufieu		
	der fuss des gewitters leuchtet	

Claus Bremer (1955)

"The base of the thunderstorm lights up." Compare Edwin Morgan's "Seven Headlines" on page 221.

rendering the legible illegible
rendering the il**legible**
rendering the illegible
rendering illegible

Claus Bremer (1963)

The German original begins *lesbares in unlesbares übersetzen*. Translated by the editor.

Claus Bremer (1964)

The German original begins *ist der text der text der ausbleibt*. Translated by the editor.

is the text the text left out
is the tex he text left out
is the te e text left out
is the t text left out
is the text left out
is the ext left out
is th xt left out
is t t left out
is left out
is left out
i eft out
ft out
t t out
th out
the out
the ut
the t t
the te
the tex t
the text xt
the text ext
the text l text
the text le text
the text lef e text
the text left he text
the text left the text
the text left o the text
the text left ou s the text
the text left out is the text

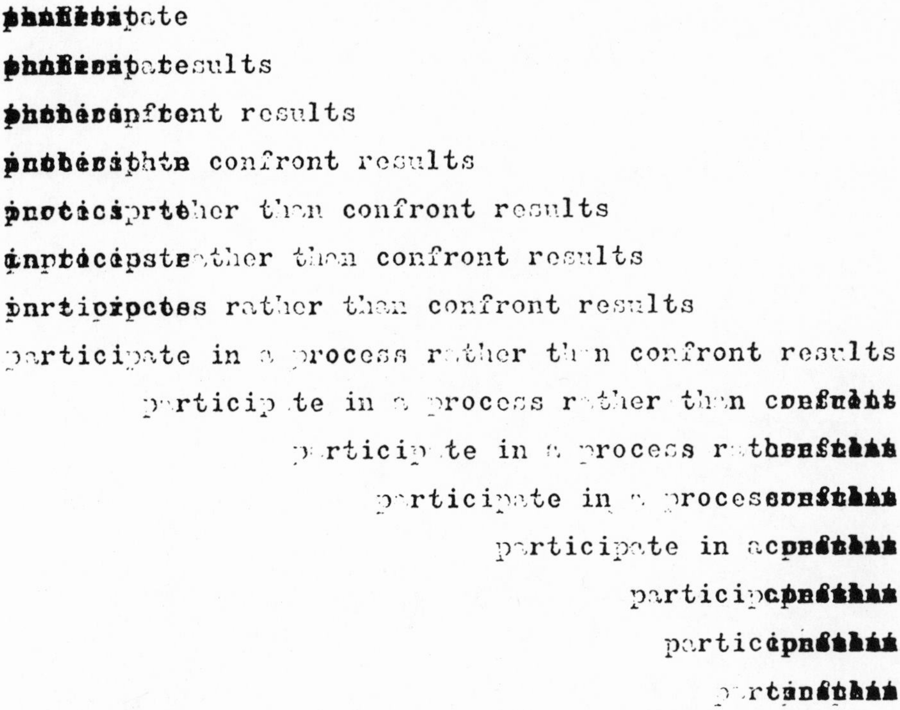
participate in a process rather than confront results

Claus Bremer (1964)

"In the first line, the text is written word over word. In the lines that follow, the last word is separated, word for word and line for line, until the text is legible. Then the process is reversed. This arrangement is intended to arouse curiosity, to reveal something, and then again to become obscure; to arouse the reader's curiosity, to reveal something to him, and then again confront him with himself. In a world in which one is constantly invited to leave one's own four walls and buy something that leads him away from himself, a world in which one is led astray from himself, concrete poetry invites the reader back to himself." (C.B.) The original German reads *keinem ergebnis gegenüberstellen sondern an einem prozess beteiligen*. Translated by Laura P. Williams.

```
was ist das
 wasistdas
  wa s as
   w   s

   d   s
  da s as
 dasistwas
das ist was
```

Claus Bremer (1964)

"This arrangement allows the reader to think about the relationship between question and answer in his own way. If I say that in this text the question 'what is that' changes into the answer 'that is what,' or that the fact of being asked makes something 'something,' or that the question is the key to things, those are my personal comments at the moment. Anyone else's comments could be quite different. Concrete poetry gives no results. It yields a process of discovery. It is motion. Its motion ends in different readers in different ways. Concrete poetry says formally what it means to say, or means to say what its form says. Its form is its meaning, its meaning its form." (C.B.)

n
ni
nic
nich
nicht
nicht
nicht n
nicht nu
nicht nur
nicht nur
nicht nur
nicht nur
nicht nur
nicht nur
nicht nur
nicht nur
nicht nur
nicht nur
nicht nur
nicht nur
nicht nur

informieren
informiere
informier
informie
informi
inform
infor
info
inf
in
i

haltungen
altungen
ltungen
tungen
ungen
ngen
gen
en
n

provozieren
provozieren
provozieren
provozieren
provozieren
provozieren
provozieren
provozieren
provozieren
provozieren
provozieren
rovozieren
ovozieren
vozieren
ozieren
zieren
ieren
eren
ren
en
n

Claus Bremer (1966)

nicht nur = not only
informieren = inform
haltungen = attitudes
provozieren = provoke

"*nicht nur informieren haltungen provozieren* is the word-material for this star-shaped construction. To understand its organization . . . . the reader must move either the poem or himself. The text reveals its word play only to those who examine the subject from the right, from above, and from the left, that is to say, from all sides. . . . . These are not engaging texts. They are engaged texts." (C.B.)

für
dich
und
für
mich

ccd
dffh
hii
mnr
ruüü

Claus Bremer (1966)

The letters of a simple text, "for you and for me," are rearranged in the last five lines according to their alphabetical priority.

immer schön in der reihe bleiben
immer schön in der reihe bleiben
immer schön in der reihe bleiben
immer schön in der reihe bleiben
immer schön in der reihe bleiben
immer schön in der reihe bleiben
immer schön in der reihe bleiben
immer schön in der reihe bleiben
immer schön in der reihe bleiben
immer schön in der reihe bleiben
immer schön in der reihe bleiben
immer schön in der reihe bleiben
immer schön in der reihe bleiben
immer schön in der reihe bleiben
immer schön in der reihe bleiben
immer schön in der reihe bleiben
immer schön in der reihe bleiben
immer schön in der reihe bleiben
immer schön in der reihe bleiben
immer schön in der reihe bleiben
immer schön in der reihe bleiben
immer schön in der reihe bleiben
immer schön in der reihe bleiben
immer schön in der reihe bleiben
immer schön in der reihe bleiben
immer schön in der reihe bleiben
immer schön in der reihe bleiben
immer schön in der reihe bleiben
immer schön in der reihe bleiben
immer schön in der reihe bleiben
immer schön in der reihe bleiben
immer schön in der reihe bleiben
immer schön in der reihe bleiben
immer schön in der reihe bleiben
immer schön in der reihe bleiben
immer schön in der reihe bleiben
immer schön in der reihe bleiben
immer schön in der reihe bleiben
immer schön in der reihe bleiben
immer schön in der reihe bleiben
immer schön in der reihe bleiben
immer schön in der reihe bleiben
immer schön in der reihe bleiben
immer schön in der reihe bleiben
immer schön in der reihe bleiben
immer schön in der reihe bleiben
immer schön in der reihe bleiben
immer schön in der reihe bleiben
immer schön in der reihe bleiben
immer schön in der reihe bleiben
immer schön in der reihe bleiben
immer schön in der reihe bleiben
immer schön in der reihe bleiben
immer schön in der reihe bleiben
immer schön in der reihe bleiben
immer schön in der reihe bleiben
immer schön in der reihe bleiben
immer schön in der reihe bleiben
immer schön in der reihe bleiben
immer schön in der reihe bleiben
immer schön in der reihe bleiben
immer schön in der reihe bleiben
immer schön in der reihe bleiben
immer schön in der reihe bleiben
immer schön in der reihe bleiben
immer schön in der reihe bleiben
immer schön in der reihe bleiben
immer schön in der reihe bleiben
immer schön in der reihe bleiben
immer schön in der reihe bleiben
immer schön in der reihe bleiben
immer schön in der reihe bleiben
immer schön in der reihe bleiben
immer schön in der reihe bleiben
immer schön in der reihe bleiben
immer schön in der reihe bleiben
immer schön in der reihe bleiben
immer schön in der reihe bleiben
immer schön in der reihe bleiben
immer schön in der reihe bleiben

Claus Bremer (1966)

"I almost didn't succeed in keeping in line and writing a page of 'keep in line' line for line one under the other but my effort spares you that of reading. For just as one can hardly write a text in this form, one can hardly read one line for line. The keep-in-line of 'keep in line' causes one not to keep in line but, on the contrary, to get out of line. This kind of organization provokes an urge for freedom and reason. This text, as do all of my engaged texts, sets the reader free in the realm of his own possibilities, the realm in which we are brothers." (C.B.)

immer schön in der reihe bleiben
immer schön in der reihe bleiben
immer schön in der reihe bleiben
immer schön in der reihe bleiben
immer schön in der reihe bleiben
immer schön in der reihe bleiben
immer schön in der reihe bleiben
immer schön in der reihe bleiben
immer schön in der reihe bleiben
immer schön in der reihe bleiben
immer schön in der reihe bleiben
immer schön in der reihe bleiben
immer schön in der reihe bleiben
immer schön in der reihe bleiben
immer schön in der reihe bleiben
immer schön in der reihe bleiben
immer schön in der reihe bleiben
immer schön in der reihe bleiben
immer schön in der reihe bleiben

eis

os

amantes *sem* parentes

senão

os corpos

irmã*um* gemeo*utrem*

cimae*u* baixe*la*

ecora*cambos*

d u p l *a m p l* i n f a n t *u n* o *(s)* e m p r e

*semen(t)*emventre

es*t*êsse *aquel*êle

*in*humen*o*utro

Augusto de Campos, "*eis os amantes*" (1953)

Translation by the author on facing page.

here
are
the
lovers *without* parents
only
the bodies
sister*one* moaning*other*
above*i* below*she*
andheart*both*
d o u b l e *w i d* e i n f a n t o *n e (a)* l w a y s
*semen(seed)*inwomb
heshe *this*that
*inone*inhume*into*other

Augusto de Campos, "here are the lovers" (1953)

"A literal translation. The original was printed in two colors, red and black. The colors were not symbolic, but were meant to provide a notation for two voice timbres, male and female. The score (the poem should be read aloud) follows Webern's *Klangfarbenmelodie* principle—a continuous melody, displaced from one instrument to another, constantly changing its color or timbre. A love ideogram." (Haroldo de Campos)

o v o
n o v e l o
novo no velho
o filho em folhos
na jaula dos joelhos
infante em fonte
f e t o f e i t o
d e n t r o d o
centro

o
p o n t o
onde se esconde
lenda ainda antes
e n t r e v e n t r e s
quando queimando
o s s e i o s s ã o
p e i t o s n o s
dedos

nu
des do nada
a t e o h u m
a n o m e r o n u
m e r o d o z e r o
crua criança incru
stada no cerne da
carne viva en
fim nada

n o
t u r n a noite
em tôrno em treva
turva sem contôrno
morte negro nó cego
sono do morcego nu
ma sombra que o pren
dia preta letra que
s e t o r n a
sol

Augusto de Campos (1955)

"A genesis poem—a child's generation and the generation of the poem. The egg and the uterus: elementary forms of birth in process. Greek *technopaegnis* revisited with a concrete sensibility for synthesis." (Haroldo de Campos)

Augusto de Campos (1957)

"'*terremoto*' (earthquake) is another generative poem, this time with cosmic and existential hints. A kind of 'portable cosmogony' in cross-word form." (Haroldo de Campos)

ovo = egg
novelo = ball of thread
novo = new
sol = sun
letra = letter (of alphabet)
estrela = star
soletra = (it) spells
so = only
terremoto = earthquake
temor = fear
morte = death
metro = meter
termometro = thermometer

```
      o
  n o v e l o
  o v o
o v o             s o l
  e               o
  l               l e t r a
  o               e
              e s t r e l a       t
              s   r               e
      s o l e t r a               r
      o   e   r                   r
      l   t   e                   e
          r   l               t e m o r
          a   a                   o
                          t       t     t
                          e     m o r t e
                t e r r e m o t o       r
                          o     r       m e t r o
                          r     t       o
                              t e r m o       m   m
                                    e       m o t o r
                                    t     m o t o r
                                    r       t o r t o
                                    o     m o r t o
                                            r   o
```

Augusto de Campos (1956)

com som = with sound
cantem = sing
contém = (it) contains
tensão = tension
também = *also*
tombem = tumble
sem som = without sound

" 'Concrete poetry: tension of things-words in space-time.' This phrase from one of Augusto de Campos' theoretical texts, later incorporated into the 'pilot plan for concrete poetry,' explains the process of this poem. Its reading is open: you may depart from wherever you wish." (Haroldo de Campos)

com
som

can
tem

con
tém

ten
são

tan
be

tom
bem

ser
sor

uma vez
uma vala
uma foz
uma vez   uma bala
uma fala   uma voz
uma foz   uma vala
uma bala   uma vez
uma voz
uma vala
uma vez

Augusto de Campos (1957)

uma vez = one time, once upon a time
uma fala = a speech, a talk
uma foz = a river-mouth
uma bala = a bullet
uma voz = a voice
uma vala = a ditch

"The reduction of a plot (love? murder?—'once upon a time . . .') to a dynamic iterative endless process." (Haroldo de Campos)
English version by Edwin Morgan.

once was
one ditch
one beach
once was   one whiz
one speech   one voice
one beach   one ditch
one whiz   once was
one voice
one ditch
once was

Augusto de Campos (1957)

"The act of vision. Its ideogram. Eye as a pivot." (Haroldo de Campos)

eixo = axis
ôlho = eye
polo = pole
fixo = fixed
flor = flower
pêso = weight
solo = soil
English version by Edwin Morgan.

eixoôlho
polofixo
eixoflor
pêsofixo
eixosolo
ôlhofixo

fixteyes
poleaxis
fixtrose
hungaxis
fixtsoil
eyesaxis

Augusto de Campos (1960)

"The masking and unmasking of the poem's process. Like a snail slowly unfolding its going." (Haroldo de Campos)

colocar a máscara = to put on the mask
mascara = mask, (it) masks
mas = but
cara = face
caracol = snail

c o l o c a r a m a s

c a r a c o l o c a r

a m a s **c a r a c o l**

o c a r a m a s **c a r**

a c o l o c a r a m a

s **c a r a c o l** o c a

r a m a s **c a r a c o**

l o c a r a m a s **c a**

r a c o l o c a r a m

a s **c a r a c o l** o c

a r a m a s **c a r a c**

o l o c a r a m a s **c**

a r a c o l o c a r a

m a s **c a r a c o l** o

c a r a m a s **c a r a**

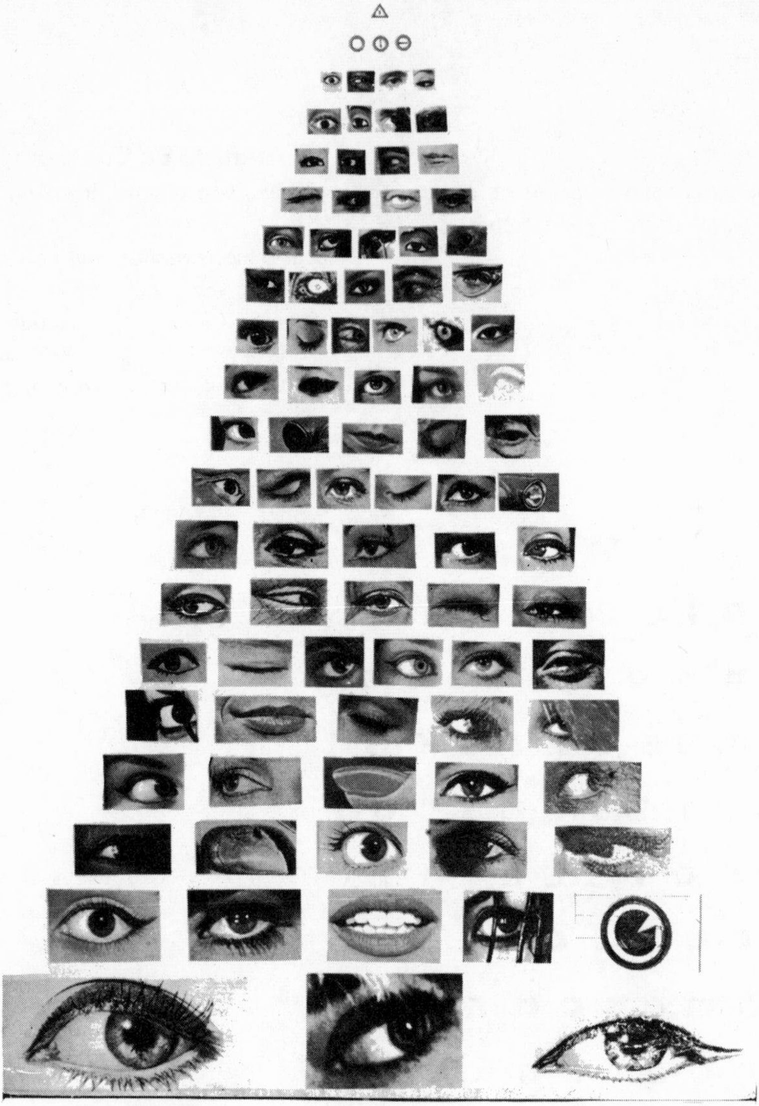

Augusto de Campos (1964)

"ôlho por ôlho" (eye for eye) is a "popcrete" poem. The original, in color, collaged from magazines, is 50 cm by 70 cm.

branco	**branco**	**branco**	**branco**
vermelho			
estanco	**vermelho**		
	espelho	**vermelho**	
		estanco	**branco**

white	white	white	white
red			
midnight	red		
	mirrored	red	
		midnight	white

Haroldo de Campos (1957)

branco = white
vermelho = red
estanco = I stanch
espelho = mirror, I mirror
English version by Edwin Morgan.

"A progression with the word *branco* (white). In counterpoint, the word *vermelho* (red). The internal rhymes provide the skeleton (*branco* / *estanco, vermelho* / *espelho*). The maximum opening of the poem coincides with the maximum blank of the page: a coinformation, at visual level, with the effect of white color over a white surface in painting, or the word white written with white ink on white paper." (H. de C.)

SI

marsupialamor   mam
ilos de lam
préias prêsas   can
ino   am
or
turris   de   talis
man
gu   (LEN)
tural   aman
te   em   te
nebras   febras
de   febr
uário   fe
mural   mor
tálamo   t'
aurifer
oz : e
foz
paz
ps

CIO

Haroldo de Campos, *"si len cio"* (1955)

"This poem opens the series ***o âmago do ômega ou fenomenologia da composicão*** (the heart of the omega or phenomenology of composition). Printed white on black. The poem is cyclical: *SI* (if) *LEN* (first syllable of *LENto*, slow) CIO (sexual union). A phenomenology of the sexual act. The poem is to be read aloud, as a quasi-litany in a pseudo-Latin. The words are fragmented and transformed kaleidoscopically, like particles floating in seminal fluid. The final *silence* disembogues into the black page—the original night, the nothingness of language, where all ceases to be." (H. de C.)

This is an example of the author's first concrete phase, very much connected with musical and aural problems. Readers who have access to Hans G. Helms' ***Fa:m'***

SI

marsupialamour mam
elle de lam
proie prise can
in am
our
tour de talis
man
gu (L E N T) t
tural aman
t en té
nèbres fièvre
de fevr
ier fem
oral mor
thalamus t'
auriféroce
noces : et
bout
chut
paix

CE
ss
e

Haroldo de Campos, *"silence ou phénoménologie de l'amour"* (1955)

Translation by the author of poem on the facing page.

Ahniesgwow (DuMont-Schauberg, Cologne 1959) should compare this poem with Helms' "Fragment II, 8."

o pavilhão da orelha ourela
o ávido pavilhão
auréola
aura
em cornu cópia
caramujo do ouvido
munge a teta
do ar
a tur
gida tôrre
de vento
labora em labirinto
o som o filisom
dos palpos dos nenh
ures ubres

Haroldo de Campos, "*o pavilhão da orelha*" (1956)

"This poem belongs to the series **the heart of the omega or phenomenology of composition**. Here, the poet tries to arrive at the *eidos* of the sound, of the sonorous texture of words. The ear is seen as a snail (*caramujo*) milking (*mungindo*) airy milk of sound from nipples of nowhere." (H. de C.)

Haroldo de Campos, "the ear's pavilion" (1956)
Translation by the author of poem on facing page.

```
the   ear's     pavilion        edging
      eager     pavilion
       aureola
       aura

                in cornu copia  ear
                   snail milks
                   teat of
                   air
                   win
                   dy tower
                   tur
                   gid
                                manages in maze
                                sound fili
                                sound
                                      from palps
                                      from nothing
                                           ness nipples
```

Haroldo de Campos (1958)

cristal = crystal
fome = hunger
forma = form
de = of

"An essay of poetic crystallography. The metaphorical hunger of form and form as a kind of hunger. Crystal as the ideogram of the process." (H. de C.)

cristal
cristal
fome
cristal
cristal
fome de forma
cristal
cristal
forma de fome
cristal
cristal
forma

se
nasce
morre nasce
morre nasce morre
renasce remorre renasce
remorre renasce
remorre
re
re
desnasce
desmorre desnasce
desmorre desnasce desmorre
nascemorrenasce
morrenasce
morre
se

Haroldo de Campos (1958)

se = if
nasce = (a human being) is born
morre = (a human being) dies
re = again
denasce = (a human being) is unborn
desmorre = (a human being) undies

"Hans Arp once made the following comparison between the poetry of the painter-poet Kandinsky and the poetry of Goethe: 'A poem by Goethe teaches the reader, in a poetical way, that death and transformation are the inclusive condition of man. Kandinsky, on the contrary, places the reader before an image of dying and transforming words, before a series of dying and transforming words . . . ' This poem wants to be an exact *presentification* of that proposition. The vital cycle (or the Joycean 'vicocycle')." (H. de C.)

PROEM

mônca ouro?
môsca fôsca.

môsca prata?
môsca preta.

môsca íris?
môsca reles.

môsca anil?
môsca vil.

môsca azul?
môsca môsca.

môsca branca?
poesia pouca.

•

o azul é puro?
o azul é pus

de barriga vazia
o verde é vivo?

o verde é virus
de barriga vazia

o amarelo é belo
o amarelo é bile

de barriga vazia

o vermelho é fúcsia?
o vermelho é fúria

de barriga vazia

a poesia é pura?
a poesia é para

de barriga vazia

•

poesia em tempo de fome
fome em tempo de poesia

poesia em lugar do homem
pronome em lugar do nome

homem em lugar de poesia
nome em lugar do pronome

poesia de dar o nome
nomear é dar o nome

nomeio o nome
nomeio o homem
no meio a fome

nomeio a fome

fly of gold?
fly gone dry.

fly of silver?
fly of cinders.

fly of rainbows?
fly of rags.

fly of indigo?
fly of indigence.

fly of blue?
fly of flies.

fly of white?
poetry no-poetry.

•

blue's pure?
blue's pus

to empty belly
green's vivid?

green's virus
to empty belly

yellow's vaunted?
yellow's vomit

to empty belly

red's fuchsia?
red's frenzy

to empty belly

poetry's pure?
poetry's purpose

to empty belly

•

poetry in time of hunger
hunger in time of poetry

poetry in place of humanity
pronoun in place of nouns

humanity in place of poetry
noun in place of pronoun

poetry of giving the name
naming is giving the noun

i name the noun
i name humanity
in mid-naming is hunger

i name it hunger

Haroldo de Campos, *Servidão de passagem* (1961)

POEM

de sol a sol
soldado
de sal a sal
salgado
de sova a sova
sovado
de suco a suco
sugado
de sono a sono
sonado

sangrado
de sangue a sangue

•

onde mói esta moagem
onde engrena esta engrenagem

moenda homem moagem
moagem homem moenda

engrenagem
gangrenagem

from sun to solar
solder
from salt to salty
saline
from stick to stone
stunned
from sap to sugar
sucked
from sleep to slip
slumped

sanguined
from seep to spurt

•

where does this grinding grind
where does this gear engage

grindstone man's grinding
grinding man's grindstone

gearchanged
gangrengaged

•

de lucro a lucro
logrado
de lôgro a lôgro
lucrado
de lado a lado
lanhado
de lôdo a lôdo
largado

sol a sal
sal a sova
sova a suco
suco a sono
sono a sangue

•

onde homem
          essa moagem
onde carne
          essa carnagem
onde osso
          essa engrenagem

•

homem forrado
homem forrado

homem rapina
homem rapado

homem surra
homem surrado

homem buraco
homem burra

•

homem senhor
homem servo

homem sôbre
homem sob

•

from profit to profit
pinched
from pinch to pinch
profited
from pole to pole
parted
from puddle to puddle
poleaxed

sun to salt
salt to stun
stun to sap
sap to sleeping
sleeping to bleeding

•

with man
          this bonegrind
with flesh
          this bloodgut
with bone
          this baregear

•

bland man
branded man

pillage man
peeled man

cudgel man
cudgelled man

sieve man
steel-safe man

•

sir man
serving man

super man
sub man

Haroldo de Campos, *Servidão de passagem* (continued from preceding page)

homem saciado
homem saqueado

homem servido
homem sôrvo

•

homem come
homem fome

homem fala
homem cala

homem sôco
homem saco

homem mó
homem pó

•

quem baraço
quem vassalo

quem cavalo
quem cavalga

quem explora
quem espólio

•

quem carrasco
quem carcassa

quem usura
quem usado

quem pilhado
quem pilhagem

•

quem uisque
quem urina
quem feriado
quem faxina
quem volúpia
quem vermina

stacked man
sacked man

served man
swallowed man

•

trencher man
empty man

yakkity man
yes man

socko man
sick man

graft man
chaff man

•

who's lord
who's lout

who's the horse
who's on horseback

who's the exploiter
who's the spoil

•

who's hangman
who's hanged man

who's usury
who's used

who's plundered
who's plundering

•

who's whisky
who's piss
who's feast-day
who's fatigue-duty
who's lust
who's lice

Haroldo de Campos, *Servidão de passagem* (continued from facing page)

•

carne carniça carnagem

sangragem sangria sangue

•

homemmoendahomemmoagem

açúar
nesse bagaço?

almíscar
nesse sovaco?

petunia
nesse melaço?

•

indigo nesse buraco?

•

ocre
acre
osga
asco

•

canga cangalho cagaço
cansaço cachaço canga
carcassa cachaça gana

•

de mingua a mingua
de magro a magro
de morgue a morgue
de morte a morte

•

só moagem
ossomoagem

•

flesh filth fury

bloodbath bleeding blood

•

grindstonemangrindingman

sugar
in these husks?

musk
in this armpit?

petunia
in these molasses?

•

indigo in this snakepit?

•

ochre
acrid
lizard
lazar

•

halter harness hot-seat
heaviness head-hot halter
hangdog half-tot anger

•

from dearth to dearth
from drouth to drouth
from deadhouse to deadhouse
from death to death

•

only grindinghood
bone-grindinghood

Haroldo de Campos, *Servidão de passagem* (continued from preceding page)

"The book **transient servitude** is composed of two parts: *'proem'* and *'poem.'* *'Proem'* contains three pieces, which develop, in a dialectical way, the linguistic and existential play between *poesia pura* (pure poetry) and *poesia para* (committed poetry, poetry with a social purpose, poetry for). The first one is the fly of blue; the second, the fly of flies. Hoelderlin: *'Und wozu Dichter in dürftiger Zeit?'* (and what is poetry for in a time of scarcity?). And Heidigger about Hoelderlin: 'Poetry is the foundation of *being* through the word.' These somewhat metaphysical statements are transformed by the poem into a physical matter of facts: hun-

sem miragem	**no mirage to brood**
selvaselvagem	**through savage wood**
•	**•**
servidão de passagem	**transient servitude**

ger in Brazilian underdeveloped regions, as a counterweight in the poet's mind, in the very act of compounding his poem: *nomeio o nome* (I name the noun), *nomeio o homem* (I name humanity), *no meio a fome* (in mid-naming is hunger); in Portuguese, by the mere cutting of the word *nomeio* is obtained non-discursively *no meio* (in the middle) which introduces 'hunger' in the very act of nominating. Feuerbach: *'Der Mensch ist was er isst'* (man is what he eats) and Brecht: *'Erst kommt das Fressen denn kommt die Moral'* (first comes grub, then comes the moral). In a circumstance of scarcity, the poet tries to give *'un sens plus POUR aux mots de la tribu.'* A committed poetry, without giving up the devices and technical achievements of concrete poetry." (H. de C.)
English version by Edwin Morgan.

viande salée	viande fraiche
viande féminine	viande masculine
viande infantile	viande ferme
viande 1° choix	viande 2° choix
viande 3° choix	viande 4° choix
viande en frigo	viande en confessionn
viande médicale	viande expérimentale
viande pustuleuse	viande saine
viande de prêtre	viande de notaire
viande de poète	viande ingénieuse
viande de vierge	viande appateuse
viande commerçante	viande alcoolisée

chut chut chut sauve garde culture bien-être soleil
puberté dans tout ça

Henri Chopin (1953)

"A pre-concrete poem written Nov. 10, 1953, after the perforation of my stomach. It is like a library for meat only." (H.C.)

dans le silence

lance l'air

dans le silence

lance l'air

dans le silence

lance l'air

dans le silence

lance l' rrrrrrrrrr

dans le silence lance l'air

dans le silence

Henri Chopin (1962)

moudur moudur moudur moudur
quiqui quiqui quiqui quiqui
???????? ???????? ????????
durmou durmou durmou durmou
durmou durmou durmou durmou
quiqui quiqui quiqui quiqui
!!!!! !!!!! !!!!! !!!!! !!!
murdou murdou murdou murdou
doumur doumur doumur doumur
??? ??? ??? ??? ??? ??? ???
gloriaàlapoésieconcrètedoux
moudur moudur moudur moudur
durmou durmou durmou durmou
???????????? ????????????
gloriaauxgouvernements?mous
etauxhommesdursettoujoursmm
durmou durmou durmou durmou
ceciestleplanquinquenal?dur
?? ?? ?? ?? ?? ?? ?? ?? ???
rourud roudur roudur roudur
poudud moudud moudud poudud
gloria gloria gloria gloria
???? ???? ???? ????
!!!!! !!!!! !!!!! !!!!! !!!!!
durmou moudur durmou moudur

Henri Chopin (1965)

"A tribute to Mondrian? No, to de Gaulle. The poem is intended to be concretized on a skyscraper to replace the Elysée Palace. The letters are windows." (H.C.)

aaaaaaaaaaaaaaaaaaaaaaaaaaa aaaaaaaaaaaaaaaaaaa aaaaaa
bbbbbbbbbbbbbbbbbbbbbbbbbbbbbbbbbbbb
cccccccc ccccccccccccc ccccccccccccccc ccccccccccccccccc
ddddddddddddddddddddd ddddddddddddddddddddddd
eeeeeeeee eeeeeeeeeeeeeeeeeee eeeeeeeeeeeeeeeeeeeeeeeeeeeeee
ffffffffff ffffffffffffffffffffffff ffffffffffffffffff ffffffffffffff
ggggggg ggggggggggggggggggg gggggggggg gggggggggg
hhhhhh hhhhhhhhhhhhhhhhhhh hhhhhhhh hhhhhhhhhhh
iiiiiiiiii iiiiiiiiiiiiiiiiiiiiiiiiiiiiiiiiiiiiiii iiiiiiiiii iiiiiiiiiiiiiiiiiii
jjjjjjjjj jjjjjjjjjjjjjjjjjjjjjjjjjjjjjjjjjjjj jjjjjjj jjjjjjjjjjjjjjjjjjjjj
kkkkk kkkkkkkkkkkkkkkkkkkkkk kk kkkkkkkkkkkkk
lllllllll lllllllllllllllllllllllllllllllllllllllllllllllllllll llllllllllllllllllllllllllllll
mmmmmmmmmmmmmmmmmmmmm mmmmmmmmmmm
nnnnnnnnnnnnnnnnnnnnnnnnnnnnn nnnnnnnnnnnnnn
ooooo ooooooooo oooooooooooooooooooo oooooooooooooo
oooo ooooooooooo ooooooooooooooooooooo oooooooooooooo
ppp pppppppppppp pppppppppppppppppp ppppppppppp
qqqqqqqqqqqqqqqqq qqqqqqqqqqqqqqqqqq qqqqqqqqqq
rrrrrrrrrrrrrrrrrrrrrrrrr rrrrrrrrrrrrrrrrrrrrrrrrr rrrrrrrrrrrrr
SSSSSSSSSSSSSSS sssssssssssssssssssss *SSSSSSS*
ttttttttttttttttttttttttt ttttttt ttttttttttttttttt ttttttttt
UUUUUUUUUUUUU UUU UUUUUUUUUUU uuuuu
vvvvvvvvvvvvvvvvvv vvv vvvvvvvvvvvvvvvvv vvvvv
wWwWwWwWwWwWwWW wW wwWwWwWwWwW WwW
xxxxxxxxxxxxxxxxxxxxxxxxx x xxxxxxxxxxxxxxxxxx xxxx
zzzzzzzzzzzzzzzzzzzzzzzzzzzzzzzzzzzzzzzzzzzzzzzzzzzzzz zzzzz

ABCDEFGHIJKLMNOPQRSTUVWXZ
il manque toujours l'y
yyyyyyyyyyyyyyyyyyyyyyyyyyyyyyyyyyyyyyyyyyyy
q u e l l e i m p o r t a n c e

Henri Chopin (1965)

First published in the *Between Poetry and Painting* catalogue of the Institute of Contemporary Arts in London in 1965, this poem has since been mounted on a gigantic canvas. It was conceived as a monument to be erected on a white wall. The original was executed in three colors.
In the French review *Approches*, the poem was printed with the title *"le dernier poème concret."*

r
rrr
règle
rrègler
rrrèglerr
rrrrèglerrr
rrrrrèglerrrr
rrrrrrèglerrrrr
rrrrrrrèglerrrrrr
rrrrrrrrèglerrrrrrr
rrrrrrrrrèglerrrrrrrr
rrrrr rrrrèglerrr rrrrr
rrrrr rrrrrèglerrrr rrrrr
rrrrr rrrrrrèglerrrrr rrrrr
rrrrr rrrrrrrèglerrrrrr rrrrr
rrrrr rrrrrrrrèglerrrrrrr rrrrr
rrrrr rrrrrrrrrèglerrrrrrrr rrrrr
rrrrr rrrrrrrrrrèglerrrrrrrrr rrrrr
rrrrrrrrrrrrrrrrèglerrrrrrrrrrrrrrrr
rrrrrrrrrrrrrrrrègle**rrrrrrrrrrrrrrrr**
rrrrr rrrrrrrrrrèglerrrrrrrrr rrrrr
rrrrr rrrrrrrrrèglerrrrrrrr rrrrr
rrrrr rrrrrrrrè**glerrrrrrr rrrrr**
rrrrr rrrrrrrèglerrrrrr rrrrr
rrrrr rrrrrrèglerrrrr rrrrr
rrrrr rrrrrèglerrrr rrrrr
rrrrr rrrrèglerrr rrrrr
rrrrr rrrèglerr rrrrr
rrrrr rrègler rrrrr
rrrrrrrèglerrrrrr
rrrrrrèglerrrrr
rrrrrèglerrrr
rrrrèglerrr
rrrèglerr
rrègler
règle
rrr
r

le vrai poème-concret

Henri Chopin, *"la règle et les règles de ma femme"* (1966)
la règle = the rule
les règles = menstrual periods
In the original, the bottom half of the poem was printed in red.

Carlfriedrich Claus, "Poetic Syntax in Relation to Prose" (1959)

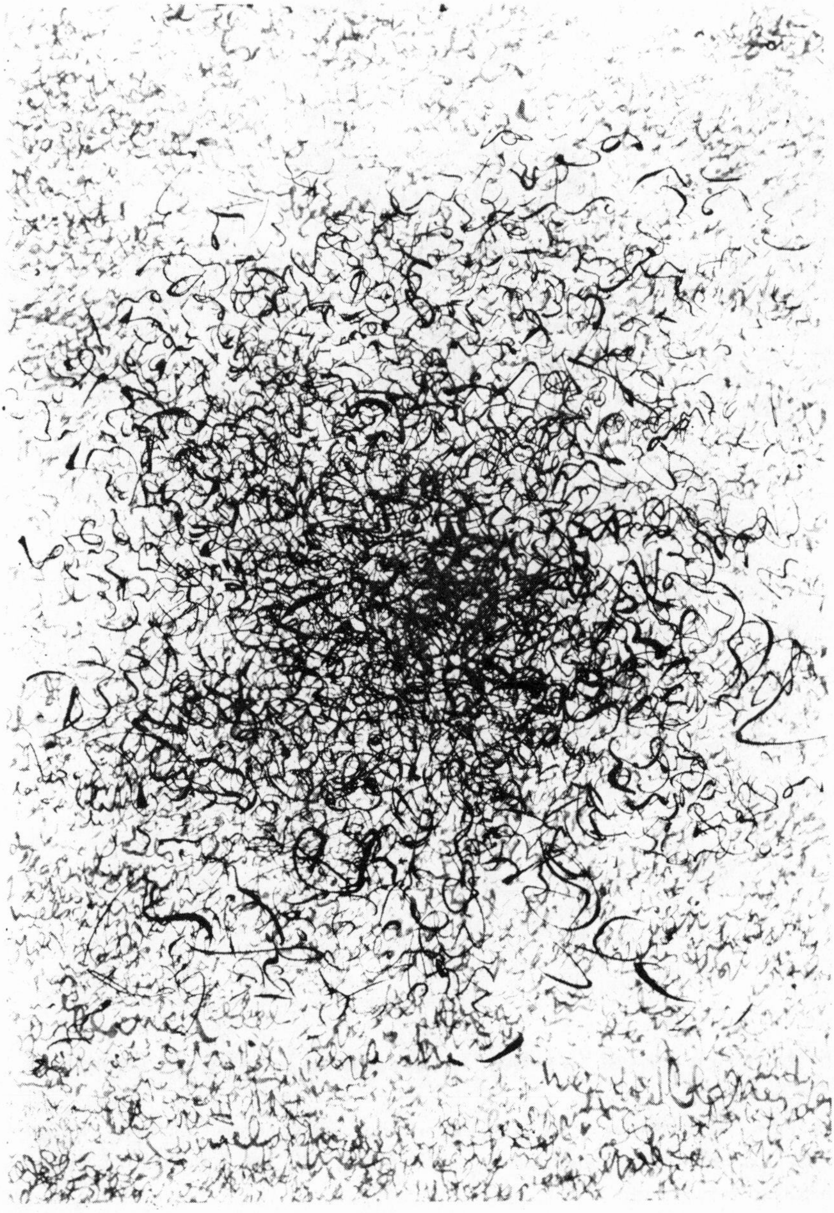

Carlfriedrich Claus, "Verbal Daydream on the Higher Threshold" (1962–63)

This reproduction shows a phase of the original, which consists of three transparent sheets, worked on front and back, and a fourth with the "nucleus" of the poem. On facing page, another phase.

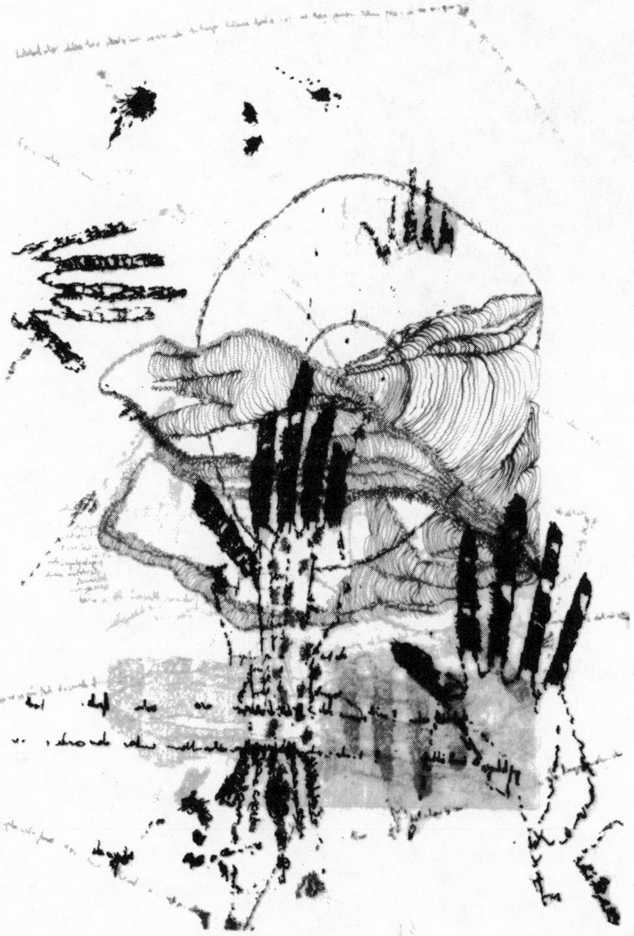

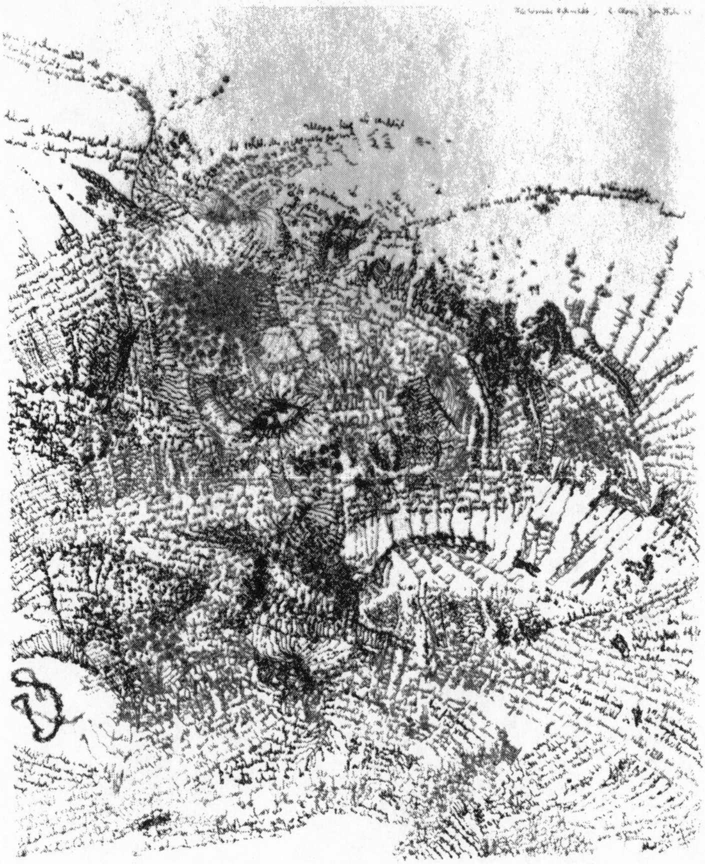

Carlfriedrich Claus, "Allegorical Essay: for Werner Schmidt" (1965)

Front-side view.

On facing page, a detail, full scale.

grin
grin
grin
grin
grim
gay green
grey green
gangrene
ganglia
grin
grin
grin

Bob Cobbing (1965)

"Bob Cobbing's poem was originally conceived in a column with all the g's justified on the left-hand side, and the bow shape was adopted later to fit the square format. The crucial point in this particular poem is the contrast in meaning between vaguely similar sounding words starting with g—grin grim, gay gray—which suggests associations with black humour. It is one of a series of poems for each letter of the alphabet, and Cobbing refers to it basically as a sound poem of which this interpretation is a visual variant." (Jasia Reichart, in introduction to **concrete poetry britain canada united states**)

wordrow   worn row
wombat tab mow
womb mow   wort row
weser re-sew
wolf flow
wolf-dog god flow
won't now
wonder red now
wordrow

drown word   drawn ward
ward draw   prawn warp
beware era web
ebor draw wardrobe
yawn way   yaws sway
yawl way   trawl wart
west india aid nit sew
wollaston not sallow
drownword

wordrow   wad daw
walhalla allah law
waler re law   waster fretsaw
war raw   warsaw was raw
wayward draw yaw   warder red raw
wordrow

drownword   wordrow
wasp saw   way yaw
walnut tun law   walton not law
west sew   wend new   wed dew
weft few   won now   wen new
wordrow   drownword

Bob Cobbing (1966)

The poem consists of four palindromes or anacyclics—"probably the 1st ever to alliterate," according to Dom Sylvester Houédard, who hails Cobbing as the major sound poet in England.

Bob Cobbing (1966)

Like the more complex poems in this genre, a deceptively simple series keeps becoming something else. Sound poets, however, are not punsters. Punsters work from the outside, imposing a touch of chaos on workaday words. The sound poet works from inside, with a stick of dynamite, and lets the pieces fall where they may, without the slightest regard for the discipline of story-telling.

wan
do
tree
fear
fife
seeks
siphon
eat
neighing
den
elephan'
twirl

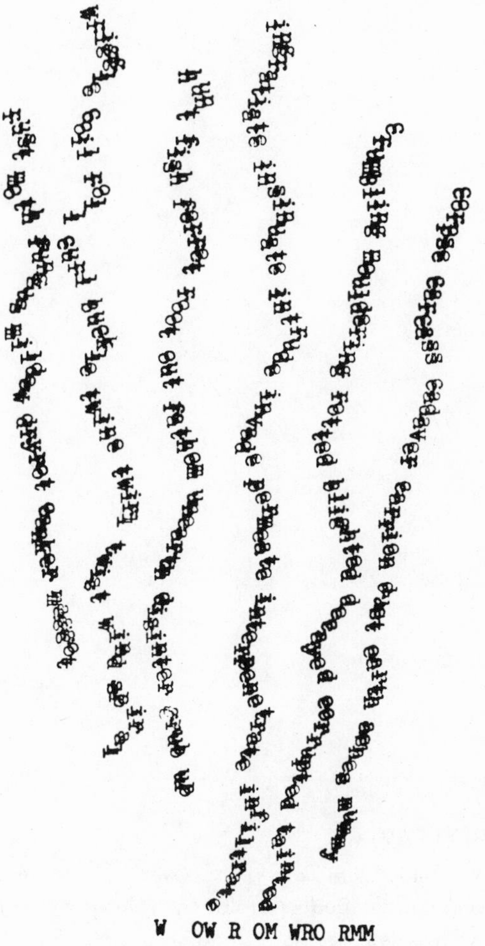
W OW R OM WRO RMM

Bob Cobbing (1966)

"eyear or 'oreil' was title i used for 1st talk (rca) in britain on concrete 1964—poetry tending to appeal between eye-ear—& cobbing's WORM (cf apollinaire's rain?) is a classic—a passion for bonamors & capuchin boneyards helps—but the converging movement down of the 6 lines already gives the inverted-delta sense of wobble—the off-register of each letter—the inweave of WOWROMWRORMM—white invading black like lumps pushed peristaltically thru—tensions between its jadelike pureform & baroque deathcult—this is one cobbing poem merits lavish production." (Dom Sylvester Houédard, in introduction to **Extra Verse No. 17**)

Reinhard Döhl (1962)

In German, *Nil* = Nile. "Nile colors," however, cannot render the *nil/nihil* relationship of the original. A rough translation, column by column: blue sea, white sea, black sea, yellow sea, red sea, dead sea; blue Nile, white Nile; blue man, white man, black man, yellow man, red man, dead man; blue skin, white skin, black skin, yellow skin, red skin, dead (flayed) skin; bluebeard, paleface, blackass, japs, redskin.

	nilfarben			
blaues meer	**blauer nil**	**blauer mann**	**blaue haut**	**blaubart**
weisses meer	**weisser nil**	**weisser mann**	**weisse haut**	**bleichgesicht**
schwarzes meer		**schwarzer mann**	**schwarze haut**	**blackarsch**
gelbes meer		**gelber mann**	**gelbe haut**	**japs**
rotes meer		**roter mann**	**rote haut**	**rothaut**
totes meer		**toter mann**	**totgehaut**	
	nihil			

pfelApfelApfelApfel
pfelApfelApfelApfelApfelA
felApfelApfelApfelApfelApfe
ApfelApfelApfelApfelApfelApf
pfelApfelApfelApfelApfelApfel
lApfelApfelApfelApfelApfelApfe
pfelApfelApfelApfelApfelApfel
ApfelApfelApfelApfelApfelApfe
felApfelApfelApfelApfelApfel
pfelApfelApfelApfelApfelAp
elApfelApfelApfelWurmAp
elApfelApfelApfelApfel
pfelApfelApfelApfel
felApfelApfelA
felApfelA

Reinhard Döhl (1965)

Pattern poem with an elusive intruder.

yretsym rettib a si evol love is a bitter mystery
tsim rettib a si evol love is a bitter mist
rettib a si evol love is a bitter
tib a si evol love is a bit
a si evol love is a
s revol lover s
hgual laugh

hgual laugh
s revol lover s
a si evol love is a
tib a si evol love is a bit
rettib a si evol love is a bitter
tsim rettib a si evol love is a bitter mist
yretsym rettib a si evol love is a bitter mystery
yretsym rettib a si evol love is a bitter mystery
tsim rettib a si evol love is a bitter mist
rettib a si evol love is a bitter
tib a si evol love is a bit
a si evol love is a
s revol lover s
hgual laugh

Reinhard Döhl (1965)

Typographically rendered by Hansjörg Mayer.

menschenskind mankind
menschenkind makind
menschekind akind
menschkind kind
mensckind mkind
menskind mekind
menkind menkind
mekind menskind
mkind mensckind
kind menschkind
mkind menschekind
makind menschenkind
mankind menschenskind

Reinhard Döhl (1966)

menschenskind = man alive!
menschenkind = mankind

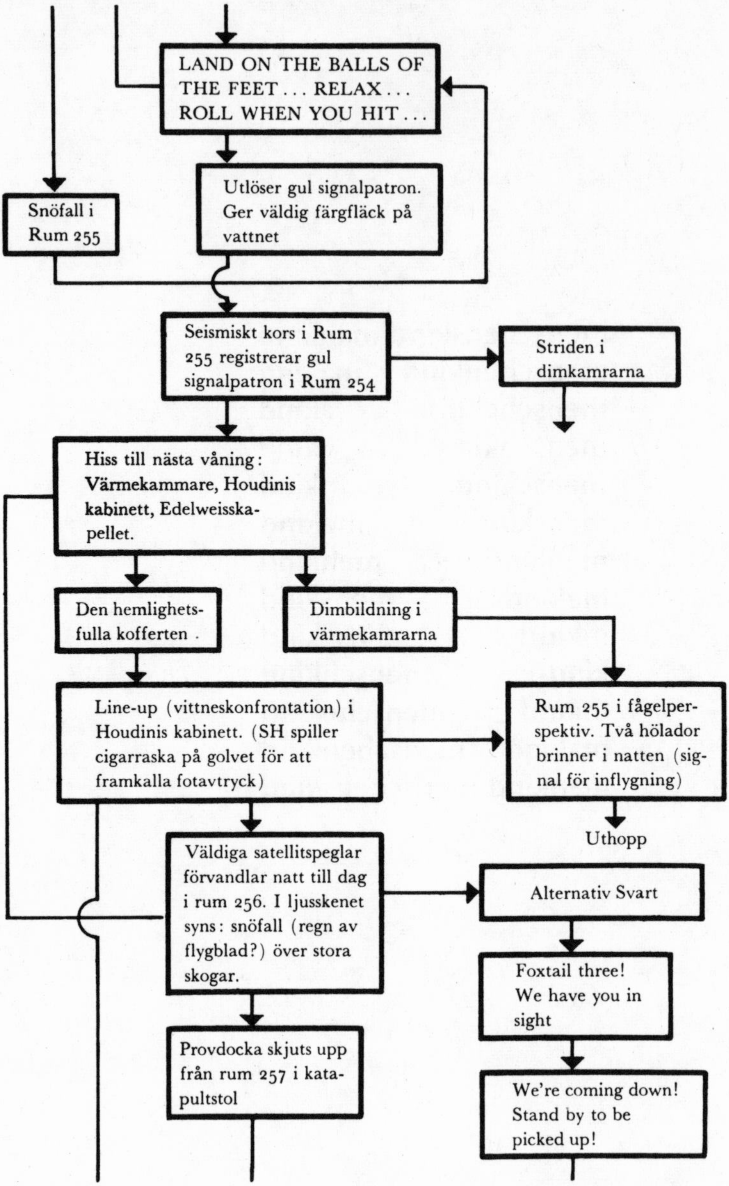
LAND ON THE BALLS OF THE FEET . . . RELAX . . . ROLL WHEN YOU HIT . . .
Snöfall i Rum 255
Utlöser gul signalpatron. Ger väldig färgfläck på vattnet
Seismiskt kors i Rum 255 registrerar gul signalpatron i Rum 254
Striden i dimkamrarna
Hiss till nästa våning: Värmekammare, Houdinis kabinett, Edelweisskapellet.
Den hemlighetsfulla kofferten .
Dimbildning i värmekamrarna
Line-up (vittneskonfrontation) i Houdinis kabinett. (SH spiller cigarraska på golvet för att framkalla fotavtryck)
Rum 255 i fågelperspektiv. Två hölador brinner i natten (signal för inflygning)
Uthopp
Väldiga satellitspeglar förvandlar natt till dag i rum 256. I ljusskenet syns: snöfall (regn av flygblad?) över stora skogar.
Alternativ Svart
Foxtail three! We have you in sight
Provdocka skjuts upp från rum 257 i katapultstol
We're coming down! Stand by to be picked up!

Torsten Ekbom (1966)

Ekbom, whose last novel was structured with fifteen game matrices elaborated by computers for two opposing powers, uses flow diagrams and other concepts borrowed from cybernetics in his work in progress, a page of which is reproduced above.

mera
mera saker
mera saker av marginalen
mera saker av marginalen som ja
mera saker av marginalen som ja och
mera saker av marginalen som ja och skallskinande
mera saker av marginalen som ja och skallskinande
mera saker av marginalen som ja och skallskinande gröda
mera saker av marginalen som ja och skallskinande gröda på
mera saker av marginalen som ja och skallskinande gröda på livsföreståndare

Öyvind Fahlström, from *Morgon* (1952)

					is- o. tå-		
			ring		pallen	u-	urr
		vilt	nära	jumper			aska
	skriv		ovana		ändar	yra	
ring	glöd	ovan				bollar	
	bollar				ovan	*nypa*	hopp
		i is-					
		o. tape-				pekoral-	
		hallen	eter	ovan		finger	
					pekoral-		
ön			bo	löst	finger		
ur	åker	askar		famnar			

	löst			ovana	BO	ändar	
närande		askar			ring		yra
	ö			*åker*		ringen	buren
			pekfing-				
			rets	*vakna*	åskådare		ovana
ovana		ur	slunga	slunga			
bo	ringa		ur			askar	
					applåd-		
eter		famnar			åska		lös
	eter	buren	om			nära	

Öyvind Fahlström, from *Nyarsklockorna* (1954)
Fragment of a permutational poem.

ithmetical poem

and three variations

meinteufel
fuego
druck
wenn
seesaw
hush
tap
\+ hugo
notit
hug
oroscopo
the
coccodrillo

---

cmoeciocnrotsodefdensruurwehhocifeuesututhotlegcnasagiuphlloknwhpotgoeo

CMO ! ECI OCN ROT SOD? EF DENSRU URWEH. HOC IF EU ESUTUT
HOT LEG. CNA ! SAG IUPHL LOKN WH POT, GO EO !

C MOE ? CIOC N ROTS. ODE F DEN SRU. UR WEH HOC IF! EU ES
U TUT HO T LEG. C...NA SAG I? UPHL LOKN WHP OT. GO! E. O...

C! MO E. CIO CN ROT. SOD EFD EN SRU. URW EH? HO CIF. E.
UES UT UT HOT L EG. CNAS A GI ? UP. HL. LOK N WHP.
OT GO E. O?

Carl Fernbach-Flarsheim (1966)

s s

r r

a a

e e

l l

s s l l

r r a a

a a s s

t h e h o r i z o n

s s

r r

a a

e e

l l

l l

o f h o l l a n d

Ian Hamilton Finlay, "The Horizon of Holland" (1963)

"The horizon of Holland 'is all ears.' Ears, or the upthrust arms of the windmills. The poem was first constructed—fifteen feet long and six high—in a garden in Easter Ross, Scotland. It had a yellowish framework, blue letters—and the air of a giraffe." (I.H.F.)

Green Waters
Blue Spray
Grayfish

Anna T
Karen B
Netta Croan

Constant Star
Daystar
Starwood

Starlit Waters
Moonlit Waters
Drift

Ian Hamilton Finlay (1963)

"The collage uses 'real' elements in an artificial art-context. Here, the poem is made entirely from the names of actual trawlers, registered at the fishing-ports of Aberdeen, Lowestoft, Milford Haven, etc. The tension is not only between the printed poem and the 'real' names but between it and the conventional sea-lyric which it almost suggests." (I.H.F.)

p l e u r e
p l e u t
p l e u r e
p l e u t
p l e u r e
p l e u t
p l e u r e
p l e u t
p l e u r e
p l e u t
p l e u r e
p l e u t
p l e u r e
+
p a r a -
p l u i e

Ian Hamilton Finlay (1963)

"It is raining, he is crying. Why? '*Ce deuil est sans raison . . .* ' as in Verlaine's *Ariettes Oubliées.*' " (I.H.F.)

The poem splashes so audibly the poet has supplied the reader with an umbrella.

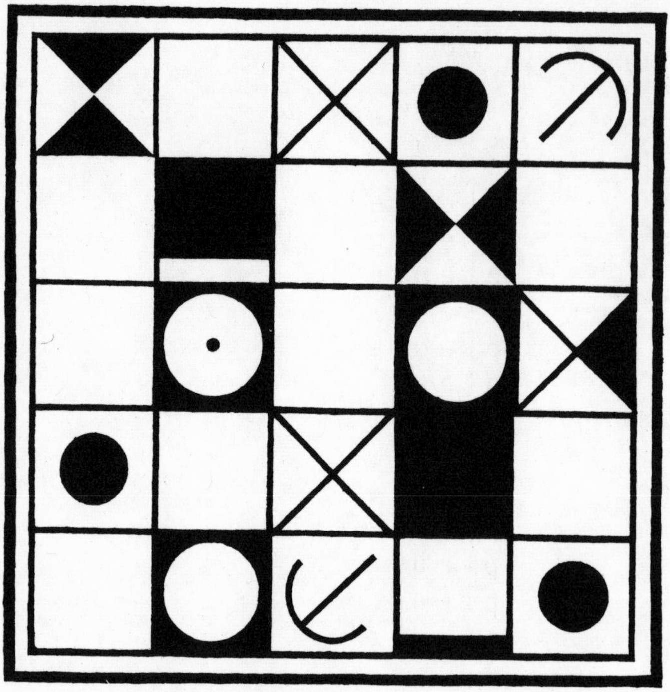

Lexical Key

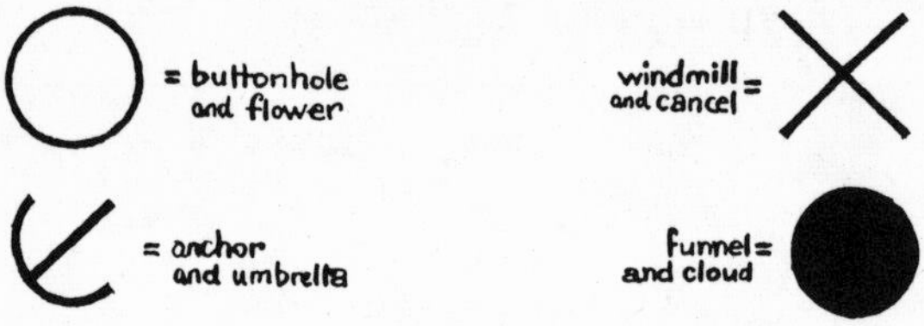
= buttonhole
and flower
windmill =
and cancel
= anchor
and umbrella
funnel =
and cloud

Ian Hamilton Finlay, "Semi-idiotic poem"

A semi-idiotic contribution to the semiotic or code-poem genre invented by Décio Pignatari and Luiz Angelo Pinto. See page 254.

Ian Hamilton Finlay (1963)

"The 'XM poem' is less concrete than 'fauve.' A little burn (stream) flows with a sound which suggests tunes on a mouth-organ. Its path is denoted by the x's and m's, the m's being the sound and the x's a windmill, as well as the conventional sign for kisses—of light on water, perhaps—and signs of happiness. Different sizes and kinds of type suggest the altering nature of the water." (I.H.F.)

m
Mm
x
m
mMm
x
m
mm
m
mm
x
MmM
mm
m
m
mm
m
x
mmm
m
m
mm
x
m
mmMm
m
x
m
mm
m
this
is
the
little
burn
that
plays
its
mm
mMm
m
mmouth-
organ
by
the
m
mm
mmm
mMm
mill
x
mm
Mmm

Ian Hamilton Finlay (1964)

"A lullaby—'a little poem to put your eyes to sleep a little.' It ends where it begins, and it is not sheep that are being counted but boats." (I.H.F.)

A

... blue boat
a brown sail

LITTLE

a brown boat
a green sail

TO PUT

a green boat
a black sail

YOUR EYES

a black boat
a blue sail

TO SLEEP

a...

LITTLE...

a a a a a
c c c c
r r r r r
o o o o
b b b b b
a a a a
t t t t t
s s s s
t t t t t
a a a a
b b b b b
o o o o
r r r r r
c c c c
a a a a a

Ian Hamilton Finlay (1964)

"Isolated, single letters are pattern but letters joined in words (as these are) are direction. Those in the 'acrobats' poem are both, behaving like the real circus acrobats who are now individual units, now—springing together—diagonals and towers. Properly, the poem should be constructed of cut-out letters, to occupy not a page but an entire wall above a children's playground." (I.H.F.)

Ian Hamilton Finlay (1964)

"The boat is at sea (ring of waves)—fishing (row of nets)—but in coastal waters (string of lights)—landing its catch from a seine-net (row of fish, ring of nets)—returning (row of roofs)—the crew taking home some fish threaded on string (string of fish). The 'ring of light' is the lamp, and culture, as opposed to nature's 'ring of waves' at the start of the poem. (A companion work, where the halos are explicit, is Marsden Hartley's 'Fishermen's Last Supper')." (I.H.F.)

ring *of* waves

row *of* nets

string *of* lights

row *of* fish

ring *of* nets

row *of* roofs

string *of* fish

ring *of* light

the little leaf *falls*
the little fish *leaps*

the little fish *falls*
the little leaf *leaps*

the little fish *leaps*
the little leaf *falls*

the little leaf *falls*
the little fish *leaps*

★

the little fish *falls*
the little fish *leaps*

the little fish *leaps*
the little leaf *falls*

the little leaf *leaps*
the little fish *falls*

the little leaf *falls*
the little fish *leaps*

★

the little fish *leaps*
the little leaf *falls*

the little fish *falls*
the little leaf *leaps*

the little leaf *leaps*
the little fish *falls*

the little leaf *falls*
the little fish *leaps*

Ian Hamilton Finlay, "3 Happenings" (1965)

"Are Happenings sometimes wearisome? This is a *plein air* or out-of-door one. A leaf falls, a fish rises. The breeze blows, the river ripples. It is all, as they say, happening—and not only once, but again and again." (I.H.F.)

star
star
star
star
star
star
star
star
star
star
star
star
steer

Ian Hamilton Finlay (1966)

There are so many stars—which single star shall we choose to steer by? The poem presents in an undidactic way the ideas of clarity, resolution, and choice." (I.H.F.)

Ian Hamilton Finlay (1966)

"The poem is one image in two parts—a mere list of nets, all but the first of which are fishing-nets; followed by the single word 'planet,' with its lonely seas, set in lonelier space." (I.H.F.)

stack net

ring net

seine net

salmon net

drift net

trawl net

herring net

planet

Ian Hamilton Finlay (1966)

"The repeated letters of 'wave' seem to move from left to right, where they meet massed letters of the word 'rock,' which emerge strongly and clearly. Where the letters meet and are superimposed they suggest the third word, 'wrack' (seaweed), and the thickened stems of the letters suggest, visually, seaweedy rocks. The poem is 'about' two opposing forces, but, being a poem, presents them in equipoise, resolved." (I.H.F.)

The poem was executed on glass. This photograph, by Patric Eager, was first published on the cover of *The Beloit Poetry Journal,* Volume 17, No. 1, Fall 1966.

rockrock
rockrockrock

Sleep	like a log	lie	sleep	to sleep
fall	like a stone	fall	to fall	to sleep
lie	like a rug	sleep	to lie	to sleep

log		tree	chair	to sleep
stone		river	garden	to sleep
rug			walk	to sleep

body	immerse	sleep	sleep	to sleep
condition	motionless	sleep	sleep	to sleep
interval	inactive	sleep	sleep	to sleep

Larry Freifeld (1966)

God bless america I love you stars & stripes forever
and why not gloom not the devil knows despair and why
not remembering for a moment the stars & stripes forever

Retreaded	the	wheels of	the tanks
beheaded	the	knight of	the time
capitulated	the	throne of	the
decapitated	the		
delirious	the		
dismal	the		daring

---

alone she says he says alone you should live not alone but
alone you know not lonely neither but "come live with me
and be my love" now not with no time for me J. not early
with nowhere to go not Peter blew my cool but cool to the
end of my cool until the hot of her uncool holds me really
he digs him turns her on really knows where its at but not
hip like desperate hip who anyone fda fbi fears knowing not
whos hip nor cool
Don't hang me love I'm cool but not <u>that</u> cool

---

the	house			
the	house	in the house		
the	house	inthe house	is a place	in her house
the	castle		is a room	in his house
			all the rooms	in that house
the	house	in he lives	the place	in which house
			is a place	
		of his house	in the bedroom	in a house
the	house	where he lives	is a bed	
the	bed	in the bed		in her bed
the	bed	in the bed	he sleeps	in his bed
the	bed	in the bed	she sleeps	in his bed
the	bed	in the bed		

Larry Freifeld (1967)

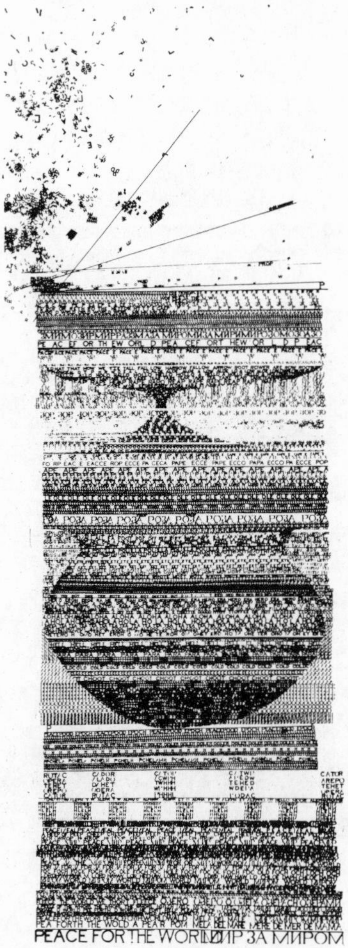
PEACE FOR THE WORLD МИР ЗА МИРОМ

John Furnival, "The Fall of the Tower of Babel" (1964)

"The first few drawings that I did around the Babel theme were architectural: composed of a single house unit which was repeated almost ad infinitum until the city itself lost its form and became megalopolis. These drawings were in the form of plans. I then decided that after all it was the confusion of noises which made Babel significant, not the mammoth architecture, although the two are infinitely related, so I started doing elevation drawings, made up of layer upon layer of

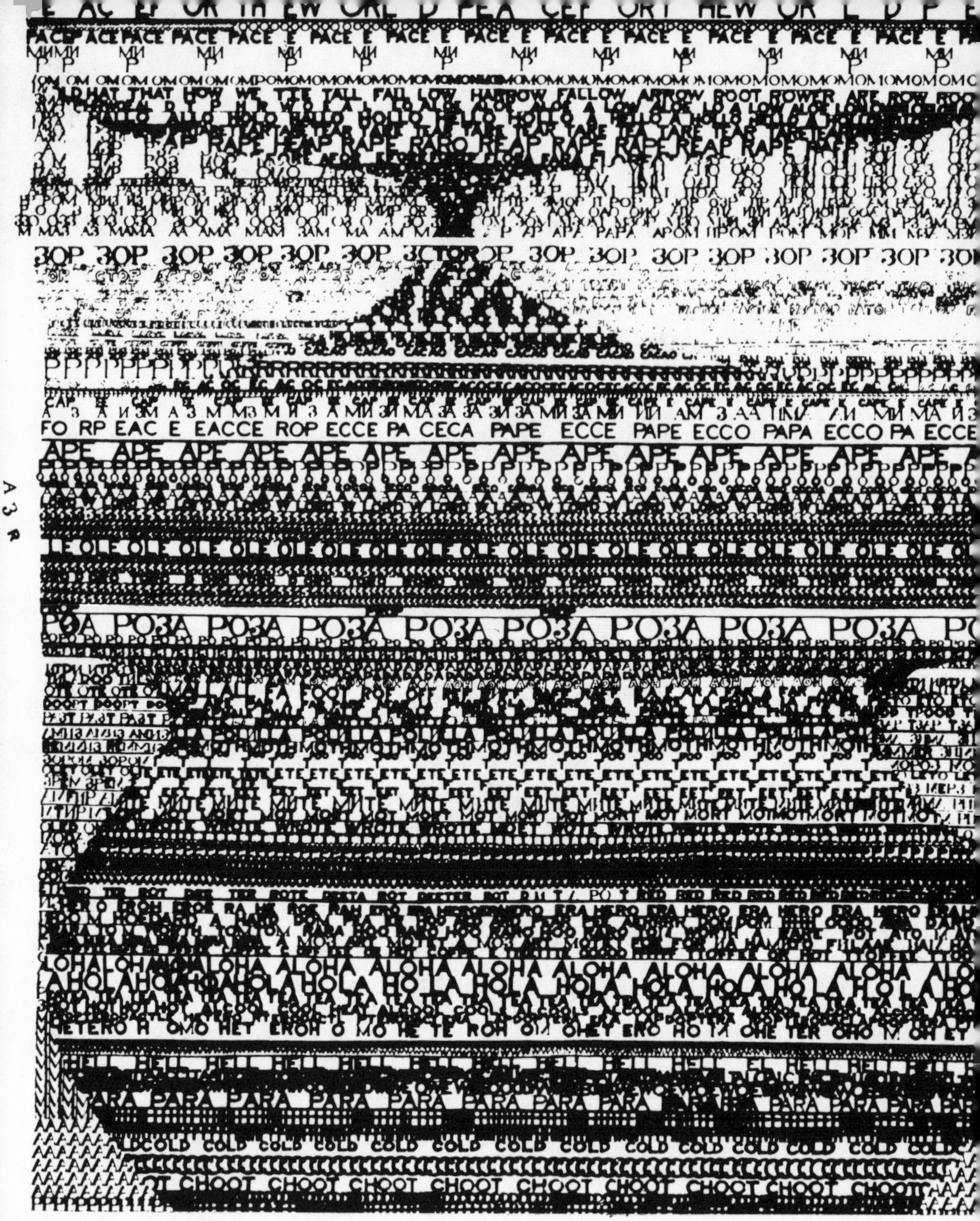
FO RP EAC E EACCE ROP ECCE PA CECA PAPE ECCE PAPE ECCO PAPA ECCO PA ECCE

John Furnival, "The Fall of the Tower of Babel" (continued from preceding page)
Close-up.

John Furnival, "The Fall of the Tower of Babel" (continued from facing page)
Detail.

visual noises. The first one that I did of this kind (**The Fall of the Tower of Babel**) was composed of the slogan 'Peace for the World' and its Russian equivalent '*Meer za Meerom*,' both of which start out at the bottom of the tower pretty clearly, but as they progress up the tower become more and more intermingled, forming odd words in other languages, or just meaningless noises, until at the top even the different characters combine and, rather than fall into a heap on the ground, eventually evaporate into nothingness."

a l l e s

Heinz Gappmayr (1962)

alles = all

"The new poetry does not describe a situation outside of language, but refers to itself, to its concepts, and to the connection between these concepts and the signs necessary to its conveyance." (H.G.)

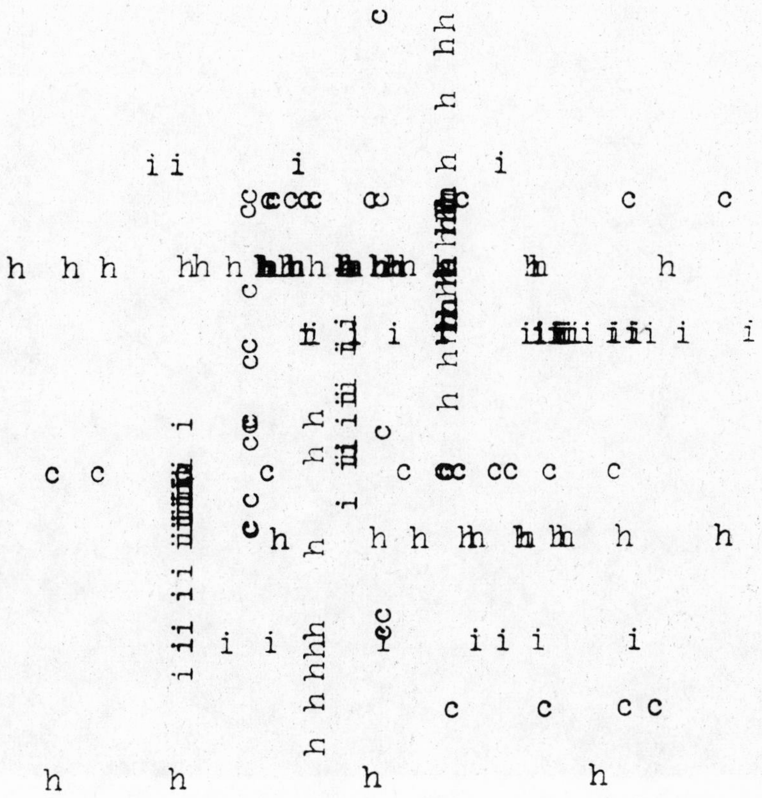

Heinz Gappmayr (1965)
One of a series of *ich* poems.

ver

Heinz Gappmayr (1966)

ver = an inseparable prefix added to German verbs, and nouns and adjectives derived from them, with the idea of removal, loss, untoward action, using up, change, reversal, etc.

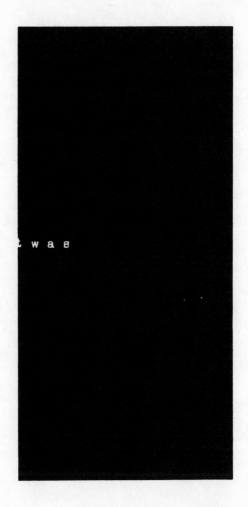
t w a s

Heinz Gappmayr (1966)

etwas = something

sind (sind)

~~sind~~

"sind"

Heinz Gappmayr (1964)

sind = first and third person plural present indicative of *sein,* to be.

"The text is a fixed connection between thought and physical reality, a unity of concept and sign, and each change of the sign (size, placement, etc.) and its material condition (color, type face, paper) changes the concept." (H.G.)

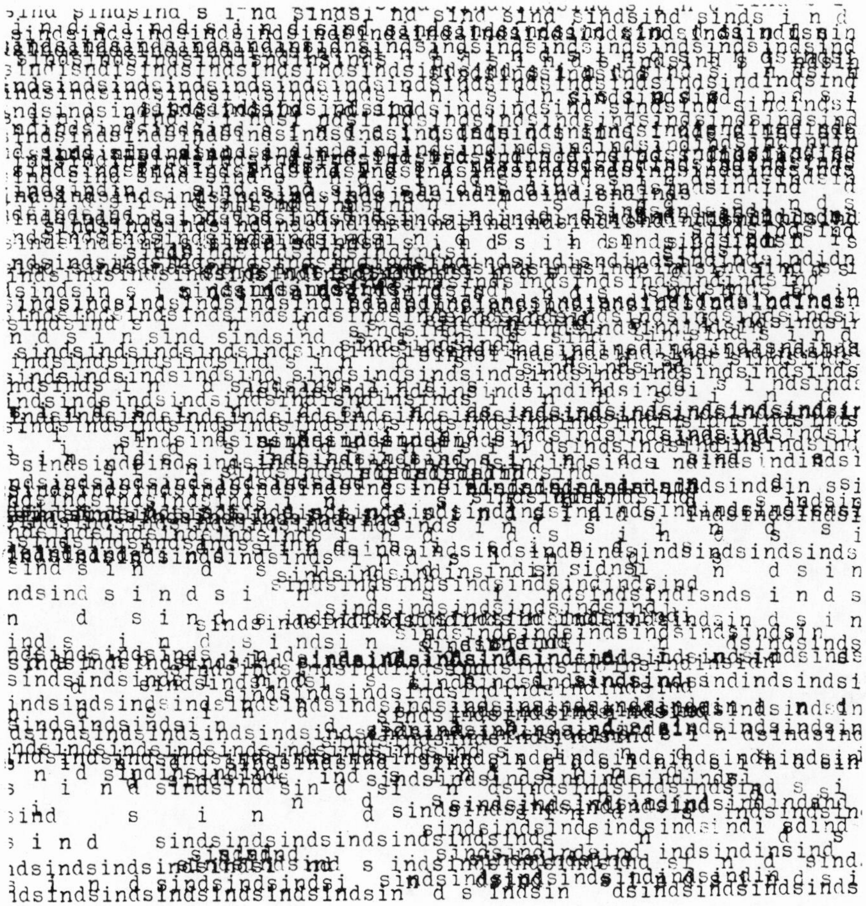

Heinz Gappmayr (1964)

SOLEIL

SOLEIL

SOLEIL

SOLEIL

SOLEIL

SOLEIL

SOLEIL

SOLEIL

SOLEIL

SOLEIL

SOLEIL

Pierre Garnier, "*Grains de Pollen*" (1962)

In this poem by the founder of the internationalist Spatialist movement, the title, "Grains de Pollen," pinpoints the activity of the sun (*soleil*).

sssssssssssssssssssssssssssssssss
sssssssssssssssssssssssssssssssss
sssssssssssssssssssssssssssssssss
sssssssssssssssssssssssssssssssss

oooooooooooooooooooooooooooo
oooooooooooooooooooooooooooo
oooooooooooooooooooooooooooo
oooooooooooooooooooooooooooo

lllllllllllllllllllllllllllllllllllllllllllll
lllllllllllllllllllllllllllllllllllllllllllll
lllllllllllllllllllllllllllllllllllllllllllll
lllllllllllllllllllllllllllllllllllllllllllll

eeeeeeeeeeeeeeeeeeeeeeeeeeeee
eeeeeeeeeeeeeeeeeeeeeeeeeeeee
eeeeeeeeeeeeeeeeeeeeeeeeeeeee
eeeeeeeeeeeeeeeeeeeeeeeeeeeee

iiiiiiiiiiiiiiiiiiiiiiiiiiiiiiiiiiiiiiiiiiiiii
iiiiiiiiiiiiiiiiiiiiiiiiiiiiiiiiiiiiiiiiiiiiii
iiiiiiiiiiiiiiiiiiiiiiiiiiiiiiiiiiiiiiiiiiiiii
iiiiiiiiiiiiiiiiiiiiiiiiiiiiiiiiiiiiiiiiiiiiii

lllllllllllllllllllllllllllllllllllllllllllll
lllllllllllllllllllllllllllllllllllllllllllll
lllllllllllllllllllllllllllllllllllllllllllll
lllllllllllllllllllllllllllllllllllllllllllll

e e e e e e e
e e e e e e e
e e e e e e e

a a a a a a a
a a a a a a a
a a a a a a a

u u u u u u u
u u u u u u u
u u u u u u u

Ilse and Pierre Garnier, *"Extension classique des mots 'soleil' et 'eau' "* (1964)

"*Wortverräumlichungen*: we habitually 'see' words as tradition hands them down to us; but if one spreads them out, or extends them, their elements are reanimated. If I write, for example, *sauleille* instead of *soleil* (sun), I shock the French reader, I take him out of his element, I force him to re-examine the language and, in this way, the world. Classical extension works in the spirit of the French language because it augments the tendency to abstraction which this language has developed strongly since the 16th century." (P.G.)

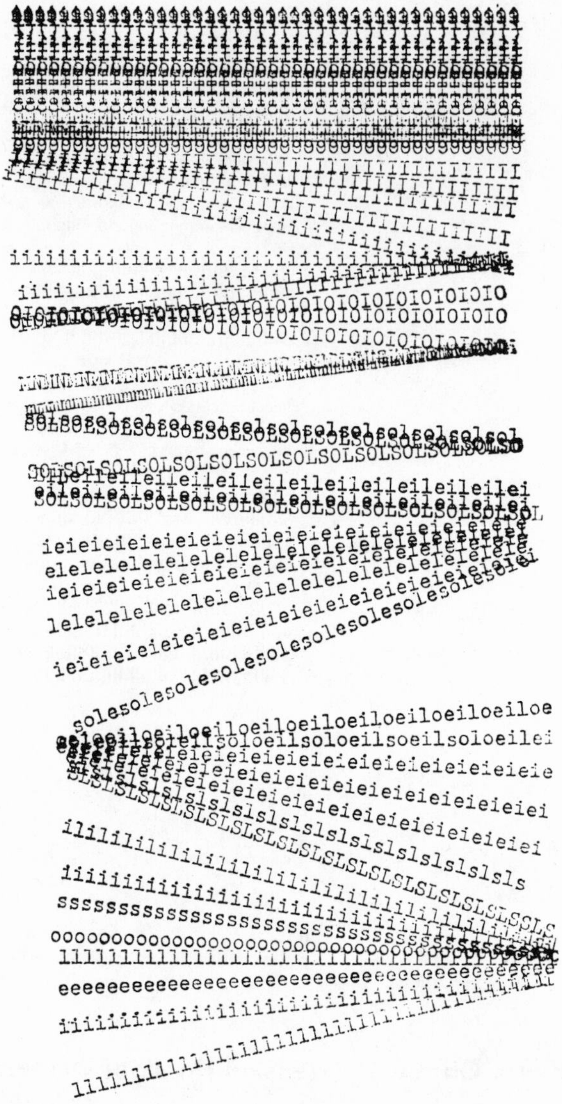

Ilse and Pierre Garnier, *"Extension 2"* (1964)

"The noun *soleil* is rich—it is one of the best for concrete poetry: the impact of its vowels, its consonants, its vibrations and scintillations, at the same time soft and violent. And from this noun spring up other nouns—*île, elle, aile, oeil, io, sol*, etc. —whence this progression radiates in space." (P.G.)

Ilse and Pierre Garnier (1965)

"Light and shadow, vertical and horizontal, the card game of creation; the *i* is the letter that stands out, rises up; the e is the gray letter, always turned in on itself. The two fields of letters confront one another across a breach, that of the 'nothingness' between existences." (P.G.)

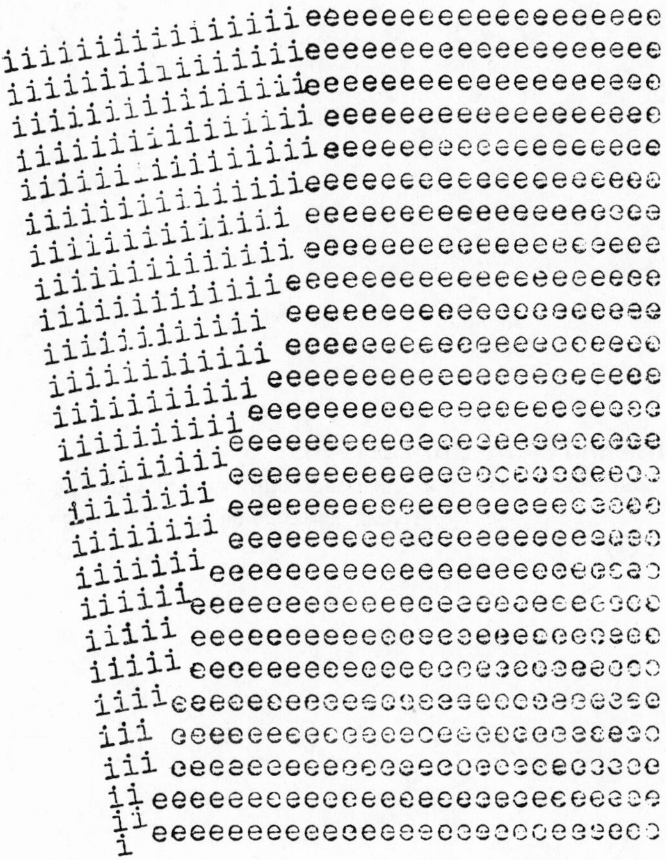

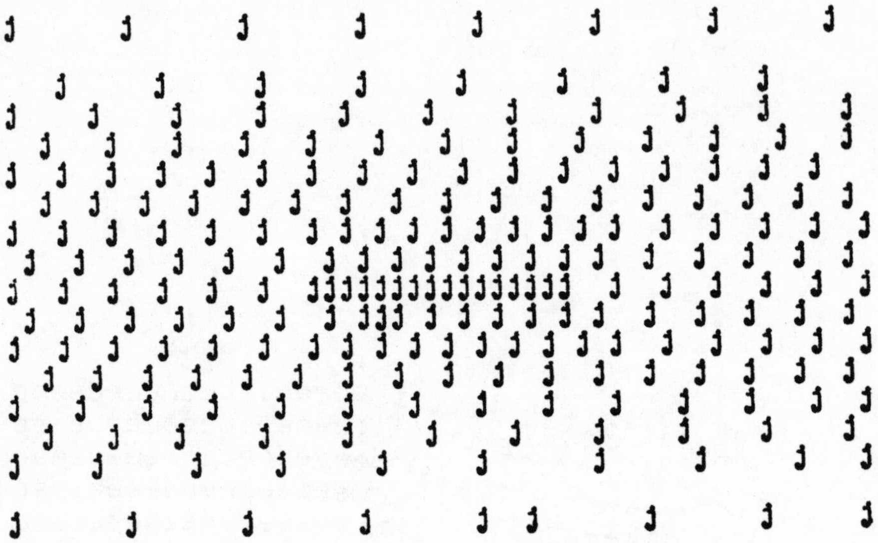

Ilse and Pierre Garnier (1965)

"Combination of *i* and e. Vegetal sign. Musical sign. Concentration and spatialization. Concretions and void. Throughout, a rhythm is given to the white page." (P.G.)

cinemacinemacinemacinemacinemacinemacinem
acinemacinemacinemacinemacinemacinemacine
macinemacinemacinemacinemacinemacinemacin
emacinemacinemacinemacinemacinemacinemaci
nemacinemacinemacinemacinemacinemacinemac
inemacinemacinemacinemacinemacinemacinema
cinemacinemacinemacinemacinemacinemacinem
acinemacinemacinemacinemacinemacinemacine
macinemacinemacinemacinemacinemacinemacin
emacinemacinemacinemacinemacinemacinemaci
nemacinemacinemacinemacinemacinemacinemac
inemacinemacinemacinemacinemacinemacinema
cinemacinemacinemacinemacinemacinemacinem
acinemacinemacinemacinemacinemacinemacine
macinemacinemacinemacinemacinemacinemacin
emacinemacinemacinemacinemacinemacinemaci
nemacinemacinemacinemacinemacinemacinemac
inemacinemacinemacinemacinemacinemacinema

Ilse and Pierre Garnier (1965)

"An attempt to render linguistically the cinematographic play of white (*cin*) and black (*ema*) and the vibration of light on the screen." (P.G.)

```
mariemariemariemariemariemariemarie
mariemariemarie     mariemariemarie
mariemariema          riemariemarie
mariemarie               mariemarie
mariema                    riemarie
marie                         marie
mariema                    riemarie
mariemarie               mariemarie
mariemariema          riemariemarie
mariemariemarie     mariemariemarie
mariemariemariemariemariemariemarie
```

Ilse and Pierre Garnier (1965)

"The name Marie here forms a religious 'ikon,' based on the softness and clarity of the syllables. The diamond shape represents femininity, and in its linguistic context evokes something soft and clear, yet solid in its permanence." (P.G.)

ik pik epeke pik epe
pik bou pik bou pik bou pi
ik bo pik bo pik bo pik bo p
pik epeke pik epeke pik epeke pik epek
pik bo pik bo pik bo pik bo pik
pik epeke pik epeke pik epeke pi
pik arbe pik arbe pik arbe pik a
bo pik bo pik bo pik bo
bo pik arbe pik bo pik bo
pik bo bo epeke pik b
peke epeke pik bo pik epeke pik
pik
ikoutchu pikoutchu pikoutchu pikoutchu pik
ik bo bo bo bo
peke bo pik pik pik
bo arbe bou bou arbe bo
bo bo pik bo pik
k bo arbe arbe
bo bou pikoutchu bo b
veur pik bo piveur piveur
bo pik bo pik
pik bo bo
pikoutchu piveur bo
bo pik bo pik
arbe arbe bo
arbe bo
ik epeke arbe pik pi
pik epeke pikoutchu b
bou pik epeke
bo pik bo bou pik epeke ep
pik epeke pik bo bou pik b
pitver pik epeke pik pik bo pik bo
pitver epeke pik epeke pi
piveur pitver pitver pitver pitv
pik bou piveur pibe
pik pik bo pik bo bou piveur bo
out chu bou bou bou bou
pik epeke pik epeke bou arbe piveur
pik bo pik epeke pik epeke pik bo pik
arbe pik bou pik epeke pi
bo bou pik bo pik bou
pikoutchu arbe pik piveur
pik bo bo pik bo
pik bo pik arb
pik

Pierre Garnier, *"Pik Bou"* (1966)

"In my Picard spatial poems I have used the dialect of my native province. In general, dialects, old languages which live despite bureaucratization, have retained important concrete reserves, while the so-called national languages have developed an abstract vocabulary. Concrete poetry is well suited to these idioms.
The text above (*pik bou* = *pivert* = green woodpecker) shows the vast difference between the Picard dialect and modern French." (P.G.)

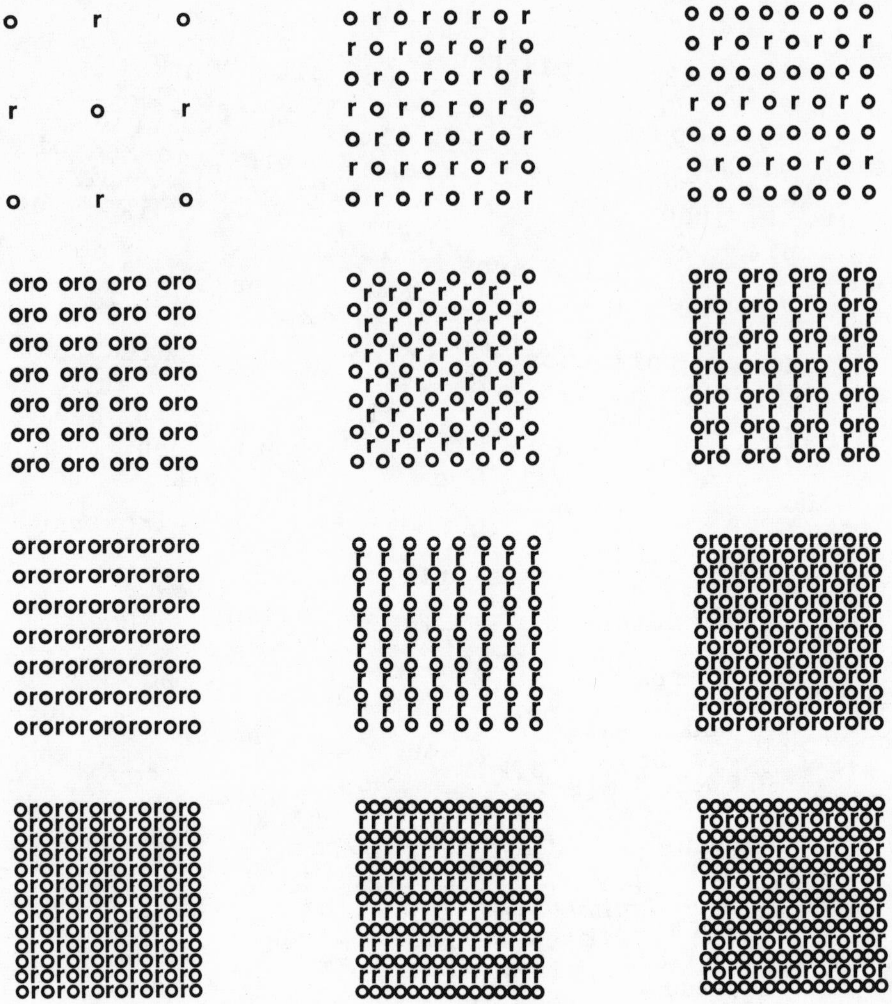

Mathias Goeritz, from *Mensajes de Oro* (1960)

Mathias Goeritz, *"el eco del oro"* (1961)
A concrete poem in iron.
Photo: Kati Horna

avenidas
avenidas y flores

flores
flores y mujeres

avenidas
avenidas y mujeres

avenidas y flores y mujeres y
un admirador

Eugen Gomringer (1951–52)

The earliest constellation by the "father" of concrete poetry, although it was written before the name concrete was applied to the new poetry.

baum
baum kind

kind
kind hund

hund
hund haus

haus
haus baum

baum kind hund haus

Eugen Gomringer (1952)

baum = tree
kind = child
hund = dog

"The constellation, the word-group, replaces the verse. Instead of syntax it is sufficient to allow two, three or more words to achieve their full effect. They seem on the surface without interrelation and sprinkled at random by a careless hand, but looked at more closely, they become the center of a field of force and define a certain scope. In finding, selecting and putting down these words (the poet) creates 'thought-objects' and leaves the task of association to the reader, who becomes a collaborator and, in a sense, the completer of the poem." (E.G.)

you blue
you red
you yellow
you black
you white
you

Eugen Gomringer (1953)

silencio	silencio	silencio
silencio	silencio	silencio
silencio		silencio
silencio	silencio	silencio
silencio	silencio	silencio

Eugen Gomringer (1954)

Eugen Gomringer (1954)

americans and apricots
american apricots
apricot americans
apricots and americans

Eugen Gomringer (1954)

o
bo
blow
blow blow
blow blow blow
blow blow
blow
bo
o o
go so
grow show
grow grow show show
grow grow grow o show show show
grow grow show show
grow show
go so
o o
lo
flow
flow flow
flow flow flow
flow flow
flow
lo
o

Eugen Gomringer (1955)

mist
mountain
butterfly

mountain
butterfly
missed

butterfly
meets
mountain

Eugen Gomringer (1956)

worte = words
sind = are
schatten = shadows
werden = become
spiele = games

worte sind schatten
schatten werden worte

worte sind spiele
spiele werden worte

sind schatten worte
werden worte spiele

sind spiele worte
werden worte schatten

sind worte schatten
werden spiele worte

sind worte spiele
werden schatten worte

b d b und b and b nid

mw mw mw mw
un

a i a i u i a u

bau d bin d b n b d

mw mw mw mw

u i u a u ida nu ai

b du baum w b wind band w

mw i a u

in a n d u m i m

bm wd

au ni

Eugen Gomringer (1960)

An "analysis" of the words *baum* (tree) and *wind* yields a field of sixty-five one-, two-, three- and four-letter groups, which in turn yield many other words and associations.

mensch hcsnem mensch hcsnem
hcsnem mensch hcsnem mensch
ɥɔsuǝɯ ɯǝusɔɥ ɥɔsuǝɯ ɯǝusɔɥ
ɯǝusɔɥ ɥɔsuǝɯ ɯǝusɔɥ ɥɔsuǝɯ

Eugen Gomringer (1960)

mensch = human being, man, person

The mechanics of this constellation reflect something of the complexity of the subject matter. In line 1, *mensch* is printed backwards, forwards, backwards, forwards, so that the first word mirrors the second, the second the third, the third the fourth, and the first and second the third and fourth. The procedure is repeated in line 2, starting off with the backwards spelling. Then, lines 3 and 4 mirror lines 1 and 2.

Eugen Gomringer (1961)

snow is english
snow is international
snow is secret
snow is small
snow is literary
snow is translatable
snow is everywhere
snow is ridiculous
snow is difficult
snow is modern
snow is hindering
snow is senseless
snow is musical
snow is gorgeous
snow is sedimentary
snow is meaningless
snow is elemental
snow is fantastic
snow is curved
snow is unauthorized
snow is disgusting
snow is ignorant
snow is irresistible
snow is rare
snow is exhausting

snow is civil
snow is smooth
snow is amusing
snow is epidemic
snow is hereditary
snow is risky
snow is analysable
snow is satisfactory
snow is catholic
snow is tasteless
snow is elegant
snow is absolute
snow is experimental
snow is neurotic
snow is instructive
snow is selfish
snow is unique
snow is prepared
snow is expensive
snow is alphabetical
snow is unsocial
snow is sexless
snow is political
snow is provisional
snow is predominant

snow is reasonable
snow is violet
snow is distracting
snow is looking
snow is utopian
snow is evangelic
snow is inevitable
snow is cheap
snow is comprehensible
snow is delicious
snow is relative
snow is norwegian
snow is military
snow is comfortable
snow is light
snow is salutary
snow is harmful
snow is cold
snow is offensive
snow is brute
snow is scientific
snow is irregular
snow is indefensible
snow is independent
snow is annoying
snow is sad

snow is enormous
snow is pale
snow is bare-footed
snow is corrupt
snow is cordial
snow is converse
snow is libidinous
snow is permitted
snow is sublime
snow is tawdry
snow is imaginable
snow is abstinent
snow is exact
snow is etymological
snow is fragmentary
snow is honourable
snow is immortal
snow is ancient
snow is illustrative
snow is aristotelian
snow is outside
snow is abstract
snow is divine
snow is white
snow is contradictory

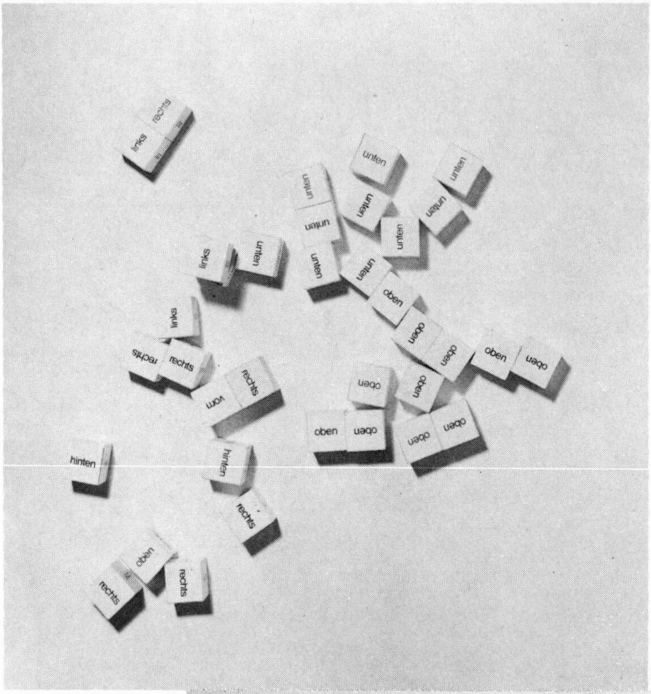

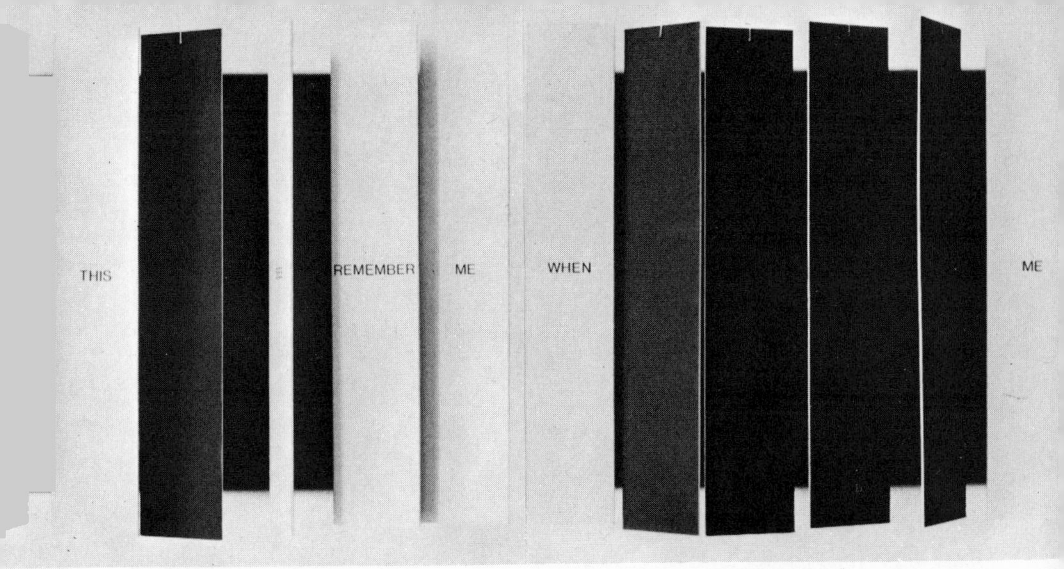
THIS
REMEMBER
ME
WHEN
ME

On facing page: Ludwig Gosewitz (1962-66)

The elements of this linguistic crap game are thirty-six 3cm cubes stamped on all sides. (*oben* = up, *unten* = down, *links* = left, *rechts* = right, *vorn* = in front, *hinten* = behind.)

Above: Ludwig Gosewitz (1966)

A text of Gertrude Stein, *when this you see remember me*, is constantly transformed as the elements turn.

Below: Ludwig Gosewitz (1966)

The method of the previous poem applied to single words, *ich* and *du*.

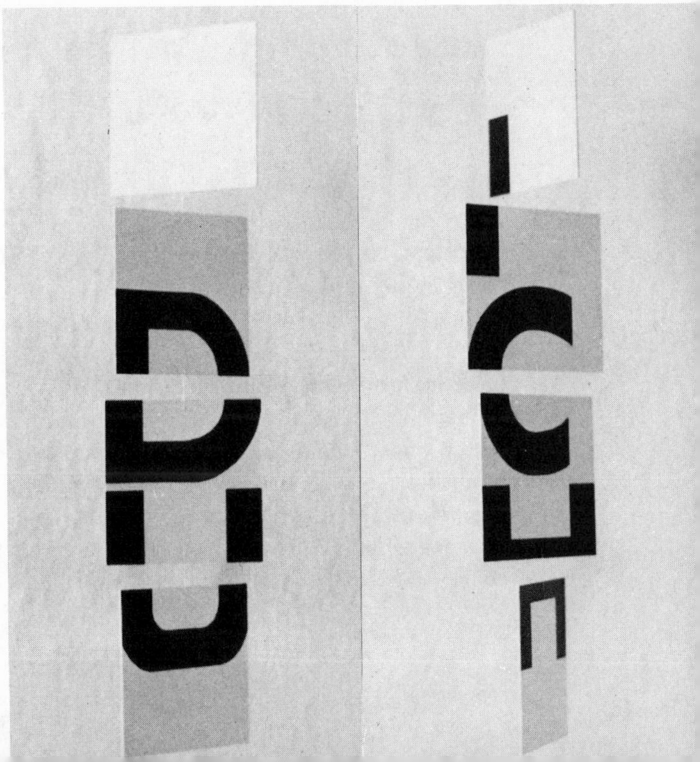

manifest

1 2 3 4 5 6 7 8 9 ; : !

q w e r t z u i o p ü

a s d f g h j k l ö ä

y x c v b n m , . - ?

Bohumila Grögerova and Josef Hiršal (1960–62)

The texts on this and the following two pages are samplings from **job boj**, a vast "workshop" in experimental poetry created by the Czech writers Bohumila Grögerova and Josef Hiršal between 1960 and 1962. This comprehensive manuscript explores the mechanics of language through a body of experiments grouped in twelve sections: the birth of a text; grammatical texts, or constellations evolved from grammatical structures, and the exploration and exploitation of the emotional and associative effect of grammatical endings; logical texts; stochastic texts, made with fragments of foreign poems and prose; syngamic texts, the interpenetration of the elements of literary works through semantics, esthetics or logic; intertexts, composed in mixed languages; linguistic objects in their plastic representation; the

S V O B O D A
V O B O D A S
O B O D A S V
B O D A S V O
O D A S V O B
D A S V O B O
A S V O B O D
F V O B O D A
V O B O D A F
O B O D A F V
B O D A F V O
O D A F V O B
D A F V O B O
A F V O B O D
F R O B O D A
R O B O D A F
O B O D A F R
B O D A F R O
O D A F R O B
D A F R O B O
A F R O B O D
F R E B O D A
R E B O D A F
E B O D A F R
B O D A F R E
O D A F R E B
D A F R E B O
A F R E B O D
F R E E O D A
R E E O D A F
E E O D A F R
E O D A F R E
O D A F R E E
D A F R E E O
A F R E E D O
F R E E D O M

Bohumila Grögerova and Josef Hiršal (1960–62)

svoboda = freedom

An "osmotic" permutational experiment renders a Czech word into an English one.

destruction of proverbs and the construction of new ones with fragments; "scores" or phonetic constellations of certain words; portraits composed with letters and syllables from the names of famous personages; micrograms, or the visual expression of the emotional and semantic effects of words; and osmosis, phenomena observed between the different elements of a language.

on
ona
on
ona
on   a   ona
on a ona
onaona
onaona onaona
onaona onaona
onaonaonaonaonaonaon
aonaonaonaonaonaonaona
onaonaonaonaonaonaonaona
onaonaonaonaonaonaonaona
onaonaonaonaonaonaonaona
onaonaonaonaonaonaonaona
ono

Bohumila Grögerova and Josef Hiršal, "*láska*" (love), 1960–62

on = he
a = and
ona = she
ono = it

¿

v e r

t i c e

d e t e v e r

r e v e r t e

d e t i

a

m i m

?

José Lino Grünewald (1956)

ver = to see

vertice = vertex

de te ver = from seeing you

rever-te = seeing you again

reverte = (it) reverts

de ti a mim = from you to me

pedra
pó pedra pó
sal pedra sal
chão pedra chão
pedra pedra pedra
grão pedra grão
cal pedra cal
só pedra só
pedra

José Lino Grünewald (1957)

pedra = stone
pó = dust
sal = salt
chão = soil, ground
grão = grain
cal = lime
só = only

preto
preto um jato
preto
preto um óleo
preto
preto um fato
preto
preto petróleo nosso
nosso
nosso
nosso
nosso
nosso
nosso
nosso petróleo

José Lino Grünewald (1957)

petróleo = petroleum
preto = black
um jato = a jet
um óleo = an oil
um fato = a fact
nosso = our

"A placard-poem, with a political commitment: the campaign for maintaining Brazilian oil under Brazilian control. Recalls Mayakovsky's agit-plakat techniques." (Haroldo de Campos)

forma
reforma
disforma
transforma
conforma
informa
forma

José Lino Grünewald (1959)

```
vai      e      vem

e                 e

vem      e      vai
```

José Lino Grünewald (1959)

vai e vem = go and come

d u r a s s o l a d o   s o l u m a n o
p e t r i f i n c a d o   c o r p u m a n o
a m a r g a m a d o   f a r d u m a n o
a g r u s u r a d o   s e r v u m a n o
c a p i t a l i e n a d o   g a d u m a n o
m a s s a m o r f a d o   d e s u m a n o

a g e r a v a g e d   m a n s o i l
s t o n e s t i f f e n e d   m a n s f l e s h
b i t t e r b e l o v e d   m a n s b u r d e n
a n g r u s u r e r e d   m a n s b o n d a g e
c a p i t a l i e n a t e d   m a n c a t t l e
m i s m a s s h a p e d   m a n l o s s

José Lino Grünewald (1961)

"Man under the 'usurocracy' of capitalism. The alienating power of money against man. All the words of this piece are grotesque portmanteau words, deformed words. The only non-deformed vocable in this wordlandscape of semantic monstrosities is—by a voluntary paradox—*desumano* (inhuman). A concrete 'usura' canto." (Haroldo de Campos)

English version by Edwin Morgan.

b o i s
b o i s

d o i s
d o i s

d o i s
b o i s

db o i s

José Lino Grünewald, "*dois bois*" (two oxen), 1964

"From digit to ideogram. *d* and *b* like two yoked oxen." (Haroldo de Campos)

I	AM	THAT	I	AM	
I	AM	I	THAT	AM	
I	AM	AM	I		THAT
I	AM	THAT	AM	I	
I	AM	I	AM	THAT	
I	AM	AM	THAT		I

AM	THAT	I	AM		I
AM	THAT		AM	I	I
AM	THAT	I	I	AM	
AM	THAT	I		I	AM
AM	THAT		AM	I	I
AM	THAT		I	AM	I

Brion Gysin (1958)

"Writing is fifty years behind painting. I propose to apply the painters' techniques to writing; things as simple and immediate as collage or montage. Cut right through the pages of any book or newsprint—lengthwise, for example—and shuffle the text. Put them together at random and read the newly constituted message. Do it for yourself. Use any system which suggests itself to you. Take your own words or the words said to be 'the very own words' of anyone else living or dead. You'll soon see that words don't belong to anyone. Words have a vitality of their own and you or anybody can make them gush into action. The repetitive poems set the words spinning off on their own; echoing out as the words of a potent phrase are permutated into an expanding ripple of meaning which they did not seem to be capable of when they were struck and stuck into that phrase. The poets are supposed to liberate the words—not to chain them in phrases. Who told poets they were supposed to think? Poets are meant to sing and to make words sing. Poets have no words 'of their very own.' Writers don't own their words. Since when do words belong to anybody? 'Your very own words' indeed! And who are 'you'?" (B.G., "Statement on the cutup method and permutated poems" (1958), first published in **Fluxus I**, New York 1965.)

THAT I AM I AM
THAT I I AM AM
THAT I AM I AM
THAT I AM AM I
THAT I I AM AM
THAT I AM AM I

I AM I AM THAT
I AM AM I THAT
I AM THAT AM I
I AM THAT I AM
I AM AM THAT I
I AM I AM THAT

AM I I THAT AM
AM I THAT AM I
AM I AM I THAT
AM I I AM THAT
AM I THAT I AM
AM I AM THAT I

THAT AM I AM I
THAT AM AM I I
THAT AM I I AM
THAT AM I I AM
THAT AM AM I I
THAT AM I AM I

AM AM I THAT I
AM AM THAT I I
AM AM I I THAT
AM AM I I THAT
AM AM THAT I I
AM AM I THAT I

I I AM THAT AM
I I THAT AM AM
I I AM THAT AM
I I AM THAT AM
I I THAT AM AM
I I AM AM THAT

NET and
favor
LATE
HEY
OH and OH and 4 1/4
ATE
or
HEY
or
in
OH
OH
LATE 3
or KILL
in
in
OH
OH
OH
OH
GOOD FOR
or
flavor
in
COOL
FIRST or
OH
COOL
in
ZO
OH
LA and
OH
OH
OH
OH
OH or FIT
in favor
OH
LALALA COOL
FIST
LA
OH
WT
EATING
flavor
ATE
and
OH

HEY
OH
SH
S
HEY
SH
OH
SH
NO
SWEETHEART
ON
S
OH
HER
HEY
SH
OH
NOW
SH
SH
HEY
HER
HEY

Al Hansen (1966)

Hansen's vocabulary and forms are limited to the words, numbers and lines (straight) on chocolate-and-silver Hershey Bar wrappers, which he transforms into dynamic visual poems.

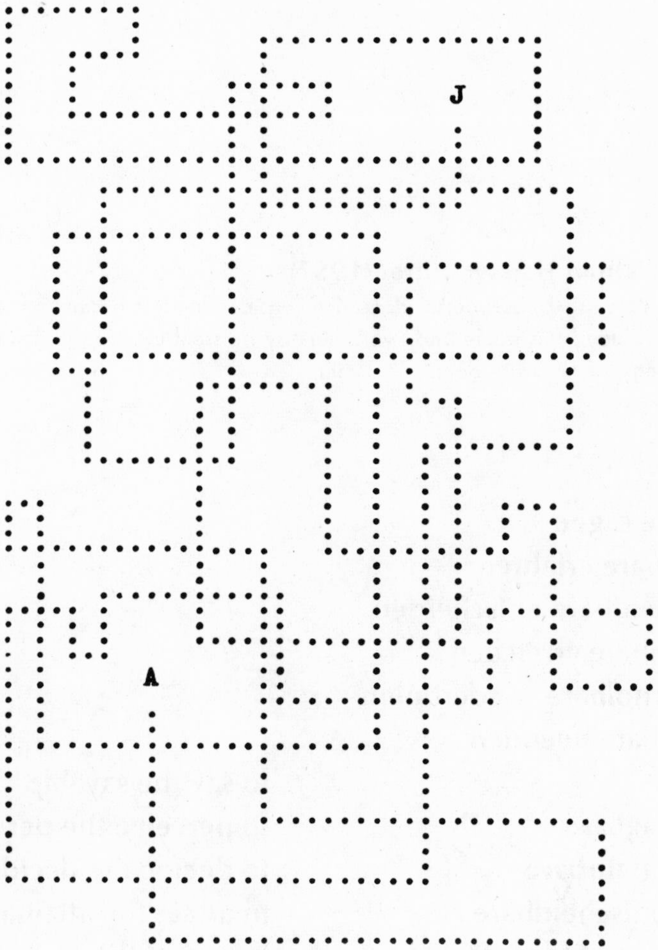
J
A

Vaclav Havel, "estrangement"
ja = I

Helmut Heissenbüttel (195?)

Although Heissenbüttel does not consider himself a concrete poet, Daniel Spoerri included this poem and two others by Heissenbüttel in the first international anthology of concrete poetry in 1958.

das sagbare sagen
das erfahrbare erfahren
das entscheidbare entscheiden
das erreichbare erreichen
das wiederholbare wiederholen
das beendbare beenden

das nicht sagbare
das nicht erfahrbare
das nicht entscheidbare
das nicht erreichbare
das nicht wiederholbare
das nicht beendbare

das nicht beendbare nicht beenden

to say the sayable
to perceive the perceivable
to decide the decidable
to attain the attainable
to repeat the repeatable
to complete the completable

the non-sayable
the non-perceivable
the non-decidable
the non-attainable
the non-repeatable
the non-completable

not to complete the non-completab

Helmut Heissenbüttel (195?)

erste	person	singular
	person	singular
erste		singular
		singular
erste	person	
erste		
	person	
		singular
	person	
	person	singular
erste		singular
	person	
		singular
erste		
erste		
		singular

Möwen und Tauben auch
Schwäne
kommen an Seen
vor und Schwalben im Sommer
Tauben im Sommer
an Seen
kommen Schwäne und
Möwen vor Tauben
und
Schwäne und auch
Möwen
kommen im Sommer
vor

Helmut Heissenbüttel (1964)

Möwen = seagulls
Tauben = doves, pigeons
Schwäne = swans
Schwalben = swallows
an Seen = by lakes
im Sommer = in summer
und = and
auch = also
kommen = come
kommen + *vor* = are found

Helmut Heissenbüttel (1964)

<table>
<tr><td>kam</td><td>nachts</td><td></td><td>es war kino</td><td>und</td><td></td><td></td><td></td></tr>
<tr><td></td><td></td><td></td><td>kein Roman</td><td></td><td></td><td></td><td></td></tr>
<tr><td></td><td></td><td></td><td>es war Kino</td><td>und</td><td>Schnee</td><td>fiel</td><td></td></tr>
<tr><td></td><td>nachts</td><td>von oben</td><td></td><td>und</td><td></td><td></td><td></td></tr>
<tr><td></td><td></td><td></td><td>kein Roman</td><td></td><td></td><td></td><td></td></tr>
<tr><td></td><td></td><td>von oben</td><td></td><td></td><td></td><td>fiel</td><td>etwas</td></tr>
<tr><td></td><td></td><td></td><td></td><td></td><td>Schnee</td><td></td><td></td></tr>
<tr><td></td><td></td><td></td><td></td><td>und</td><td></td><td></td><td></td></tr>
<tr><td>kam</td><td>nachts</td><td></td><td></td><td>und</td><td></td><td></td><td>etwas</td></tr>
<tr><td></td><td></td><td></td><td></td><td></td><td>Schnee</td><td>fiel</td><td></td></tr>
<tr><td></td><td></td><td>von oben</td><td></td><td></td><td></td><td></td><td></td></tr>
</table>

Åke Hodell, from *General Bussig* (1964)

Hodell has recorded selections from this "picture-sound-poem."

DO-X-5000

64	44
07	39
32	30
24	40
00	74
50	24
22	27

ROLLERI

R—R

ITZI

IKKO

COOP

ITZI

UCCE

IKKO

itzi

iiiiiiiiiiiiiiiiiiiiiiiiiiiiiiiiiiiiiiiiiiiiiiiiiiiiiiiiiiiiiiiiiiiiiiiiiiiiiiiiiiiiiiiiiiiiiiiiiiiiiiiiiiiiiiiiiiiiiiiiiiiiiiiiiiiii
iiiiiiiiiiiiiiiiiiiiiiiiiiiiiiiiiiiiiiiiiiiiiiiiiiiiiiiiiiiiiiiiiiiiiiiiiiiiiiiiiiiiiiiiiiiiiiiiiiiiiiiiiiiiiiiiiiiiiiiiiiiiiiiiiiiii
iiiiiiiiiiiiiiiiiiiiiiiiiiiiiiiiiiiiiiiiiiiiiiiiiiiiiiiiiiiiiiiiiiiiiiiiiiiiiiiiiiiiiiiiiiiiiiiiiiiiiiiiiiiiiiiiiiiiiiiiiiiiiiiiiiiii
iiiiiiiiiiiiiiiiiiiiiiiiiiiiiiiiiiiiiiiiiiiiiiiiiiiiiiiiiiiiiiiiiiiiiiiiiiiiiiiiiiiiiiiiiiiiiiiiiiiiiiiiiiiiiiiiiiiiiiiiiiiiiiiiiiiii
iiiiiiiiiiiiiiiiiiiiiiiiiiiiiiiiiiiiiiiiiiiiiiiiiiiiiiiiiiiiiiiiiiiiiiiiiiiiiiiiiiiiiiiiiiiiiiiiiiiiiiiiiiiiiiiiiiiiiiiiiiiiiiiiiiiii
iiiiiiiiiiiiiiiiiiiiiiiiiiiiiiiiiiiiiiiiiiiiiiiiiiiiiiiiiiiiiiiiiiiiiiiiiiiiiiiiiiiiiiiiiiiiiiiiiiiiiiiiiiiiiiiiiiiiiiiiiiiiiiiiiiiii
iiiiiiiiiiiiiiiiiiiiiiiiiiiiiiiiiiiiiiiiiiiiiiiiiiiiiiiiiiiiiiiiiiiiiiiiiiiiiiiiiiiiiiiiiiiiiiiiiiiiiiiiiiiiiiiiiiiiiiiiiiiiiiiiiiiii
iiiiiiiiiiiiiiiiiiiiiiiiiiiiiiiiiiiiiiiiiiiiiiiiiiiiiiiiiiiiiiiiiiiiiiiiiiiiiiiiiiiiiiiiiiiiiiiiiiiiiiiiiiiiiiiiiiiiiiiiiiiiiiiiiiiii
iiiiiiiiiiiiiiiiiiiiiiiiiiiiiiiiiiiiiiiiiiiiiiiiiiiiigevää
ää
ää
ää
ää
ää
ää
ää
ää
ää
ää
ää
ää
ää

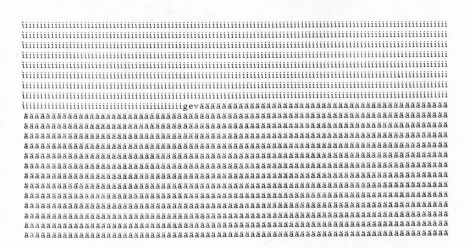

Åke Hodell, from *igevär* (1963)

igevär = shoulder arms

Page 13, the "crossover" point, of a long sound poem.

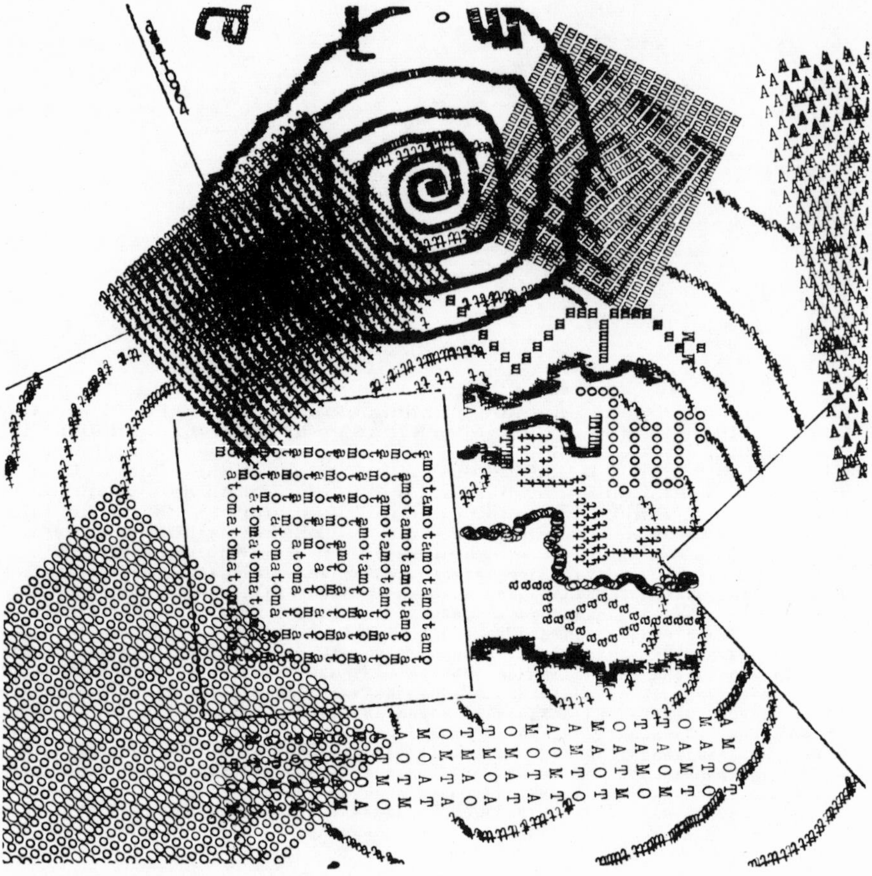

Dom Sylvester Houédard (1964)

"my own typestracts (so named by edwin morgan) are all produced on a portable olivetti lettera 22 (olivetti himself/themselves show sofar a total non interest in this fact) there are 86 typeunits available on my machine for use w/2-colour or no ribbon—or with carbons of various colours—the maximum size surface w/out folding is abt 10" diagonal—the ribbons may be of various ages—several ribbons may be used on a single typestract—inked-ribbon & manifold (carbon) can be combined on same typestract—pressures may be varied—overprints & semioverprints (½ back or ½ forward) are available—stencils may be cut & masks used—precise placing of the typestract units is possible thru spacebar & ratcheted-roller—or roller may be disengaged." (D.S.H.)

a n u r o s a n u
h o s a r o r o n
l u m u s a r o s
a h u m a n u s a
o l o l a n u r o
h u m o l u s a r
m a h u m a h o n
o l u m o l a h u

Dom Sylvester Houédard, "for raoul hausmann"

A "machine mantra"

"RAOULHAUSMANN RLHSMN aou

alphabetically HLM NRS AOU UOA
permute each 3-letter group into 4 columns of 6x3
infold cols 1/3 (A-O-U-A-O-. .)
2/4 (-U-O-A-U-O. .)
order rhopallically each resulting column of 36 letters
1/3—1-8
2/4—8-1
read w/ caesura to mark tumescence/detumescence (anabasis/katabasis) kinetically: 1/3 can move in 8 steps thru 2/4 (left-right) . . . 2/4 can move in 8 steps thru 2/4 (downwards) . . . 2/4 can move in 8 steps thru 1/3 (diagonally)" (D.S.H.)

eu	eu	eu
reu	reu	reu
kreu	kreu	kreu
z	z	z
reu	reu	reu
z	z	
eu	eu	eu
z		
kreu	kreu	kreu
z	z	z
reu	reu	
z	z	z
eu		
z	z	z
kreu	kreu	kreu
reu	reu	reu
eu	eu	eu

Ernst Jandl, "*kreuz*" (1957)

"A poem of interpenetrating triangular and quadrangular formations, a cross as a window through which the word *kreuz* (cross) can be seen in its parts: Greek *eu* (good), German *reu* (as in *Reue*, repentance) and *bereuen* (repent); Vienna dialect *kreu* (creep!, imperative; cp. German *zu Kreuz kriechen*, to humble oneself); z, suggesting the end, as well as a German interjection expressing a kind of sympathetic disapproval." (E.J.)

g o tt

p

q

r

adam s
ripp e
a
dam
ipp et
am a d
pp e
m u
a d a
p e

eva d a m

Ernst Jandl, *"erschaffung der eva"* (1957)

" 'creation of eve' is a narrative poem based on the Bible, retelling the story of the creation of Eve in terms of visual poetry: God extended horizontally, above the creation, the central *o* forming God's mouth, from which vertically downward issues God's breath, alphabetically; *a* being the first letter moving matter, by forming the genitive of Adam, *adam s*; as the alphabet moves toward the letter *v*, essential to the creation of *eva*, *adams rippe* (Adam's rib) gradually dissolves, only the e of *rippe* being retained as the first letter of *eva*; Adam himself is changed by the process, disappearing in his smaller form as the man living alone, and built up in a bigger form, as the man joined to woman, through the letter *a*." (E.J.)

Ernst Jandl (1964)

"This poem is a film. There are two actors, *i* and *l*. The action starts in line 5 and ends in the 5th line from the bottom. *i* is alone, changes position 3 times, disappears, *l* appears disappears, *i* appears disappears, both appear together changing position, like dancing; then *i* disappears for a long time, which, after stunning *l*, makes *l* restless, then immobile, like resignation; when at last *i* reappears, the dancelike jumping about and out of the picture and back again is resumed for a longer stretch than the first time. This state is final. It is the happy ending of the film. (*flim*, if you like, is the weightier half of the German *flimmern*, to flicker.)" (E.J.)

film
film
film
film
fi m
f im
fi m
f im
f m
fl m
f im
f m
flim
film
flim
film
f lm
f lm
fl m
f lm
fl m
f m
f lm
fl m
f m
f lm
f m
fl m
f lm
fl m
fl m
fl m
fl m
fl m
fl m
flim
film
flim
film
flim
film
flim
f m
film
f m
flim
film
flim
film
film
film
film
film

e

ee

eee

oooooooooööööooooooo

oooooooööööööooooooo

ooooooöööööööooooooo

oooooööööööööooooooo

ooooöööööööööooooooo

oooööööööööööooooooo

ooöööööööööööooooooo

oööööööööööööooooooo

ööööööööööööööooooooo

eöööööööööööööooooooo

eeöööööööööööööooooooo

eeeeeeeeeeeeeeee

Ernst Jandl (1964)

"This is an altogether German poem, of which Norbert Lynton remarked in *Art International* (IX/9-10, 1965, page 24): 'A very nice visual-cum-linguistic joke is Ernst Jandl's filtering of a column of e's through a battalion of o's: where e and o meet they become, of course, ö.' Which is about all you could say about this poem." (E.J.)

Bengt Emil Johnson, "Homage to John Cage" (1964)

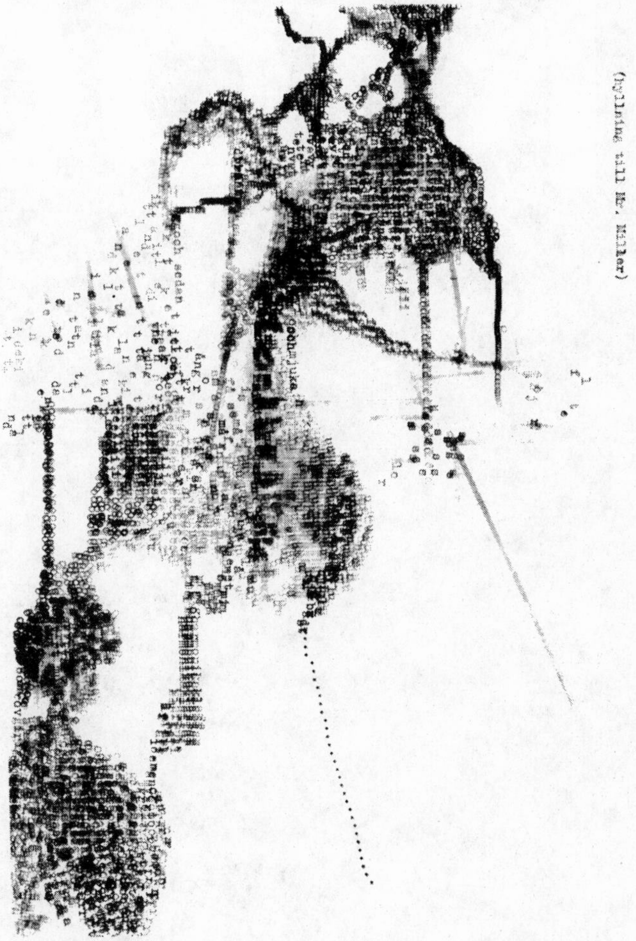
(hyllning till Hr. Müller)

Bengt Emil Johnson (1963)

One of a series of essays on ***Bror Barsk*** (untranslatable).

MOO

Ronald Johnson, Io and the Ox-Eye Daisy (1965)

Io was written in London in 1965. It was printed by the Wild Hawthorn Press as an issue of Poor.Old.Tired.Horse. (published by Ian Hamilton Finlay). The lettering was done by John Furnival.

"**Io** is a poem meant to be read by moonlight, a book of magical changes and transformations on the two letters 'I' and 'o.' 'I' is also *eye* and 'o' the real moon which can rise over the word moon. The first word is a phosphorescent moo into

MOON

the darkness, so it is apparent that Hera has already transformed Io into a white heifer. (One remembers also that the hundred-eyed Argus had been sent to watch over her which probably explains the excesses of moons, 'o's,' eyes in these skies.) The next is a moon rising over the horizon—or the word moon caught in the process of creating the actual thing. Next, Io and Ox—both ideograms which have been constructed so their 'o's' could be suspended (as in Io) or lifted aloft (as in

Io

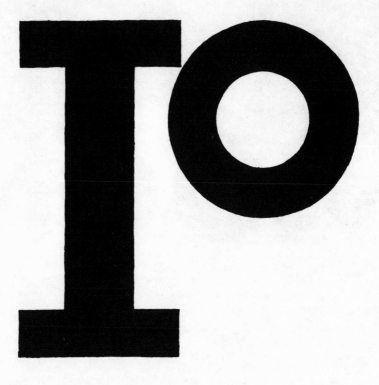

Ronald Johnson, Io and the Ox-Eye Daisy (continued from preceding page)

O

X

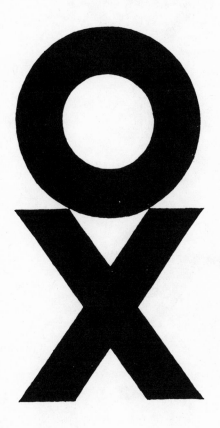

Ox). In the word eye the 'e' also imitates the rising of a moon so that it comes from below to above the 'V' to make the word. Daze is a pun on *dais*-y and is completed on the next page with (I). This is, I suppose, the confrontation of Io with the Ox-eye Daisy—the white heifer and glowing flower which floats in the night like one of Redon's giant eyes. The 'daze' or dazzle of the meeting is enforced by returning to white on black as if the moonlit world were suddenly

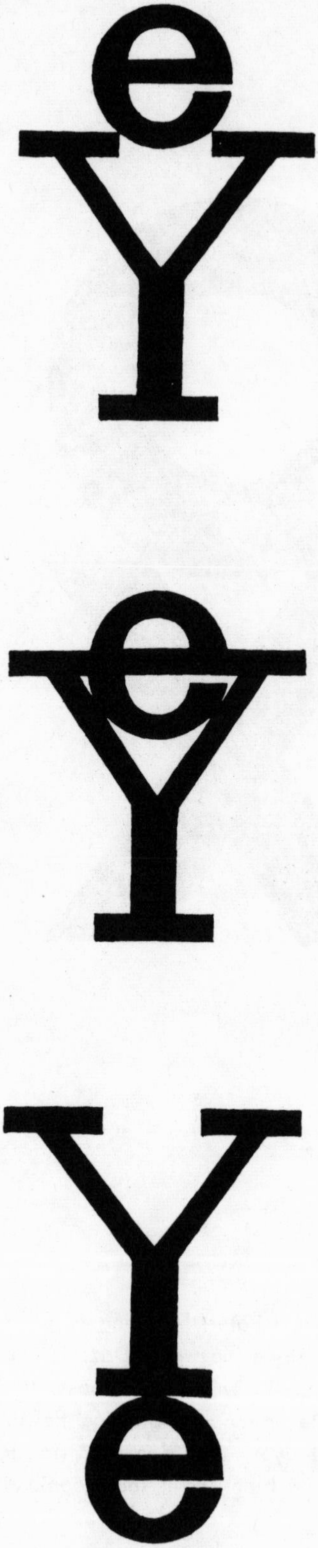

daze

Ronald Johnson, Io and the Ox-Eye Daisy **(continued from facing page)**

reversed like a photographic negative. Then the 'I' in parenthesis which both completes the word daisy and begins the word Io with its 'o' following also in paren-

(I)

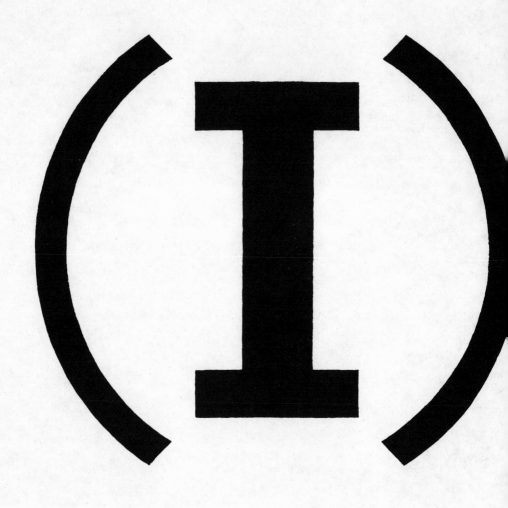

Ronald Johnson, Io and the Ox-Eye Daisy (continued from preceding page)

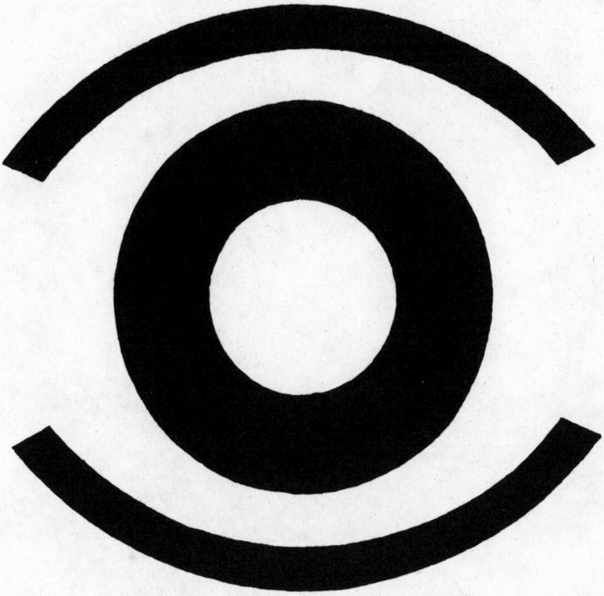

thesis. A freudian critic would point out that in this union, after all, Io, as a heifer, is meeting Ox-eye Daisy—but that is another story . . . The (I) is, again, an eye as in the  which transforms the pun even further by turning on its side to make a m

o

o

picture of an eye. Then moon and moons return again, and the darkness of night, to bring the poem itself back to a circle: MOO/MOON IO OX-EYE DAISY IO MOO/MOON." (R.J.)

o
o
n
s

Ronald Johnson, Io and the Ox-Eye Daisy (concluded)

Hiro Kamimura (1966)

Transliteration and translation on facing page.

あか

あかざ
あかがわ
あかだま
あかばら
あかばな
あかはら
あかはだ
あかはた

ああ　あまたな
あか
あかが
あかあか

aka

akaza
akagawa
akadama
akabara
akabana
akahara
akahada
akahata

aa amatana
aka
akaga
akaaka

red

red flower
red leather
red ball
red rose
red nose
red belly
red skin
red flag

oh so much
red
red is
red red

Hiro Kamimura
translation of poem on facing page

単調な空間

北園克衛

白い四角	**shiroi shikaku**	**white square**
のなか	**no naka**	**within**
の白い四角	**no shiroi shikaku**	**white square**
のなか	**no naka**	**within**
の黒い四角	**no kuroi shikaku**	**yellow square**
のなか	**no naka**	**within**
の黒い四角	**no kuroi shikaku**	**yellow square**
のなか	**no naka**	**within**
の黄いろい四角	**no kiiroi shikaku**	**black square**
のなか	**no naka**	**within**
の黄いろい四角	**no kiiroi shikaku**	**black square**
のなか	**no naka**	**within**
の白い四角	**no shiroi shikaku**	**white square**
のなか	**no naka**	**within**
の白い四角	**no shiroi shikaku**	**white square**

Kitasono Katue, *tanchona kukan* — part 1 (1957)

tanchona kukan (monotony of void space) was the first Japanese concrete poem. (See K.K.'s biography.) Haroldo de Campos, who translated the poem for this anthology, comments: "Looking at this poem, I remember Malevich's 'White on White' painting and Albers' 'Homage to the Square' series. With some hints (part 3) of a very peculiar Japanese kind of visual surrealism. The Japanese text combines cleverly the typographic resources of Nippon (*hiragana, katakana*—phonetic alphabets—and *kanji*—ideogram). Its sound is also suited to its development; see part 2, for instance."

白	**shiro**	**white**
の中の白	**nonaka no shiro**	**within the white**
の中の黒	**nonaka no kuro**	**within the yellow**
の中の黒	**nonaka no kuro**	**within the yellow**
の中の黄	**nonaka no kiiro**	**within the black**
の中の黄	**nonaka no kiiro**	**within the black**
の中の白	**nonaka no shiro**	**within the white**
の中の白	**nonaka no shiro**	**within the white**

Kitasono Katue, *tanchona kukan*—part 2

Kitasono Katue, *tanchona kukan*—part 3

青	ao	glass
の三角	no sankaku	of
の髭	no hige	beard of
の	no	blue
ガラス	garas	triangle

白	shiro	parasol
の三角	no sankaku	of
の馬	no uma	horse of
の	no	white
パラソル	parasoru	triangle

黒	kuro	building
の三角	no sankaku	of
の煙草	no tabako	smoke of
の	no	black
ビルディング	birudingu	triangle

黄	kiiro	scarf
の三角	no sankaku	of
の星	no hoshi	star of
の	no	yellow
ハンカチィフ	hankachiifu	triangle

Kitasono Katue, *tanchona kukan*—part 4

白い四角	shiroi shikaku	white square
のなか	no naka	within
の白い四角	no shiroi shikaku	white square
のなか	no naka	within
の白い四角	no shiroi shikaku	white square
のなか	no naka	within
の白い四角	no shiroi shikaku	white square
のなか	no naka	within
の白い四角	no shiroi shikaku	white square

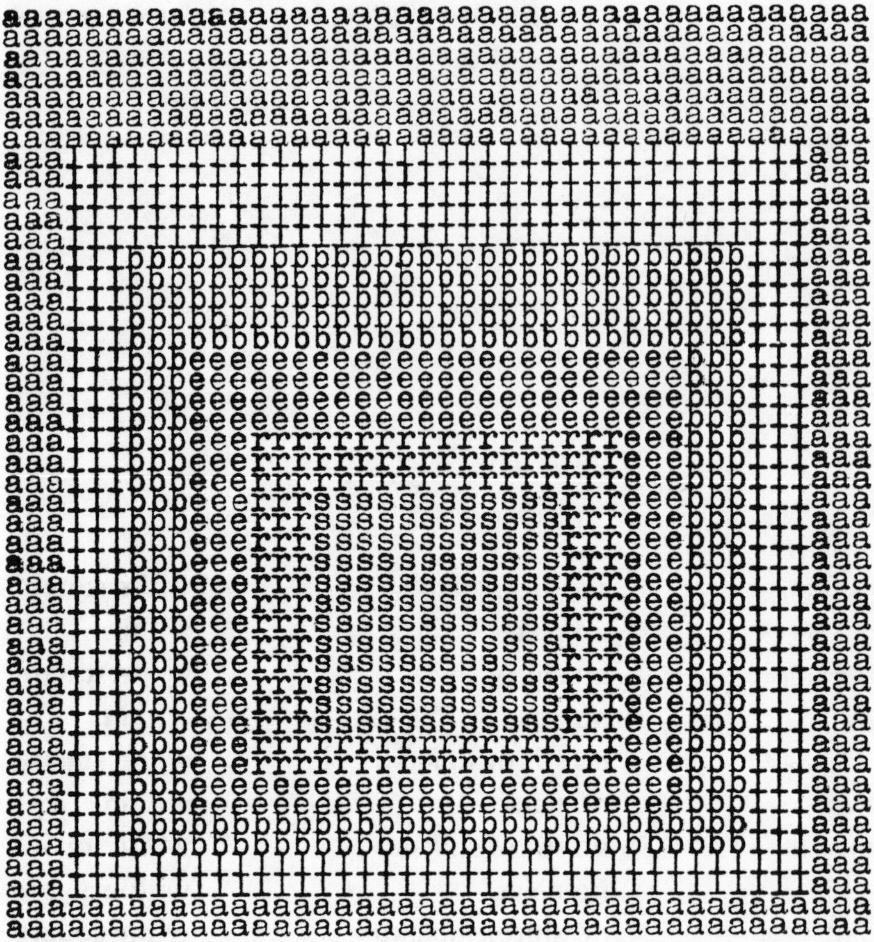

Jiří Kolář (1962)

"'Evident poetry' is all poetry that eschews the written word as the mainstay of creation and communication. The word, according to Kolár, should remain within, instigating a monologue." (Introduction to **Signboard for Gersaint**, Artia, Prague 1966.)

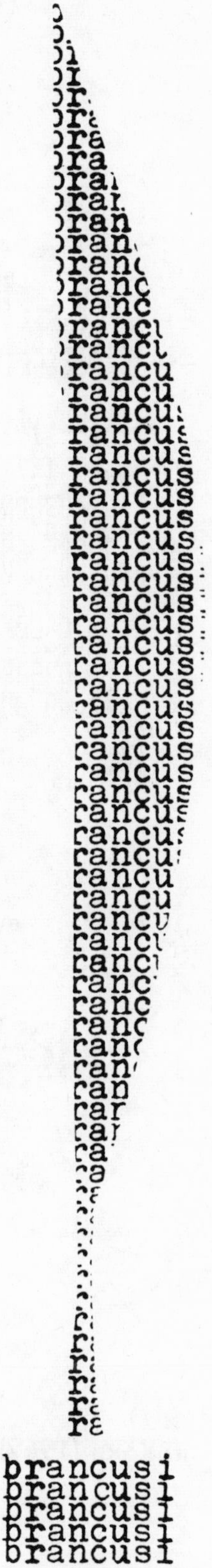
brancusi
brancusi
brancusi
brancusi
brancusi

Jiří Kolář (1962)

TINGUELY

Jiří Kolář (1962)

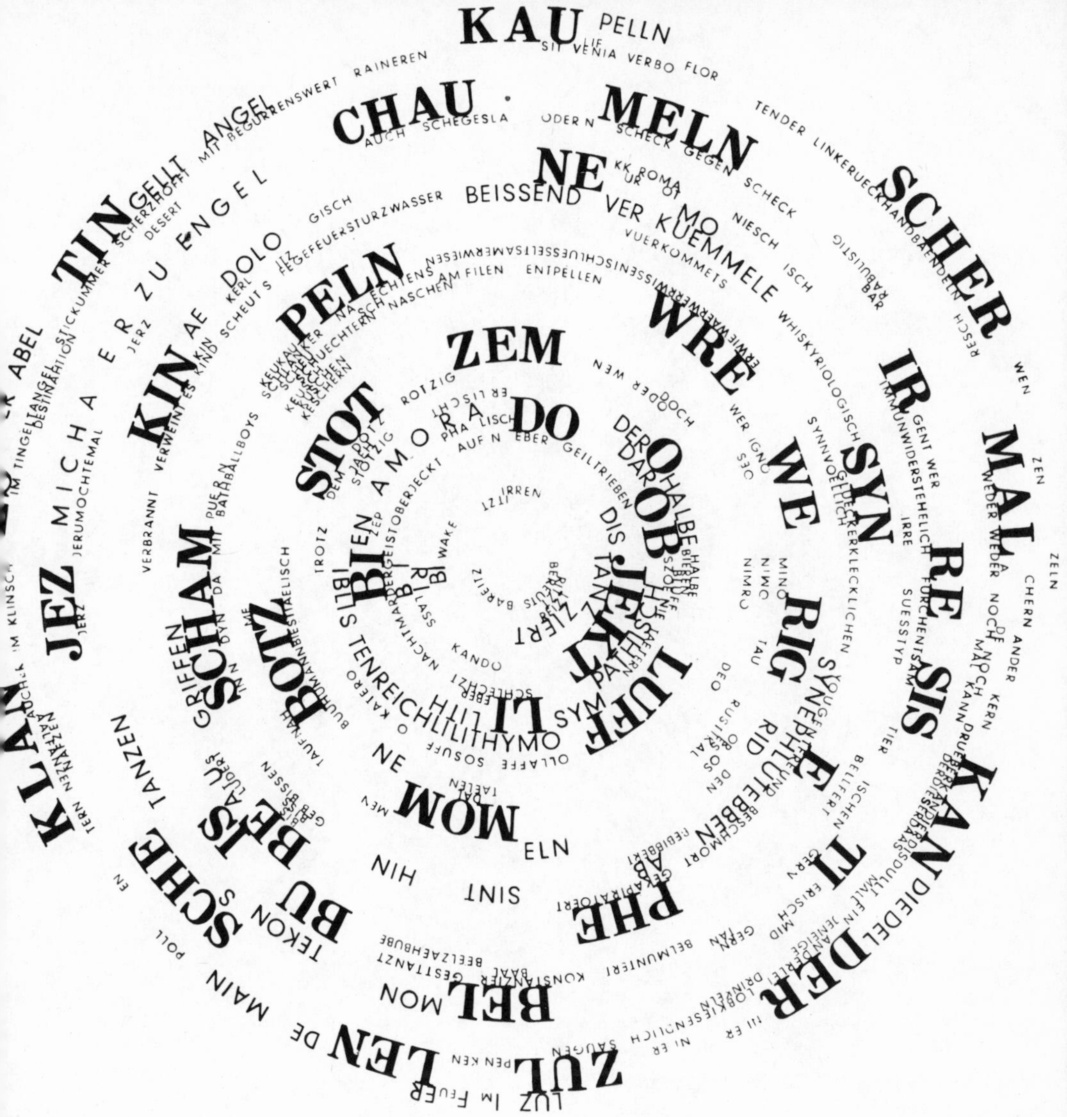
KAU
PELLN
CHAU
MELN
NE
SCHER
TIN
WRE
PELN
ZEM
KIN
STOT
DO
IR
MAL
SYN
WE
RE
JEZ
SCHAM
BOTZ
RIG
SIS
LUF
KAN
MOW
TI
PHE
DER
BEL
ZUL
LEN

Ferdinand Kriwet, "Type Is Honey" (1962)

Rundscheibe VI is constructed of 105 concentric circles—fifteen 20mm circles, thirty 10mm and sixty 5mm. The larger circles are read from left to right, the two smaller series from right to left and reverse. In his book ***leserattenfaenge*** Kriwet has written a circle-for-circle, word-for-word analysis of this and his other visual texts.

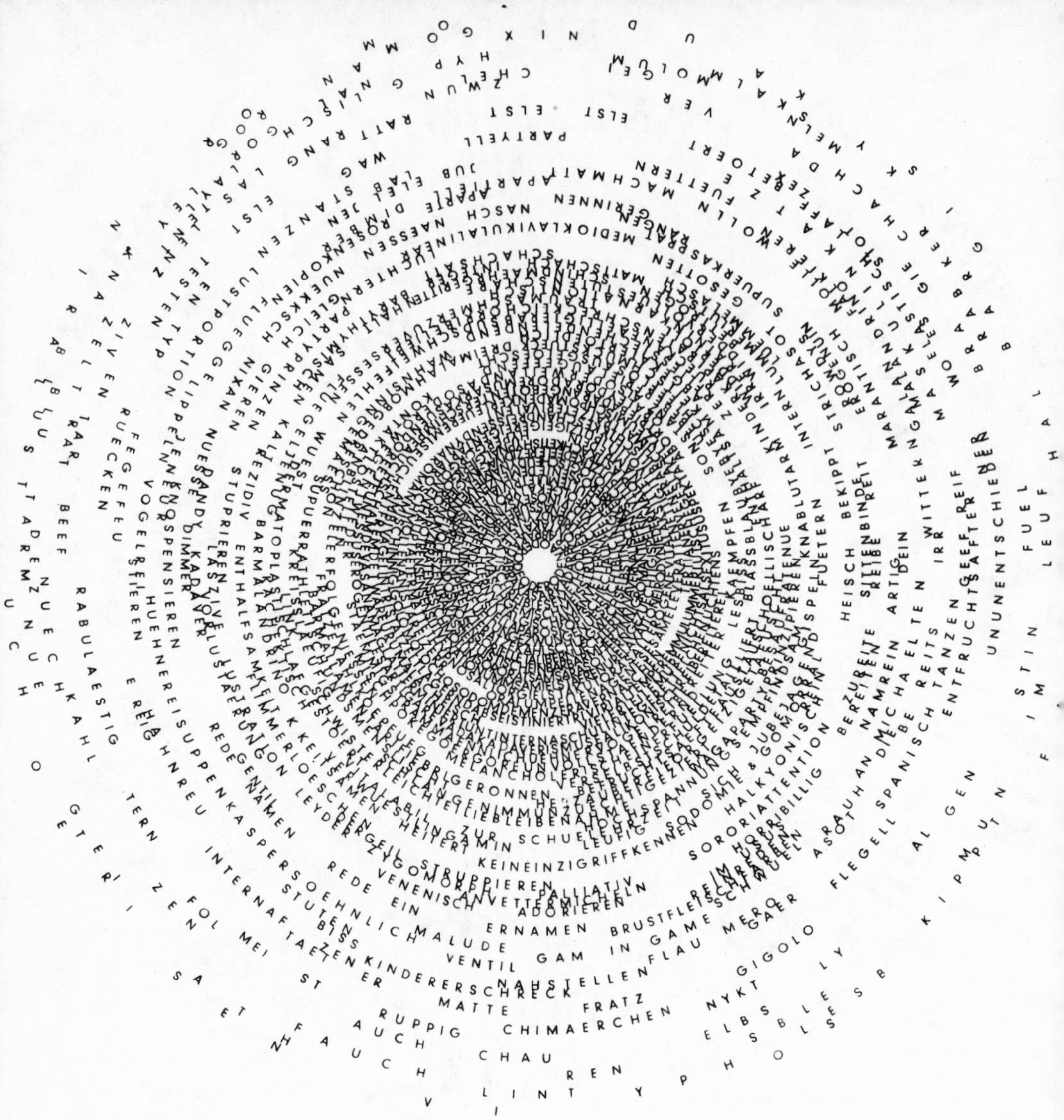

Ferdinand Kriwet, *"ZUVERSPAETCETERANDFIGURINNENNENS-WERT OLLOS"* (1962)

The text *Rundscheibe* VII unfolds in 59 concentric circles, from the center out. These 59 circles are divided into six states—circles 1 to 12, 13 to 19, 20 to 28, 29 to 40, 41 to 51, and 52 to 59. On the facing page, a detail of this *Rundscheibe* is shown full-size.

Ferdinand Kriwet, "*ZUVERSPAETCETERANDFIGURINNENNENS-WERT OLLOS*" (1962)

A detail, full-scale.

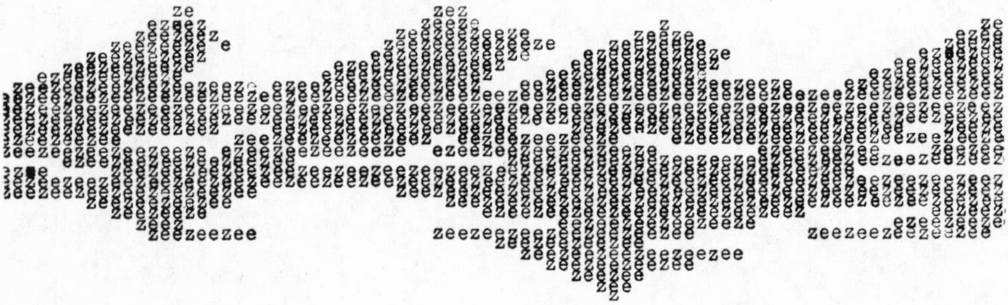

Frans van der Linde (1964)

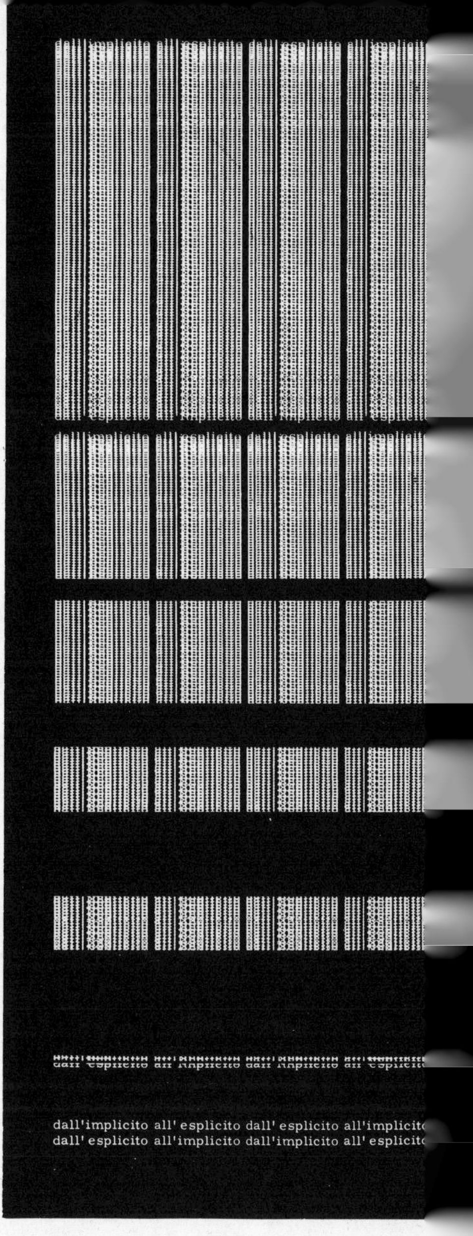
dall'implicito all' esplicito dall' esplicito all'implicit
dall' esplicito all'implicito dall'implicito all' esplicit

Arrigo Lora-Totino (1966)

Arrigo Lora-Totino (1966)

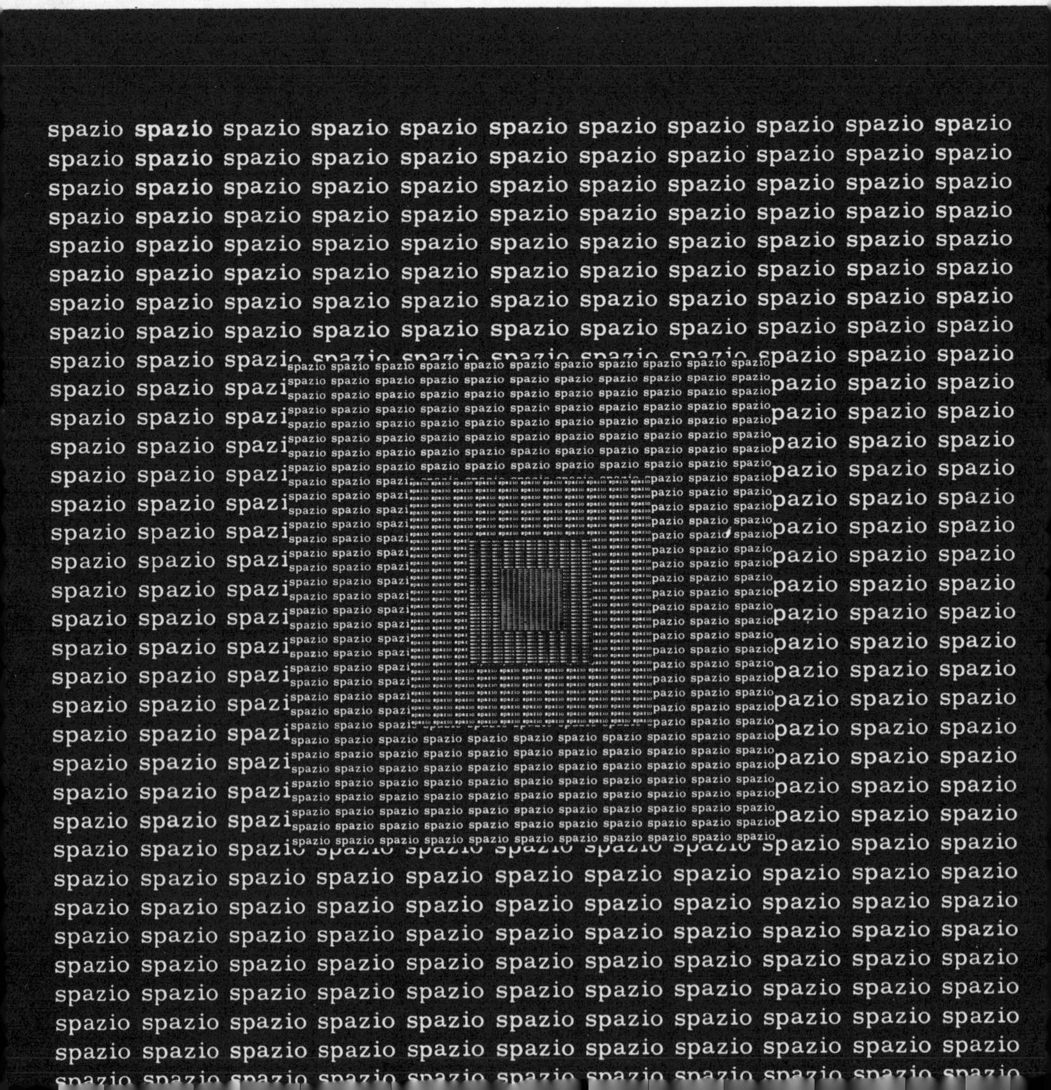

```
no no no no no no no no no no no no no no
no                                      no
no    no no no no no no no no no no    no
no    no                         no    no
no    no    no no no no no no    no    no
no    no    no             no    no    no
no    no    no    no no    no    no    no
no    no    no       no    no    no    no
no    no    no no no no    no    no    no
no    no                   no    no    no
no    no no no no no no no no    no    no
no                               no    no
no no no no no no no no no no no no    no
                                       no
                                       si
si si si si si si si si si si si si    si
si                               si    si
si    si si si si si si si si    si    si
si    si                   si    si    si
si    si    si si si si    si    si    si
si    si    si       si    si    si    si
si    si    si    si si    si    si    si
si    si    si             si    si    si
si    si    si si si si si si    si    si
si    si                         si    si
si    si si si si si si si si si si    si
si                                      si
si si si si si si si si si si si si si si
```

Arrigo Lora-Totino (1966)

5. 2. 3. 6. 5., THE 3RD BIBLICAL POEM

sustenance/_____/and/_____//_____/
/_____//_____/
/_____//_____/bullock,
of twenty/_____//_____//_____/children
hands, /_____/came and/_____/

/_____/weight threescore/_____/the
upon/_____/
Shechem/_____//_____/
/_____//_____/he/_____/his against
/_____//_____/Jephthah, cities/_____/

/_____//_____//_____/not children
/_____/thee?
ten the/_____/
/_____/said for eater But/_____/
/_____//_____/done to and

in pray/_____/sons, /_____/
they this
/_____/the Ephraim,
man/_____//_____/young/_____/unto
/_____/now up/_____/Israel

/_____/in men of/_____/
we/_____/
/_____//_____//_____/
/_____//_____/unto/_____//_____/man
prayed/_____//_____//_____//_____/

Judges 6:4—1st Samuel 1:10
January 1st, 1955

Jackson Mac Low, from 5 biblical poems (1955)

The **5 biblical poems** were the first works Mac Low composed by chance operations and the first to incorporate silences of appreciable duration and a significant degree of indeterminacy in performance. The unit is the "event" rather than the foot or syllable. These "events" are either single words or silences, each equal in duration to any word and thus indeterminate in length. The integers in the title indicate its verse structure: thus, *5.2.3.6.5.* shows that the first line in each stanza contains 5 events; the second line, 2; the third line, 3, etc. Musical or other non-verbal sounds may be produced at the ends of lines and stanzas to make the verse structure audible.

printed:	read:
	/new enjoy work.ins. K. one young/
new enjoy work.	new enjoy work./ins. K. one young/
	/new enjoy work.ins. K. one young/
	/new enjoy work.ins. K. one young/
enjoy not Jacobins.	enjoy not Jacobins./K. one young/
	/enjoy not Jacobins. K. one young/
one young	/enjoy not Jacobins. K./one young
	/enjoy not Jacobins. K. one young/
work.	work./not Jacobins. K. one young/
	/work. not Jacobins. K. one young/
one re-	/work./ one re-/ins. K. one young/
forms	/work. one re/forms/ K. one young/
K.	/work. one re-forms/K./one young/

Jackson Mac Low, "Asymmetry 147" (1960)

Mac Low's **Asymmetries** are poems of which the words, punctuation, typography and spacing on the page are determined by chance operations. They may be performed by seven different methods (some employing tones), singly or several poems simultaneously. A basic method underlies the others and is followed when all or most of the others are ruled out by circumstances. Example of reading "Asymmetry 147" by basic method: In version at right, silent words are printed between "/"'s. Spoken words are underlined for clarity only, not to indicate loud speech. They are spoken as at left: all moderately, except "K.", which is loud or shouted. At right, some words are shifted a few spaces to the right to show how the poem is read.

Jackson Mac Low, from Letters for Iris Numbers for Silence (1961)

Letters and numbers are randomly placed and each card may be held in any position. Readers pronounce for each letter any phone (falling within any phoneme(s) of any language(s) which may be represented by the letter). Names of letters should not be pronounced unless they happen to be single phones represented by the letters. Letters may be pronounced shortly or for any duration up to that of a breath. For each integer, readers are to be silent that number of seconds or of slow counts. All letters on each card are to be pronounced, once each, in any order. Amplitude, pitch, timbre, tempo and changes in all parameters are free. However, regular rhythms, tonal melodies and the like should be avoided.

JAYBIRD POEM

BIRD

NEST

TREE

A BIRD

A NEST

A TREE

Jackson Mac Low

"This poem was found in my file at the office of the Something Else Press. I don't at all* remember writing it, but external evidence, including the particular kind of yellowed file card on which it is typed, the typing, & the irrelevant specificity of the 'Jaybird' in the title, makes me believe that this was one of several works that I copied onto such cards in the summer of 1962 or 1963 & sent to various friends & strangers (mostly composers and poets) all over the world." (Jackson Mac Low 3/28/67)

* Jap. *zenzen*

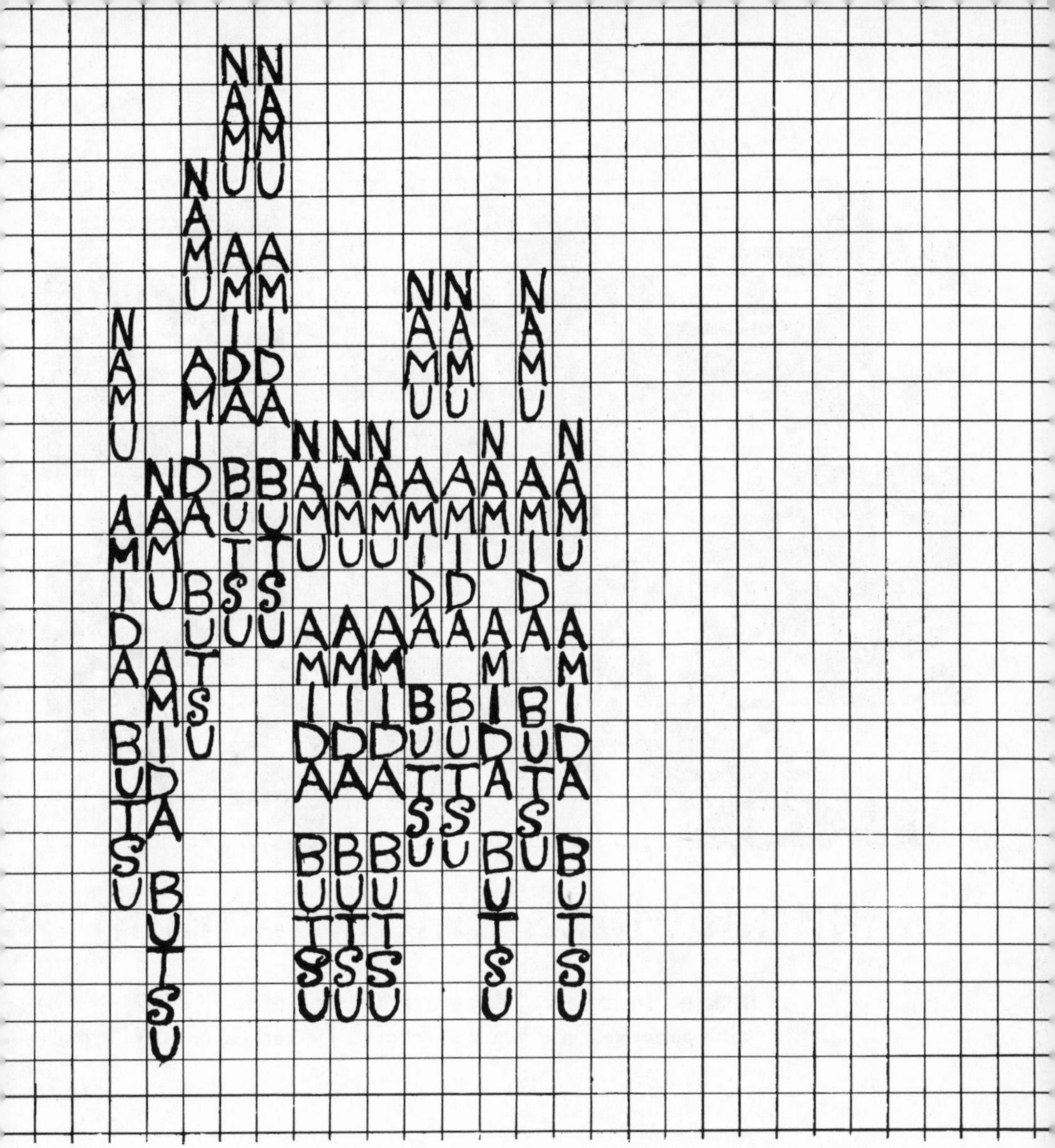

Jackson Mac Low, *"2nd Gatha"* (1961)

The reader begins at any square (empty squares are silences). He moves to any adjacent square horizontally, vertically or diagonally, and continues this process until the end of the piece. Letters are read as any sound they can stand for in any language. When letters are repeated in a number of adjacent squares their sound may be continued for the duration thought of as equivalent to that number of squares, or they may be reiterated the same number of times as of squares. Letters can be read occasionally as one-letter words denoting the letters (e.g., "D" as "Dee"). Groups of adjacent letters can be read as syllables, words, word-groups and complete sentences. The following six possibilities should be produced by each performer during the piece: silences, phones, syllables, words, word-groups, and sentences (e.g., *Namu Amida Butsu*).

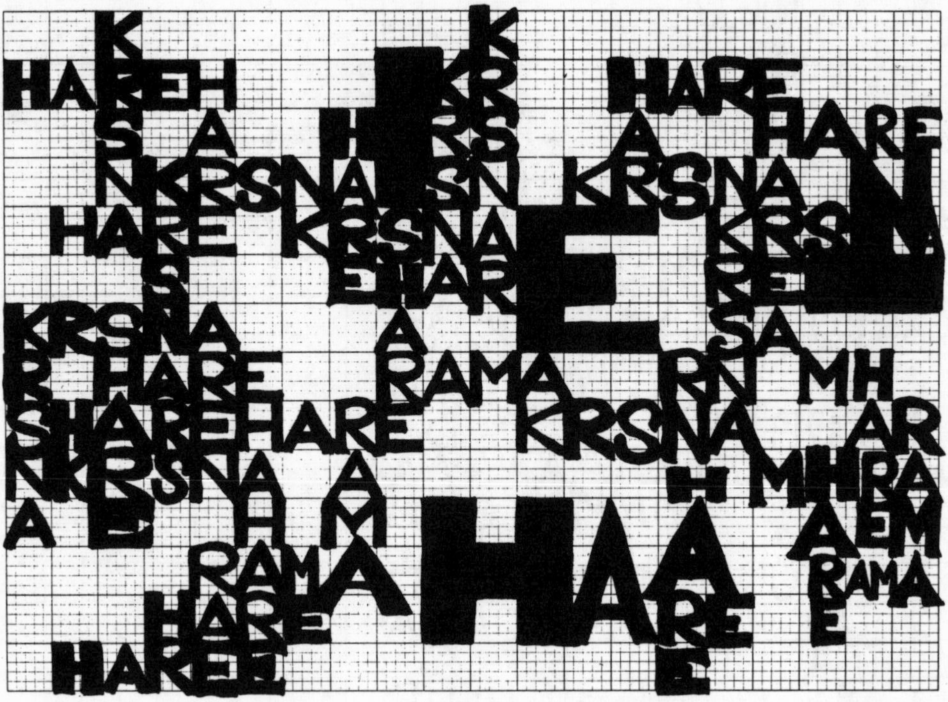

Jackson Mac Low, *"4th Hare Krsna Gatha"* (1967)

To be performed in a manner similar to the *2nd Gatha*, but "flying."

Jackson Mac Low, *"7th Hare Krsna Gatha"* (1967)

See previous note, and underline *flying*.

JAIL BREAK (for Emmett Williams & John Cage) September 1963, April & August 1966

Tear now jails down all.
Tear all now down jails.
Tear now all jails down.
Tear jails now all down.
Tear jails now down all.
Tear now jails all down.
Tear now down all jails.
Tear all down jails now.
Tear jails down all now.
Tear jails all down now.
Tear all jails down now.
Tear jails all now down.
Tear jails down now all.
Tear down now all jails.
Tear now all down jails.
Tear down now jails all.
Tear now down jails all.
Tear down all jails now.
Tear down jails all now.
Tear all jails now down.
Tear all now jails down.
Tear all down now jails.
Tear down jails now all.
Tear down all now jails.

All jails now down tear.
All now tear down jails.
All jails down tear now.
All now jails down tear.
All now down tear jails.
All jails now tear down.
All tear now jails down.
All jails down now tear.
All down now tear jails.
All tear down jails now.
All tear jails down now.
All now down jails tear.
All down tear now jails.
All down tear jails now.
All down now jails tear.
All down jails now tear.
All down jails tear now.
All tear jails now down.
All now tear jails down.
All tear down now jails.
all jails tear now down.
All now jails tear down.
All jails tear down now.
All tear now down jails.

Jails tear down all now.
Jails tear down now all.
Jails down now all tear.
Jails now tear down all.
Jails now tear all down.
Jails tear now down all.
Jails tear now all down.
Jails all tear now down.
Jails tear all now down.
Jails all tear down now.
Jails all down tear now.
Jails now down all tear.
Jails tear all down now.
Jails down all tear now.
Jails down now tear all.
Jails now all tear down.
Jails down tear all now.
Jails now all down tear.
Jails down tear now all.
Jails all now tear down.
Jails down all now tear.
Jails all now down tear.
Jails now down tear all.
Jails all down now tear.

PEOPLE: Five who speak clearly, listen closely to each other & all environing sounds, & let what they hear modify how they speak. In Way 1 they must be able to improvise together, let performance flow & their own impulses determine how they speak. Way 2 needs a precise conductor & 5 speakers who follow him accurately. MATERIALS: 120 small cards, 5 equal squares of poster board (8 to 28 inches a side), paint/ink, pen/brush; for Way 1, 10 envelopes each large enough to hold 24 cards with room for easy removal & insertion of cards.

PREPARATION: Type permutations on cards. Experiment to find size of sign easiest to handle; size, colors, letter shapes most visible in performance situation. Make 5 square signs, each with one of the 5 words on it. For Way 1 attach 2 envelopes to each sign back & put the 24 cards whose texts begin with the sign's word in one. PERFORMANCE: Way 1: The speakers line up, holding signs parallel in the order TEAR DOWN ALL JAILS NOW. Each draws a card, listens closely to other speakers & environment until he & the situation are ready, then speaks the words as a connected sentence making good sense. Speed, loudness & voice coloration are free. He puts the card in the empty envelope & draws another, &c., until he's read each card once. It ends after last speaker finishes. Way 2: Lined up as above, speakers face conductor, who shuffles the 120 cards & draws one, pointing in turn, in the permutation's order, to each word's bearer, who says the word, connecting it with the others so the sentence makes sense tho said by 5. Way 2 needs long intense rehearsal; ends when all 120 permutations are read. Way 2 performed (2nd Jail Poets' Reading, Living Theatre, 9 Sept. 1963) by Judith Malina, Tom Cornell, Paul Prensky, & 2 others, conducted by JML. Way 1 1st performed in rain (reading against USSR jailing of writers, 30 April 1966: WIN, II, 9: 6-7) by JML, Blackburn, Rothenberg, Antin, & the Rt. Revd. Michael F. Itkin.

Down tear now jails all.
Down now tear jails all.
Down tear all jails now.
Down all now tear jails.
Down jails tear all now.
Down jails all tear now.
Down now all jails tear.
Down all jails now tear.
Down all tear now jails.
Down jails now tear all.
Down now jails all tear.
Down jails now all tear.
Down tear jails now all.
Down tear all now jails.
Down now jails tear all.
Down now tear all jails.
Down jails tear now all.
Down all tear jails now.
Down tear jails all now.
Down all jails tear now.
Down tear now all jails.
Down all now jails tear.
Down jails all now tear.
Down now all tear jails.

Now all down tear jails.
Now down all tear jails.
Now tear down jails all.
Now jails all down tear.
Now jails all tear down.
Now jails tear down all.
Now down jails all tear.
Now all tear jails down.
Now all tear down jails.
Now down all jails tear.
Now jails down all tear.
Now tear down all jails.
Now tear all down jails.
Now all down jails tear.
Now tear jails down all.
Now jails down tear all.
Now down tear all jails.
Now tear all jails down.
Now all jails down tear.
Now tear jails all down.
Now jails tear all down.
Now down tear jails all.
Now down jails tear all.
Now all jails tear down.

Jackson Mac Low

Hansjörg Mayer, from *alphabet* (1963)

Hansjörg Mayer, from *fortführungen* (1964)

s a u
a u s
u s a

Hansjörg Mayer (1965)

d
c
b
a
h
g
f
e
d
c
b
a
a

Hansjörg Mayer, from *alphabetenquadratbuch* 1 (1964–65)

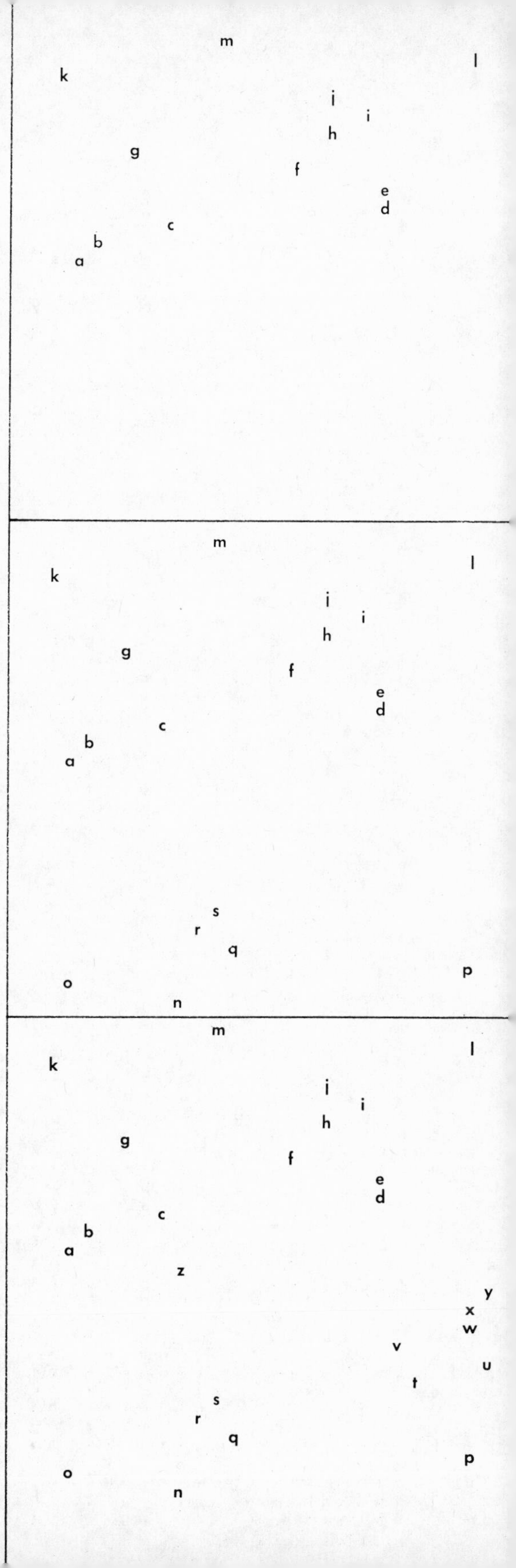

m
l
k
j
i
h
g
f
e
d
c
b
a
m
l
k
j
i
h
g
f
e
d
c
b
a
s
r
q
p
o
n
m
l
k
j
i
h
g
f
e
d
c
b
a
z
y
x
w
v
u
t
s
r
q
p
o
n

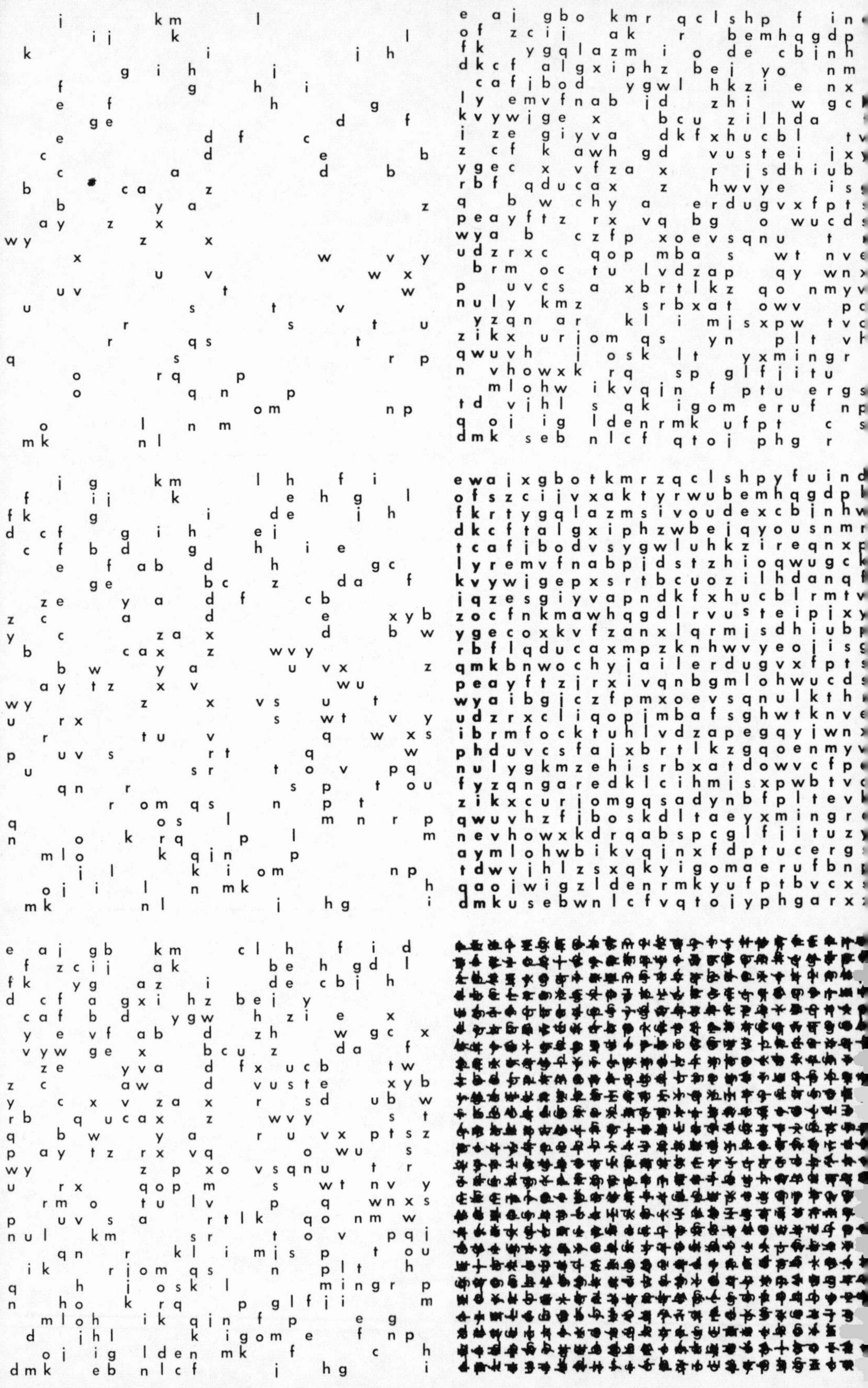

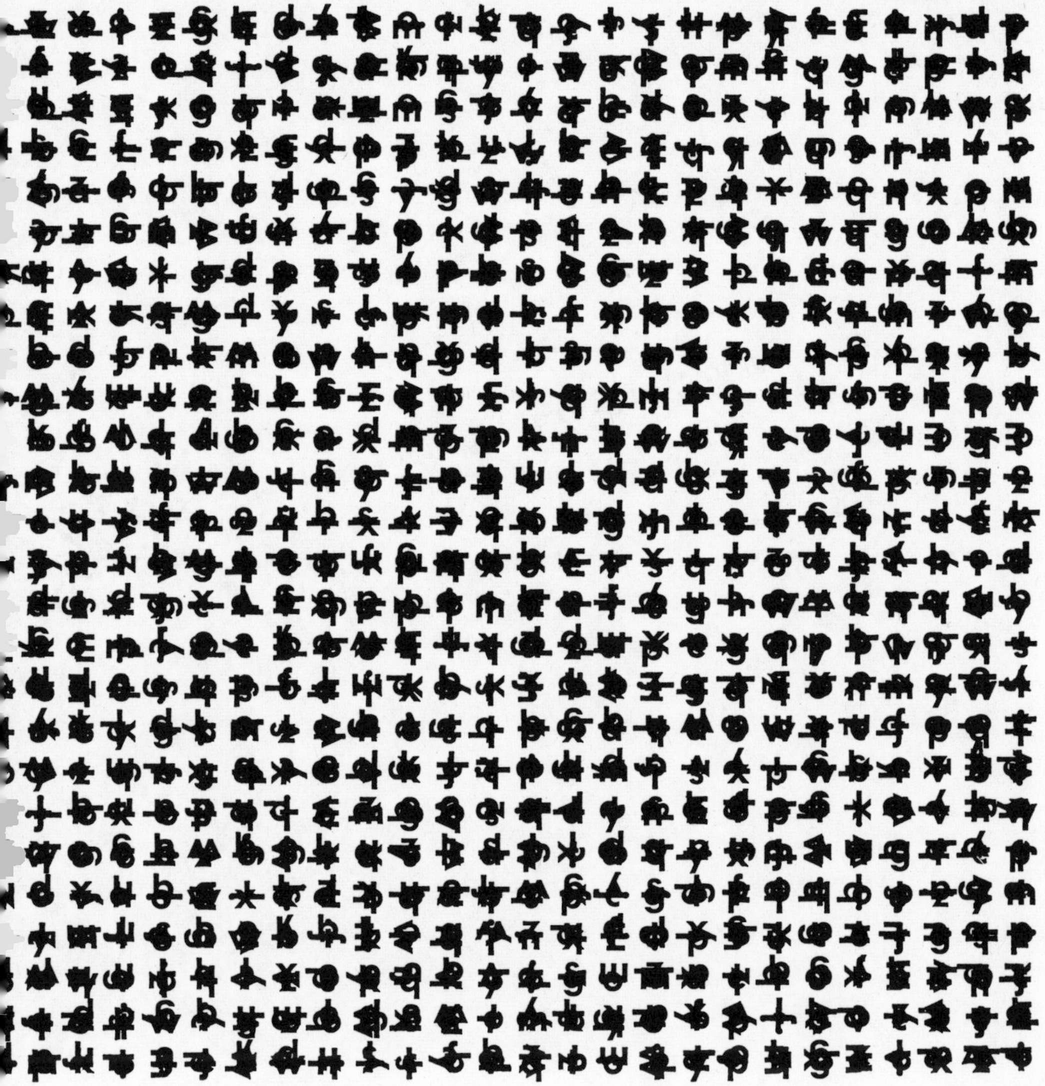

Hansjörg Mayer, from *alphabetenquadratbuch* 1

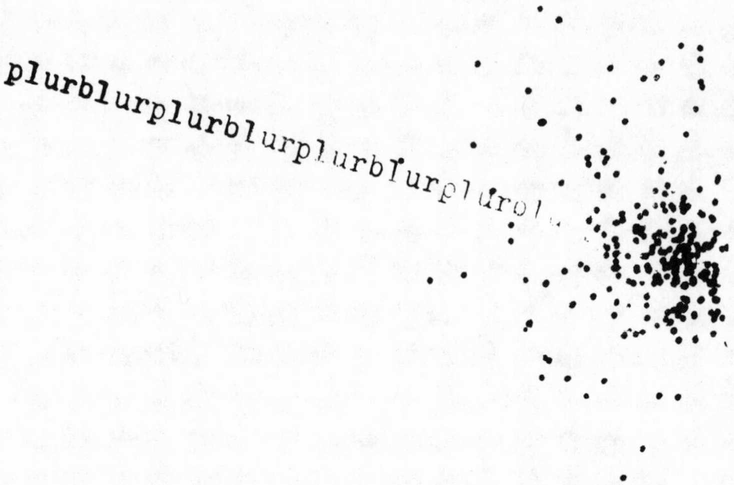
plurblurplurblurplurblurpl

Cavan McCarthy (1965)

"These poems are an attempt to catch a situation and put it onto paper; especially so with 'Plurble Poem.' This developed into a tendency to take the label or name from something and to expand it, use it as a building block to express what I felt about the thing, or how the person felt-looked-reacted-was-is." (C.M.)

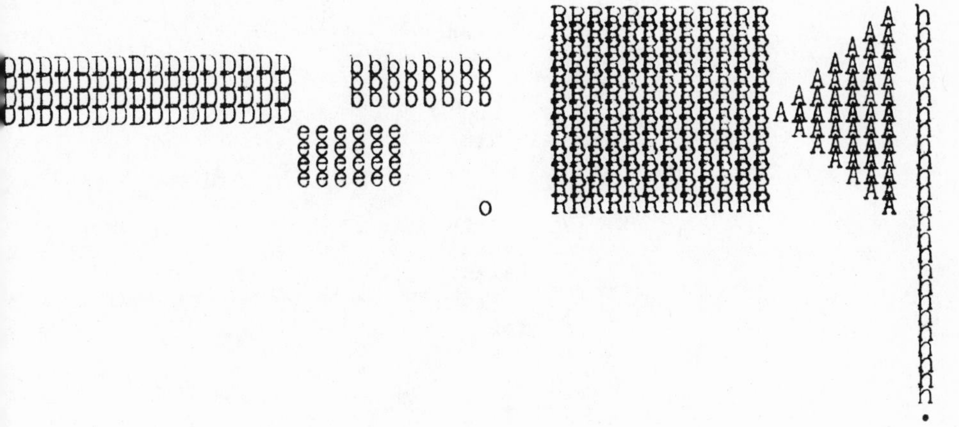

Cavan McCarthy "Poem for Deborah" (1965)

sinks
inks
sink
nks
sin
ks
s n
s s
linkssekssinks sint sud sas sa s sol sols slos slost slos los lss ls
sa
as
sak
kas
saks
kasa
akse
naks
kseno
okse
okt
kto
okto
kton
nokt
okton
nokto
okto
kto
tok
kot

Franz Mon (1959)

Through the process of what the author calls "articulative permutations," the words *sinks* and *links* (left) are transformed into a series of articulations with many semantic associations. The key words reflect the activity of the reader's eye on the page. When *links* is read, the eye is at the left. The eye *sinks* as it goes down the vertical column. Where the vertical and horizontal meet, only the *s* of the original two words remains. As the eye sinks further, new articulations suggest other words: *sak* = *sack* = dress; *kas* = *käse* = cheese; *akse* = *achse* = axis; *kseno* = *xenos* = stranger; *okto* = *acht* = eight; *nokt* = *nacht* = night, etc.

a u s d e n a u g e n a u s d e m r e g e n

a u s d e m r e g e n a u s d e m s i n n

aauussddeenmaruegg eennaauussddeemmrseignenn

aauu ee a ue ee aauu ee ei e

ssdd nm r gg nn ssdd mmrs gn nn

aa n a nnaa n nn

uu ee ue ee uu ee e e

ss gg ss s g

dd dd i

ss ee ee ss ee se e

n r nn r n nn

m mm

dd r dd r

uu u gg uu g

aa a aa i

Franz Mon (1960)

Lines 1 and 2, "out of sight out of the rain / out of the rain out of mind," are added together. Line 3 is the sum of lines 1 and 2. In line 4 are the vowels, extracted from line 3; in line 5, the consonants, also extracted from line 3. Line 6 begins a construction made by extracting the first and last letters from lines 1 and 2, and all recurrences of these letters within the lines; line 7, the second and next to last letters, and their recurrences; line 8, the third and third from last, and their recurrences; and so on. For the mixing up of proverbs in the basic text, see note on page 213.

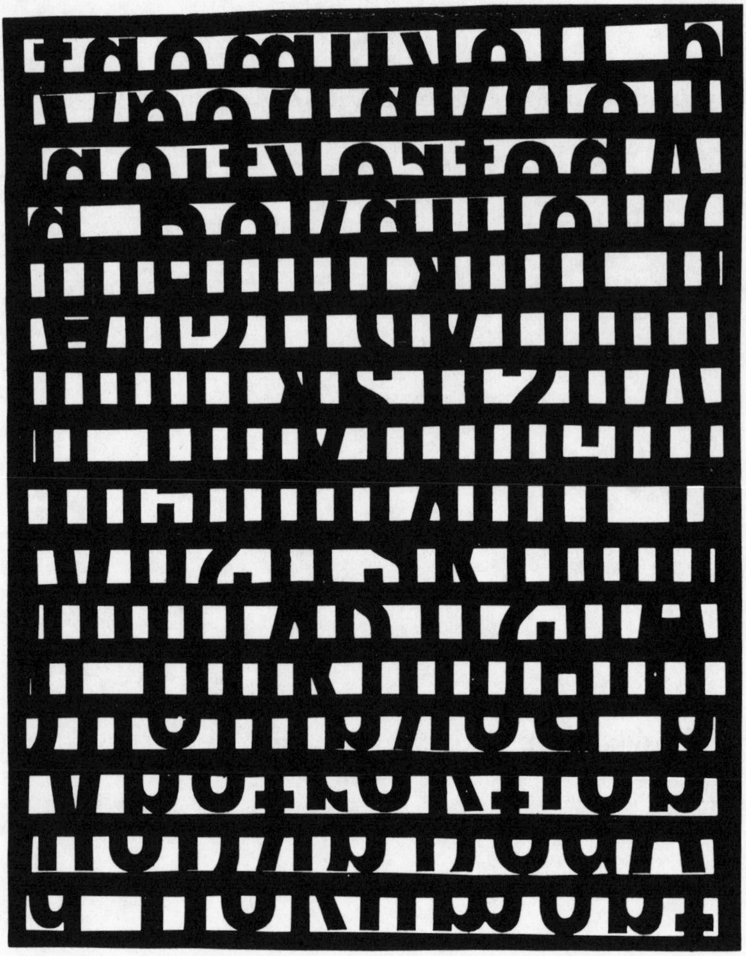

Franz Mon, *"Schriftcollage"* (1963)

aus den augen aus dem regen
aus dem regen aus der traum
aus der traum aus dem sinn
aus dem sinn aus den augen
aus den augen aus der traum
aus der traum aus dem regen
aus dem regen aus dem sinn
aus dem sinn aus der traum
aus der traum aus den augen
aus den augen aus dem sinn
aus dem sinn aus dem regen
aus dem regen aus den augen

Franz Mon (1966)

A permutation of four elements all introduced by the preposition *aus* (out of). The elements are part of German proverbs: 1 and 4 make *aus den augen, aus dem sinn*—out of sight, out of mind; the second belongs to *aus dem regen* (rain), *in die traufe* (gutter)—literally, "out of the rain, into the gutter," equivalent to the English "out of the frying pan into the fire." The third, *aus der traum* (dream) implies the end of an illusion. The elements are combined as follows: 1-2, 2-3, 3-4, 4-1, 1-3, 3-2, 2-4, 4-3, 3-1, 1-4, 4-2, 2-1.

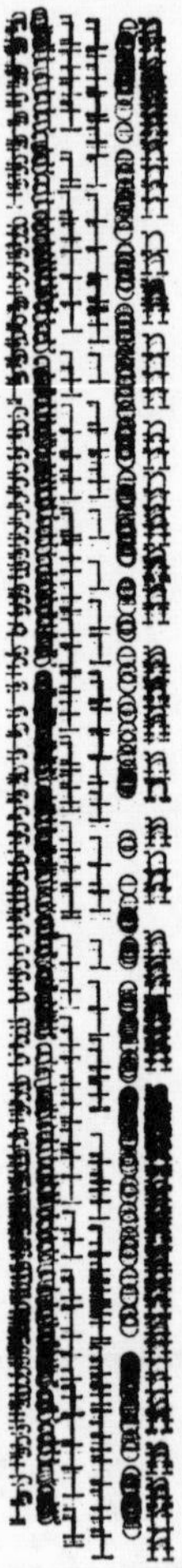

Franz Mon (1966)
fallen = to fall

jollymerry
hollyberry
jollyberry
merryholly
happyjolly
jollyjelly
jellybelly
bellymerry
hollyheppy
jollyMolly
marryJerry
merryHarry
hoppyBarry
heppyJarry
boppyheppy
berryjorry
jorryjolly
moppyjelly
Mollymerry
Jerryjolly
bellyboppy
jorryhoppy
hollymoppy
Barrymerry
Jarryhappy
happyboppy
boppyjolly
jollymerry
merrymerry
merrymerry
merryChris
ammerryasa
Chrismerry
asMERRYCHR
YSANTHEMUM

Edwin Morgan (1963)

"Permutational. All words chosen to have similar *structure* of consonant/vowel/double consonant/y, and to be working in similar *semantic* area of Christmas cheer, joy, parties, drinking, etc. The computer's final triumphant solution is relevant though wrong. 'Jerry' is a Scots word for a kind of earthenware marble used in children's games." (E.M.)

starryveldt
  slave
southvenus
  serve
SHARPEVILLE
  shove
shriekvolley
  swerve
shootvillage
  save
spoorvengeance
  stave
spadevoice
  starve
strikevault
  strive
subvert
  starve
smashverwoerd
  strive
scattervoortrekker
  starve
spadevow
  strive
sunvast
  starve
survive
  strive
so: VAEVICTIS

Edwin Morgan, "*Starryveldt*" (1964)

"The 'grid' pattern of S and V in alternating dissyllables and monosyllables is meant to build up an atmosphere of pounding menace." (E.M.)

pomander
open pomander
open poem and her
open poem and him
o p en poem and hymn
hymn and hymen leander
high man pen meander
o pen poem me and h e r
pen me poem me and him
om mane padme hum
pad me home panda hand
o p en up o holy panhandler
ample panda pen or bamboo pond
ponder a bonny poem pomander opener
open banned peon penman hum and banter
open hymn and pompom band and panda hamper
o i am a pen open man or happener
i am open manner happener
happy are we open
poem a nd a p o m
poem a nd a pan d a
poem and aplomb

Edwin Morgan (1964)

"It would take too long to expound all the references and associations here, but briefly, they are all meant to be in the area of 'opening up' something sweet and fresh like an old-fashioned pomander (I have in mind the sort that opened up in segments from the top, like the liths of an orange), whether it is the 'jewel in the lotus' (*Om Mane Padme Hum*) or a panda in a hamper, or a South American writer under the censors, or the whole conception of language in Spatialist poetry. It is both *visual* (in the shape of a pomander) and a *sound poem* in which I use a restricted range of letters and sounds to knit the wide variety of allusions together." (E.M.)

Blythsome the lovers. Brown the glove. Golden the jug. Sorrowful the bridal.
Brown the lovers. Blythsome the glove. Sorrowful the jug. Golden the bridal.
Golden the lovers. Sorrowful the glove. Brown the jug. Blythsome the bridal.
Sorrowful the lovers. Golden the glove. Blythsome the jug. Brown the bridal.

The glove lovers. The blythsome brown. The sorrowful golden. The bridal jug.
The jug lovers. The sorrowful brown. The blythsome golden. The bridal glove.
The glove jug. The brown blythsome. The golden brown. The bridal lovers.
The jug jug. The brown brown. The sorrowful sorrowful. The lovers lovers.

Sorrowful the brown glove lovers. Blythsome the golden bridal jug.

The sorrowful lovers. The brown jug. The golden glove. The blythsome bridal.

Edwin Morgan, "From an Old Scottish Chapbook" (1965)

"Permutations of the titles of four old Scottish songs, taken directly from a chapbook. The titles come clear in the last line. It's really a poem about 'chance': the chance juxtaposition of these titles seemed at once to be interesting and on the verge of meaningful. My permutations could be seen as one way of trying to find out *why* this should be so." (E.M.)

```
                         chaffinch
                  chaffinchaffinch
           chaffinchaffinchaffinch
           chaffinchaffinchaffinch
                  chaffinchaffinch
                         chaffinch
                         chaffie     chye    chaffiechaffie
                         chaffie      chye   chaffiechaffie
                                       chye  chaffie
                               chaffiechaffiechaffie
                               chaffiechaffiechaffie
                                      chaffiechaffie
                                      chaffiechaffie
                                      chaffiechaffie
                                      chaffiechaffie

                                 shillyshelly
                     shelfyshilfyshellyshilly
                           shelfyshillyshilly
                           shilfyshellyshelly
                     shilfyshelfyshelly
                                 shellyfaw
                           shielyshellyfaw
             shilfy  shielyshiely
       shilfyshelfy        shielychaffie
 shilfyshelfyshelfy        chaffiechaffie
       chaffiechaffie
       chaffiechaffie
 shilfyshilfyshilfyshelfyshelfy
chaffieshilfyshilfyshelfyshelfyshelfyshelfy
chaffieshilfyshilfyshelfyshelfyshelfyshelfyshelfy
 shilfyshilfyshilfyshelfy     shelfyshelfy
 shilfy      shilfy
             shilfy
             shilfyshelfy

       brichtie
```

Edwin Morgan, "The Chaffinch Map of Scotland" (1965)

"All these words are local terms for 'chaffinch' in various parts of Scotland; I have simply built up my map from their actual geographical distribution. In the title there's a pun on *chaffinch/half-inch*—it works in Scots and American, though not in English!" (E.M.)

the golden flood   the weightless seat
the cabin song   the pitch black
the growing beard   the floating crumb
the shining rendezvous   the orbit wisecrack
the hot spacesuit   the smuggled mouth-organ
the imaginary somersault   the visionary sunrise
the turning continents   the space debris
the golden lifeline   the space walk
the crawling deltas   the camera moon
the pitch velvet   the rough sleep
the crackling headphone   the space silence
the turning earth   the lifeline continents
the cabin sunrise   the hot flood
the shining spacesuit   the growing moon
the crackling somersault   the smuggled orbit
the rough moon   the visionary rendezvous
the weightless headphone   the cabin debris
the floating lifeline   the pitch sleep
the crawling camera   the turning silence
the space crumb   the crackling beard
the orbit mouth-organ   the floating song

Edwin Morgan, "Off Course" (1966)

"Movement from clear components to permutations of them is meant to bring out the developing theme of the rocket-ship off course, confusion, and disaster. This is one of a group of 'soundpoems' which I have had produced by the B.B.C. with radiophonic effects." (E.M.)

Edwin Morgan, "Seven Headlines" (1966)

"One of a group of 'emergent' poems, where everything comes out of, but at the same time mounts towards, the last line. The line in this poem is from Rimbaud's *Une Saison en Enfer.*" (E.M.)

Compare with Claus Bremer's "*der fuss des gewitters leuchtet*" on page 38.

```
                ol        d
               sol  e   m    n
                o         de
               sol        d
   f            o           r
   f    e            n    der
i         r     o            n
              b ol        d
         tre         n    d
i                    n
 l      et            t    er
                      t  o
               sol       o
          re a            der
    a     r    so    n
i                            n
              b ol    t
   f      r     o  m
              b  lu e
    a         bs    ent
   f            o        od
              b   u       d
   f            o u  n    d
     ut  t e                r
   f    e r        ment
i                    n
          re a so    n
         t e a     m
   f    e  e              d
    a t                 modern
                 l       ode
                     n   o
   f    et            t    er
   f            o           r
             absolu   t    e
                   m     odern
                   men
il faut être absolument moderne
```

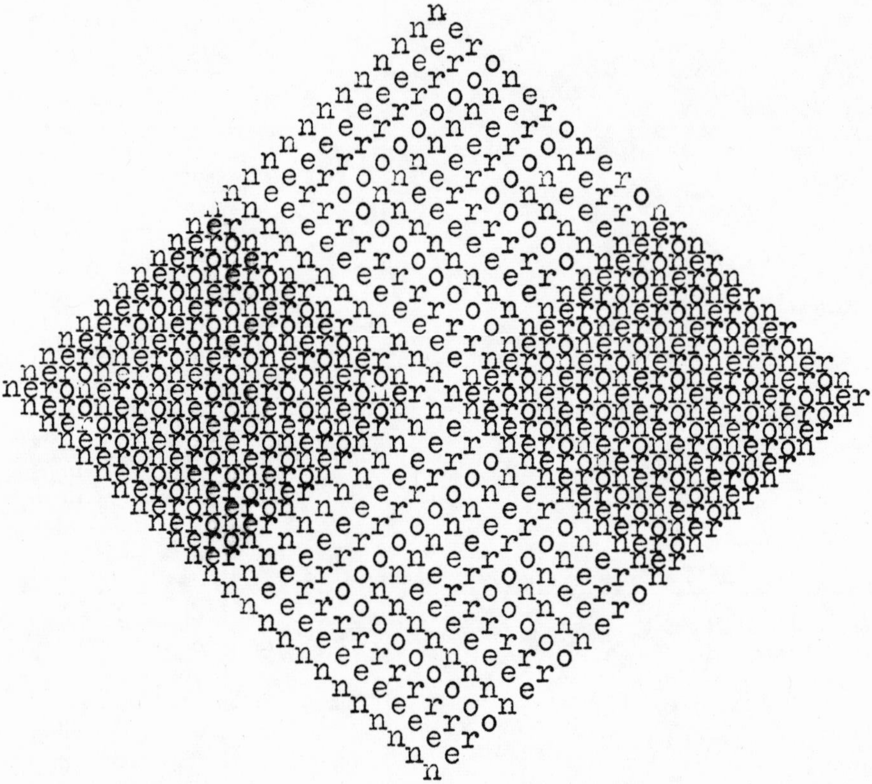

Maurizio Nannucci (1964)

nero = black

Maurizio Nannucci (1965)

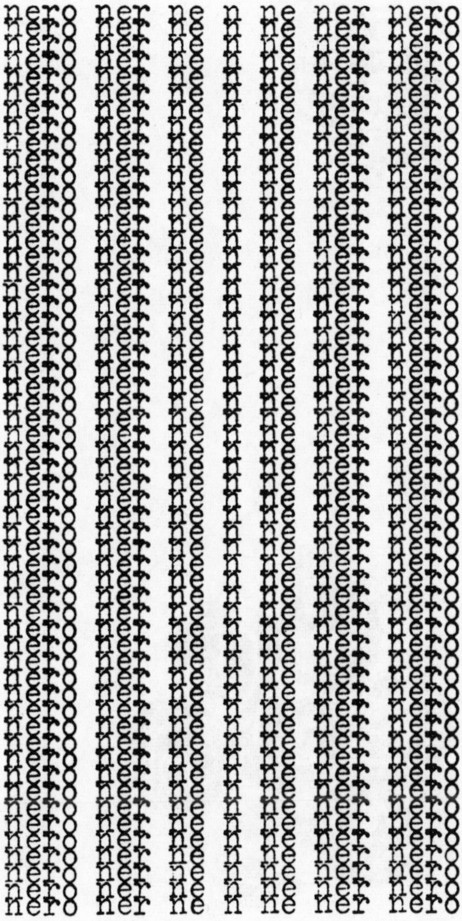
nero ner ne n ne ner nero

bp Nichol, eyes (1967)

"tight imagistic things. intended for what they teach the eye on one looking tho some tend to be pleasing if looked at a few times. executed as a unit which has become my standard concrete composing form. seldom singly. not meant as pictures but as syllabic and sub-syllabic messages for who care to listen." (bp N.)

LINE

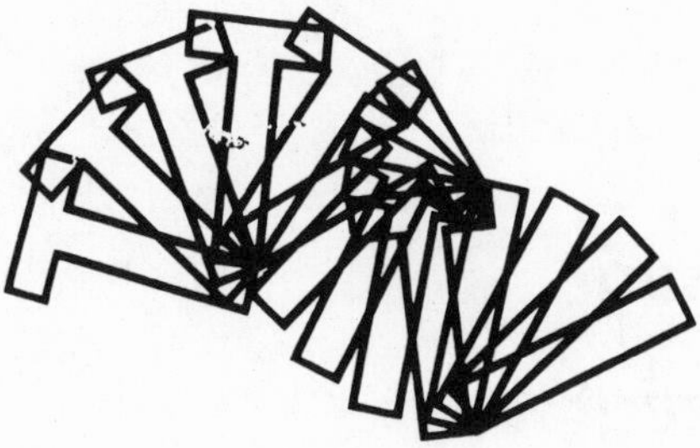

bp Nichol, eyes (continued)

" . . . i chose this unit **EYES**, which not too coincidentally is the most recent, as the best thing i've done . . . with CONCRETE i tend to think of only the most recent things as mine. all the rest go into a literary LIMBO." (bp N., in a letter to the editor.)

```
sagt
sagt som sagt
     som sagt som sagt
              som sagt sagt
                       sagt
```

Hans-Jørgen Nielsen (1965)
sagt = said
som = as

Hans-Jørgen Nielsen (1965)

midt = in the middle

m   i   d   t

            m   i   d   t

m   i   d   t

m   i   d   t

m   i   d   t

m   i   d   t

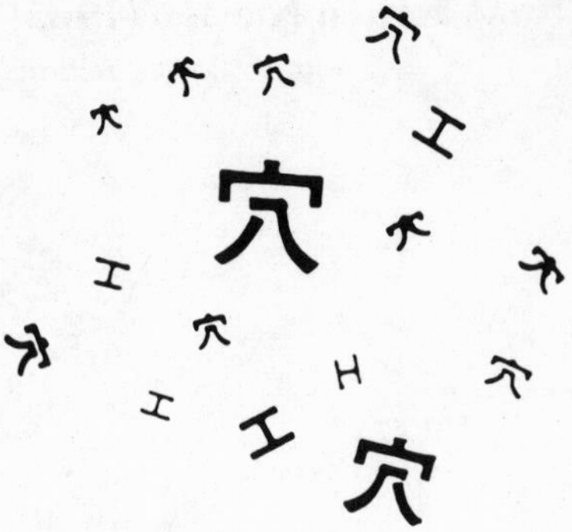

穴 工 穴 工 穴 工 穴 工 穴 工 穴 工 穴 工 穴

空

鍬

Seiichi Niikuni

穴	*ana* = orifice
工	*ko* = technique
空 穴+工=空 }	*sora* = sky
鋤	*suki* = a spade

川川川川川川川川川川川川川川川川川川川
川川川川川川川川川川川川川川川川川川州
川川川川川川川川川川川川川川川川川州州
川川川川川川川川川川川川川川川川州州州
川川川川川川川川川川川川川川川州州州州
川川川川川川川川川川川川川川州州州州州
川川川川川川川川川川川川川州州州州州州
川川川川川川川川川川川川州州州州州州州
川川川川川川川川川川川州州州州州州州州
川川川川川川川川川川州州州州州州州州州
川川川川川川川川川州州州州州州州州州州
川川川川川川川川州州州州州州州州州州州
川川川川川川川州州州州州州州州州州州州
川川川川川川州州州州州州州州州州州州州
川川川川川州州州州州州州州州州州州州州
川川川川州州州州州州州州州州州州州州州
川川川州州州州州州州州州州州州州州州州
川川州州州州州州州州州州州州州州州州州
川州州州州州州州州州州州州州州州州州州
州州州州州州州州州州州州州州州州州州州

Seiichi Niikuni

kawa = river

sasu = sand-bank

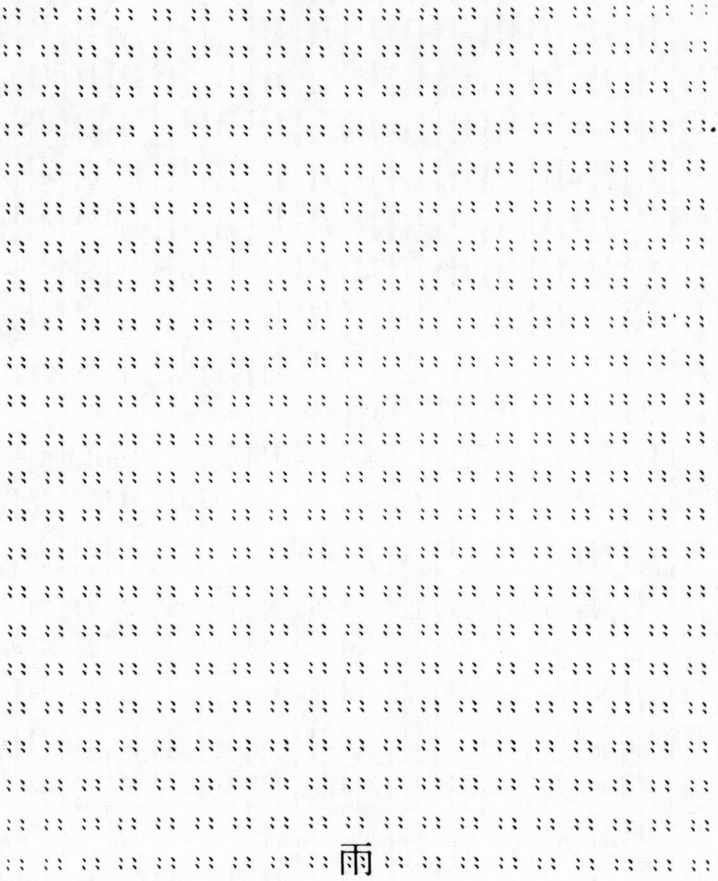
雨

Seiichi Niikuni

雨 = *ame* = rain

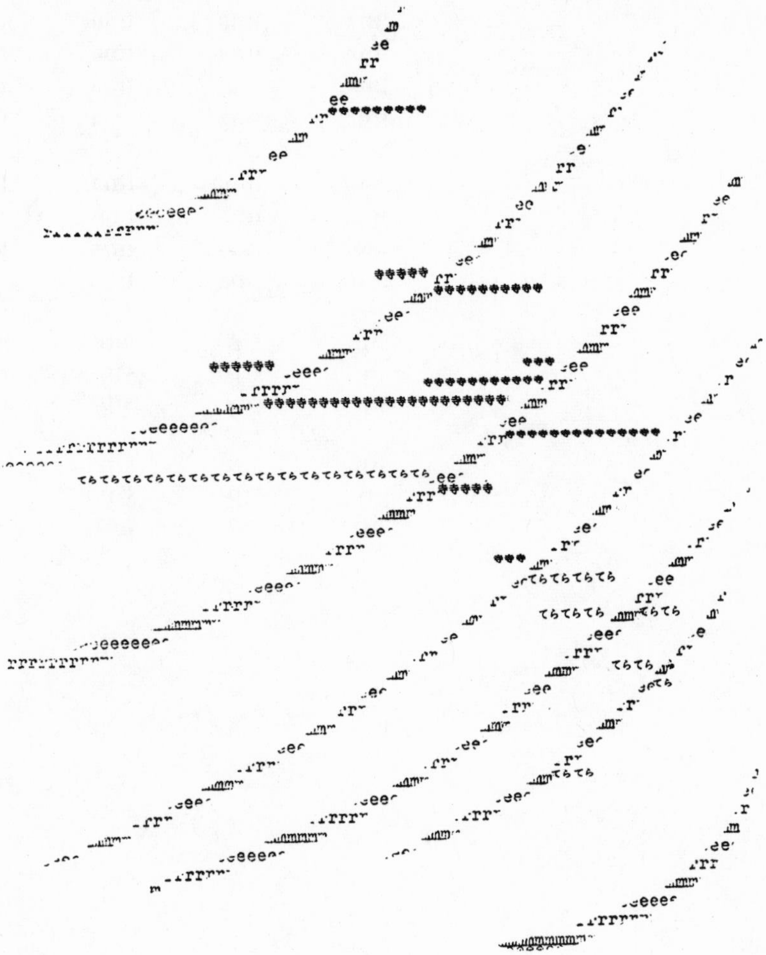

Seiichi Niikuni and Pierre Garnier, from *Poèmes franco-japonais* (1966)

"This text, done in collaboration with Seiichi Niikuni, is an attempt, in the perspective of concrete poetry, to join the French and Japanese languages together in a linguistic reality. To do this, we have had to 'file down,' as it were, the French vocabulary and letters to give them a plasticity approximating that of oriental characters, the same approach we used in our French-Japanese phonetic poems." (Pierre Garnier)

tma tma tma tam
tma tma tma tma
tma tam tma tma
tma tma tma tma

tma hma tma tma
tma tma tám tma
tam tma tma tma
tma tma tma tam

srp srp srp srp
srp srp srp prs
srp prs srp srp

srp srp srp srp
prs srp srp srp
srp srp pes srp

Ladislav Novák, from *sklenená laboratoř* (1959–63)

A poem about "*kouzlo letni noci*" (magic of a summer night).
tma = darkness
tam = there
hma-tám = I touch
srp = sickle
pes = dog

Ladislav Novák

A poem that seems to demand translation into architecture.

O

GL RIA

Ladislav Novák, from *sklenená laboratoř* (1959–63)

The poem "zakletá" (bewitched) is an incantation of *láska* (love) among the *skála* (rocks).

s k á l a s k á l a s k á l a s k á l a

s k á l a s k á l a s k á l a s k á l a

s k á l a s k á l a s k á l a s k á l a

s k á l a s k á l a s k a l á s k a l a

s k á l a s k á l a s k á l a s k á l a

y	y	y
ya	ya	ya
yar	yar	yar
yari	yarı	yari
yarim	yarım	yarim
yari	yarı	yari
yar	yar	yar
ya	ya	ya
y	y	y
m	m	m
im	mı	im
rim	mır	rim
arim	mıra	arim
yarim	mıray	yarim
arim	mıra	arim
rim	mır	rim
im	mı	im
m	m	m

Yüksel Pazarkaya, "*yarim yarim*" (1964)

ya = affirmation
yar = beloved
yari = his sweetheart
yarı = middle
yarim = my beloved
yarım = unfinished
mir = master
mira = girl's name
my = moon
mirai = family name

der esel ist eine wurst
der esel ist einewurst
der esel isteinewurst
der eselisteinewurst
dereselisteinewurst

Yüksel Pazarkaya, *the donkey cycle*: 1

Pazarkaya's donkey cycle is based on a legend from eastern Turkey. There was a man whose only possession was an old donkey. He decided to sell it, and, to get as much as possible out of the sale, he painted it to make it look young. He found a buyer—his own father. The father was swindled, but, not stupid, made the best of the bargain and converted the old donkey into sausage. Since that time, says the legend, the city of Kayseri has been famous for its sausages.

In part 1 of the cycle, the sentence *der esel ist eine wurst* (the donkey is a sausage) is transformed sausage-fashion. Part 2, a formation composed of *farb* (color) and *esel* (donkey), suggests *farb* as a synonym for the uniform, which, like the fresh paint on the old donkey, makes the wearer *look* better than he really is. Part 3

	fa esel rb	
	fa esel rb	
farbesel	fa esel rb	eselfarb
farbese	eselfarb	eselfar
farbes	farbesel	eselfa
farbe	es farb el	eself
farb	es farb el	esel
far	es farb el	ese
fa		es
f		e

Yüksel Pazarkaya, *the donkey cycle*: 2

pits the German *esel* against the Turkish *esek*. In part 4, the proposition "anybody who wants to be a donkey can be one" is tempered by a construction of *nicht leicht* (not easy) which, with the systematic subtraction of letters, becomes *leicht* (easy), until the final *t* marches off to fill the space of the original proposition.

Yüksel Pazarkaya, *the donkey cycle*: 3

esek esel esek esel esek esel esek esel esek ese
esek esel esek esel esek esel esek esel esek ese
sek sek sel sel sek sek sel sel sek sek
ek ek el el ek ek el el ek ek
k k l l k k l l k k
e e e e e e e e e e
es es es es es es es es es es
ese ese ese ese ese ese ese ese ese ese
esek esel esek esel esek esel esek esel esek ese
esek esel esek esel esek esel esek esel esek ese
sel sel sek sek sel sel sek sek sel sel
el el ek ek el el ek ek el el
l l k k l l k k l l
e e e e e e e e e e
es es es es es es es es es es
ese ese ese ese ese ese ese ese ese ese
esek esel esek esel esek esel esek esel esek ese
esek esel esek esel esek esel esek esel esek ese
sek sek sel sel sek sek sel sel sek sek
ek ek el el ek ek el el ek ek
k k l l k k l l k k
e e e e e e e e e e
es es es es es es es es es es
ese ese ese ese ese ese ese ese ese ese
esek esel esek esel esek esel esek esel esek ese
esek esel esek esel esek esel esek esel esek ese

Yüksel Pazarkaya, *the donkey cycle*: 4

eselsein werwill
eselsein werwill
eselsein werwill
eselsein werwill
eselsein werwill
eselsein werwill
eselsein werwill

nichtleichtnichtle
ichtnichtleichtni
chtleichtnichtl
eichtnichtlei
chtnichtleic
htnichtlei
chtnichtl
eichtni
chtlei
chtn
icht
lei
ch
tttttttttttttttttttttttt

Décio Pignatari (1956)

"Around the axial line of *mm*, words and segments of words constellate themselves, making a kind of verbal *mobile*." (Haroldo de Campos)

Word for word translation: a/move/ment/compounding/behind/the/cloud/a/field/of/battle/mira/ge/ire/of/a/pure/horizon/at/a/live/mo/ment

```
      u m
        m o v i
        m e n t o
    c o m p o n d o
  a l é m
                d a
n u v e m
      u m
    c a m p o
          d e
    c o m b a t e

        m i r a
    g e m
          i r a
                d e
      u m
          h o r i z o n t e
p u r o
    n u m
        m o
        m e n t o
v i v o
```

beba coca cola
babe cola
beba coca
babe cola caco
caco
cola

cloaca

Décio Pignatari (1957)
beba = to drink
babe = to slob
cola = glue
caco = pieces

"An early committed concrete poem. A kind of anti-advertisement. Against the reification of the mind through slogans, demistifying of the 'artificial paradise' promised by mass-persuasion techniques. *Cloaca* is made out of the same letters as *Coca-Cola*." (Haroldo de Campos)

Décio Pignatari (1958)

"A cine-poem. The progression of the letters corresponds to the progression of their traces. The word is reorganized following the visual crescendo of its letters' features. With four traces we have a nucleus, where all letters are condensed and resumed. By a coincidence, this nucleus is also the Chinese ideogram for sun (*jih;* Japanese *hi*), the vital principle. After this, the nucleus explodes, producing the word LIFE. The poem develops the passage from the digital unit to the semantic corpus (word), and from the ideogram (analogical) to the phonetic word (digital), suggesting some unexpected links between both processes." (Haroldo de Campos)

L

Décio Pignatari (continued from facing page)

F

Décio Pignatari (continued from preceding page)

E

Décio Pignatari (continued from facing page)

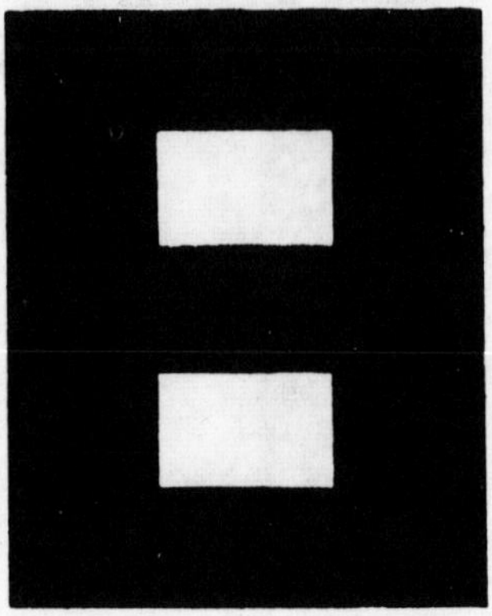

Décio Pignatari (continued from preceding page)

LIFE

Décio Pignatari (concluded)

ra terra ter
rat erra ter
rate rra ter
rater ra ter
raterr a ter
raterra terr
araterra ter
raraterra te
rraraterra t
erraraterra
terraraterra

Décio Pignatari (1956)

"This poem is a typical meta-poem or poem-about-the-poem. Its structure is based on the repetition of only one word—*terra* (earth)—as it occurs with letters of a newsreel on a luminous screen. This word is fragmented until the production (line 7) of a kind of 'error'—the duplication of the syllable *ra* (terr / *ara*). This self-correcting error feeds back the machine-poem (like in cybernetics), and gives it its semantical optimum level. By this process, the poem engenders phrases like *ara a terra* (ploughs the land) *ter rara terra* (to have a rare land), *errar a terra* (to be mistaken about the land), *terra ara terra* (land ploughs land) and, implicitly, *terra terra* (a plain thing). All these syntagmatic elements converge to the semantic matrix of the poem: the idea of a self-regulating poem, like a rare land which ploughs itself, and the creative 'error' (*errar* = to make a mistake and to roam). Visually, this concrete 'georgic' is reinforced by the blanks reproducing the furrows of the plough." (Haroldo de Campos)

h o m b r e	h o m b r e	h o m b r e
h a m b r e		h e m b r a
	h a m b r e	
h e m b r a	h e m b r a	h a m b r e

Décio Pignatari (1957)

"Concrete lyricism: a love poem made out of a paronomasia. The topology of the words on the page conveys the message—when *hombre* (man) and *hembra* (female) are placed together, *hambre* (hunger), in its figurative meaning (appetite, desire), is removed." (Haroldo de Campos) o organism o quer perdurar

o organismo quer repet

o organismo quer re

o organismo quer

o organism

Décio Pignatari, '*organismo*' (1960)

"'*organismo*' (organism): cine-poem first published as a booklet in 1960, a kind of erotic piece dealing with the transformation of a *sign* (the letter and Portuguese article O) into a biological signal." (Haroldo de Campos)

o organismo quer perdurar = the organism wants to endure

o organismo quer repet (ir) = the organism wants to repe (at)

O

o o

orgasm

```
S   O   L   I   D   A

S   O   L   I   D   A   O

S   O

        L   I   D   A

S   O   L

S                   A

            I   D

    O

                D   A

        L   I   D   A

                D

    O

                D

            I       A
```

Wlademir Dias Pino, from *solida* (1957)

solida = solid
solidão = solitude
so = only
lida = works (third person singular)
sol = sun
saido = gone out
da lido do dia = from the day's labor

```
S   O   L   I   D   A

,   ,   ,   ,   ,   ,   O

,   ,

        ,   ,   ,   ,

,   ,   ,

,                   ,

            ,   ,

    ,

                ,   ,

        ,   ,   ,   ,

                ,

    ,

                ,

            ,       ,
```

Wlademir Dias Pino, from *solida* (1957)

Second phase of poem on facing page.

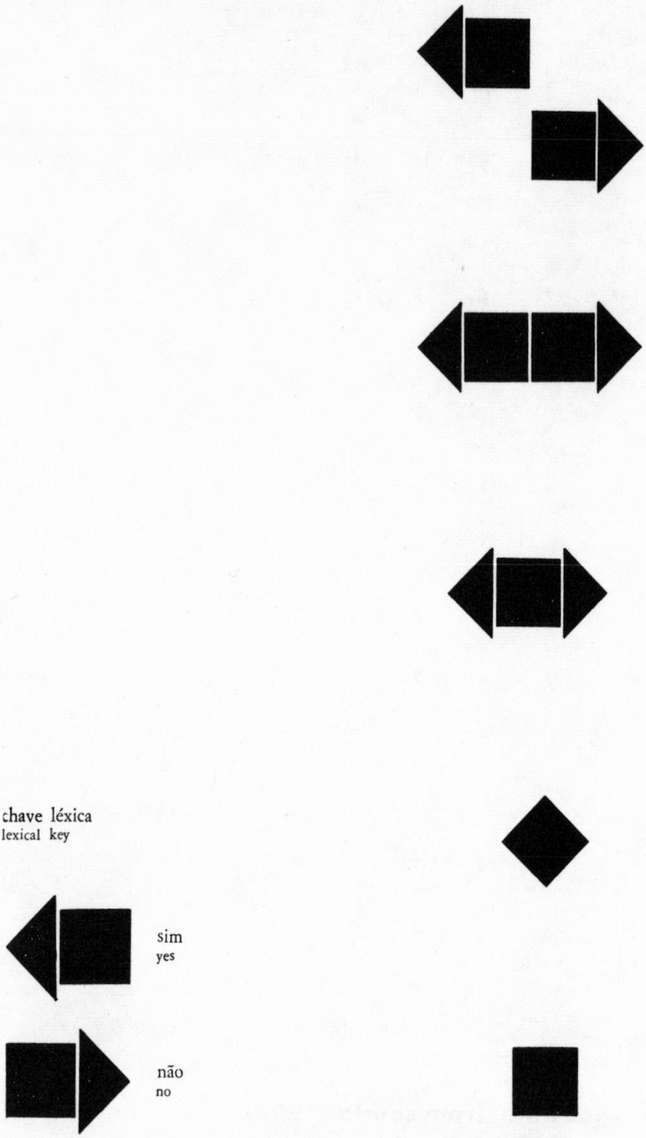
chave léxica
lexical key
sim
yes
não
no

Luiz Angelo Pinto (1964)

A semiotic or "code" poem.

" . . . the idea of a language in which the form of the signs might be designed so as to determine the syntax, giving new communications possibilities. For this, it is necessary that a set of signs (and the signs themselves) be dynamic, that is, manageable, changeable, according to the needs of each text." (From the semiotic poetry manifesto of Pinto and Décio Pignatari, *Invenção* No. 4, 1965.)

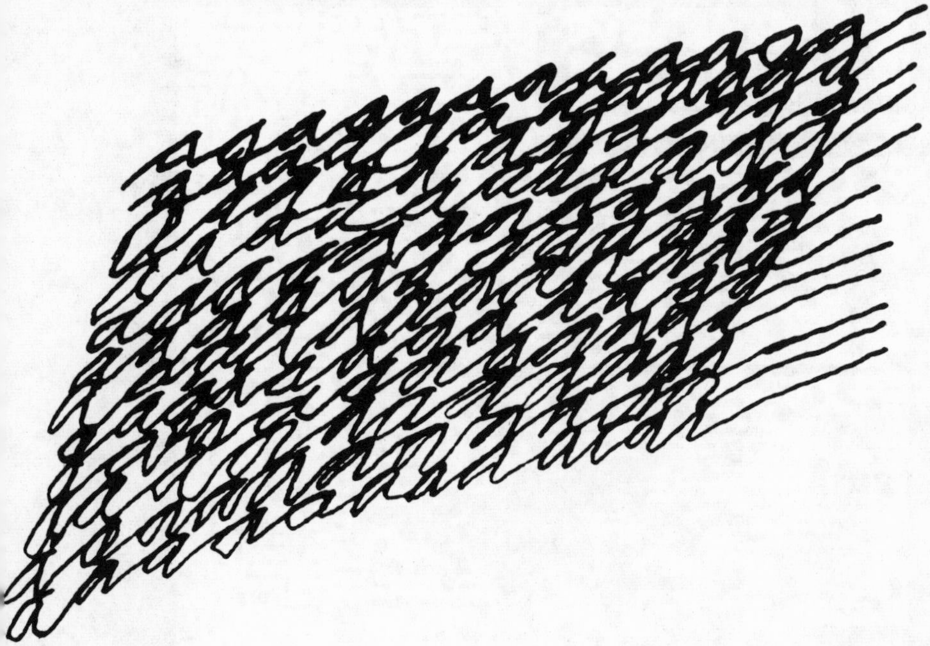

Carl Fredrik Reuterswärd, *"The Poem A"* (1954)

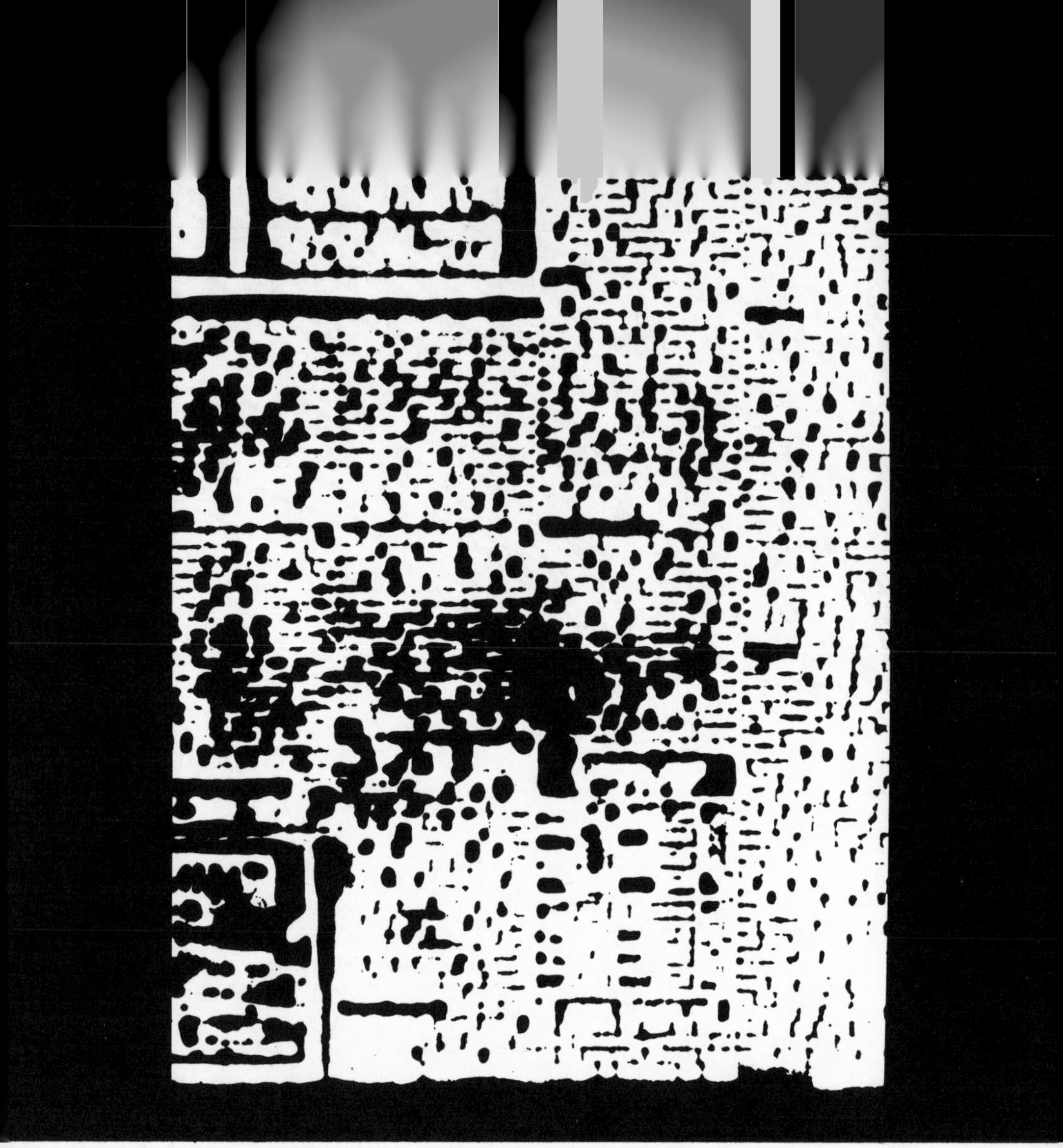

Carl Fredrik Reuterswärd (1955–56)

The **France-Soir Story** series are drawings of the spaces between words, punctuation and drawings on pages of *France-Soir*. There are 'chapters' on cuisine, murder, love, etc. This one is called "Politics."

Carl Fredrik Reuterswärd, from *Prix Nobel* (1960)

"The use of punctuation marks in a text forces them to a 'neutral value.' The word 'colon' does not correspond to any 'colon concepts.' Do you have any colon concepts? The text apparatus satisfies a demand of that kind. The position or placing

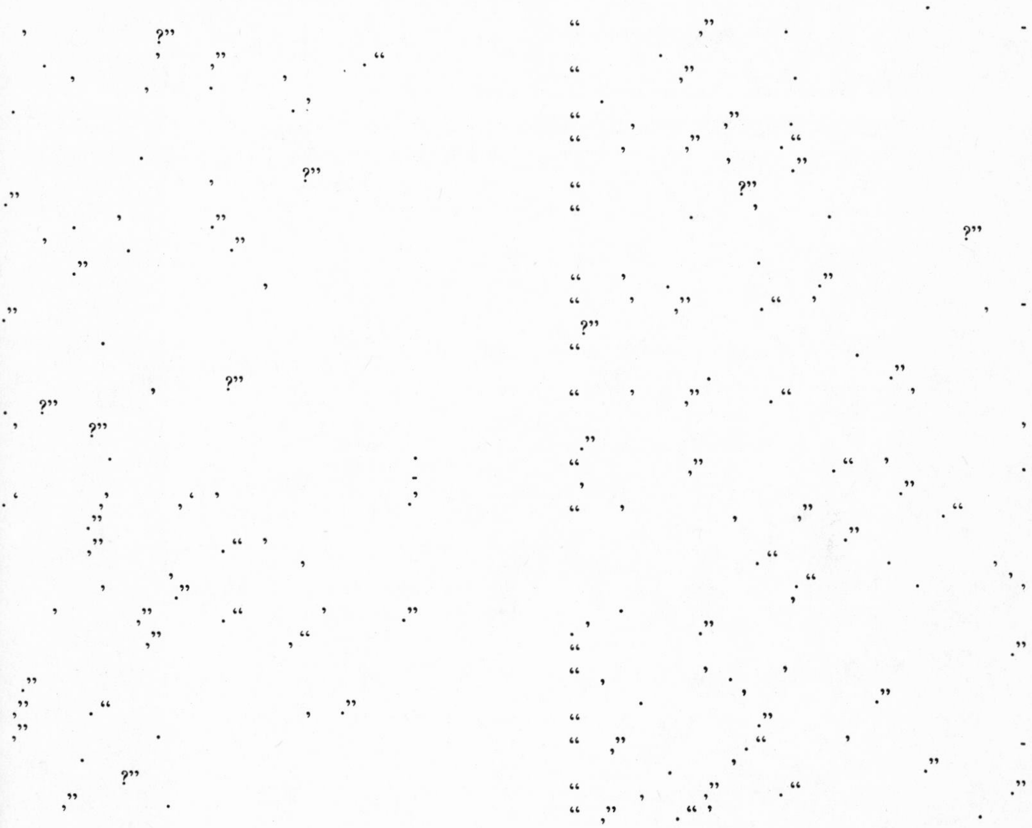

of a punctuation mark does not decide its *own* meaning. (An exclamation mark in the middle of a sentence does not distort the mark itself but does distort the emphasis of the sentence.) Nor is there any mutual order of rank; a period is not superior to a parenthesis. It is in such neutral and equal linguistic attributes that I see an interesting alternative: not to ignore a syntax but certainly to forego 'the preserved meanings of others.' The 'absence' that occurs is not mute. For want of 'governing concepts' punctuation marks lose their neutral value. They begin to speak an unuttered language out of that already expressed. This cannot help producing a 'colon concept' in you, a need of exclamation, of pauses, of periods, of parenthesis. But a state that has come about at the expense of the noble prize: out of its *own idea*. (C.F.R., introduction to ***Prix Nobel***.)

t

u

u

u

t tu

u

u

t ut

u

t t

t

Diter Rot (1956)

"The review **material**, as its name implies, was intended to propagate concrete poetry, in which I myself was interested at the time. Its aim was to eliminate the subjective point of view of the author, and present poetic material that the reader could do with as he saw fit. Some of the texts, 'ideograms,' appealed to the optical sense by their typographic arrangement. Here is an example by Diter Rot, who composed the second number of the review. Two squares, interlocking, form at their intersection the two little words ut and tu. A possible interpretation would be that there is no meeting without reciprocal influences." (Daniel Spoerri, **An Anecdoted Topography of Chance**)

Diter Rot (1956)

"two as one, one as two." (D.R.)

(See note on next page.)

Diter Rot (continued)

"I like your selection, but I thought we should add some of the pieces which are concerned with a relation of more than just one page—so I added the piece with the cross (a vertical line on the one side and a horizontal line on the other). . . . and a two-page piece where I have, so to speak, translated a grouping of lines into a grouping of words." (D.R.) (See following two pages.)

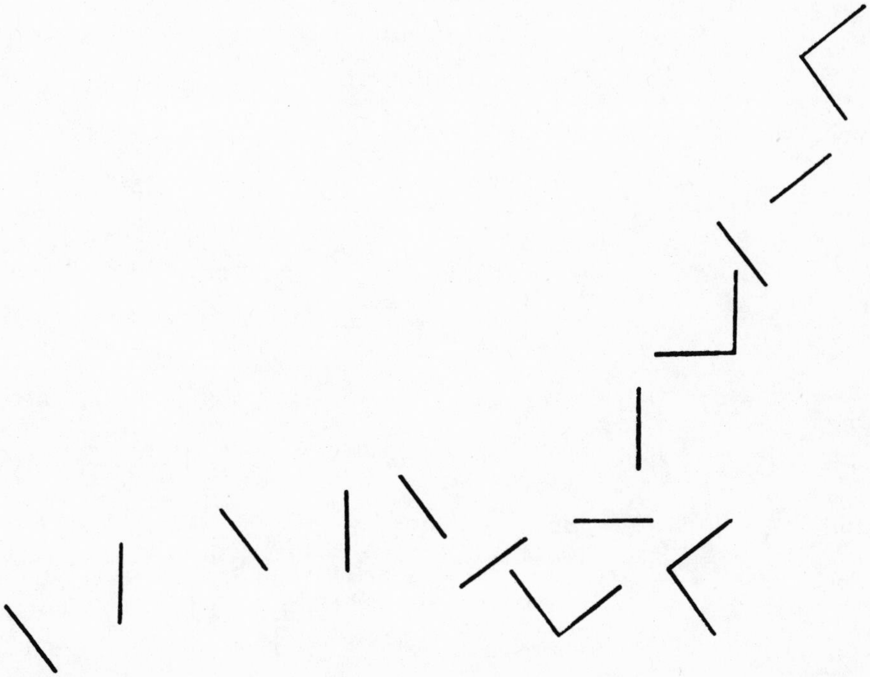

Diter Rot, "two-sided translation" (1957)
(See "translation" on next page.)

ba

fua

ba

auf

ba

ba

ba

auf auf auf auf ab fua ab fua

ba

ba

auf

Diter Rot (continued)

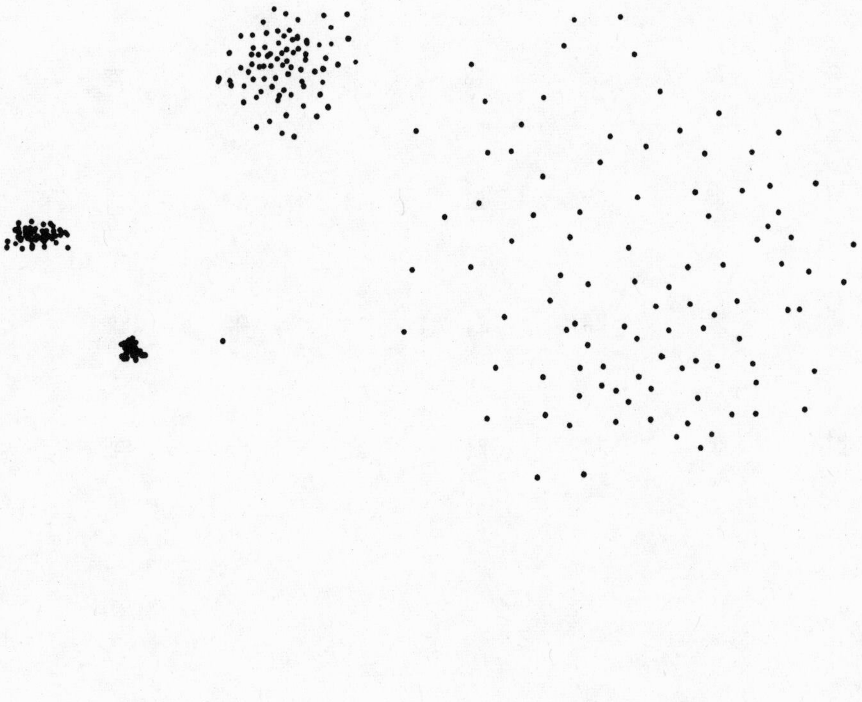

Diter Rot (1958)

"All as one? one as all?" (D.R.)

A prototype of non-semantic concretizing.

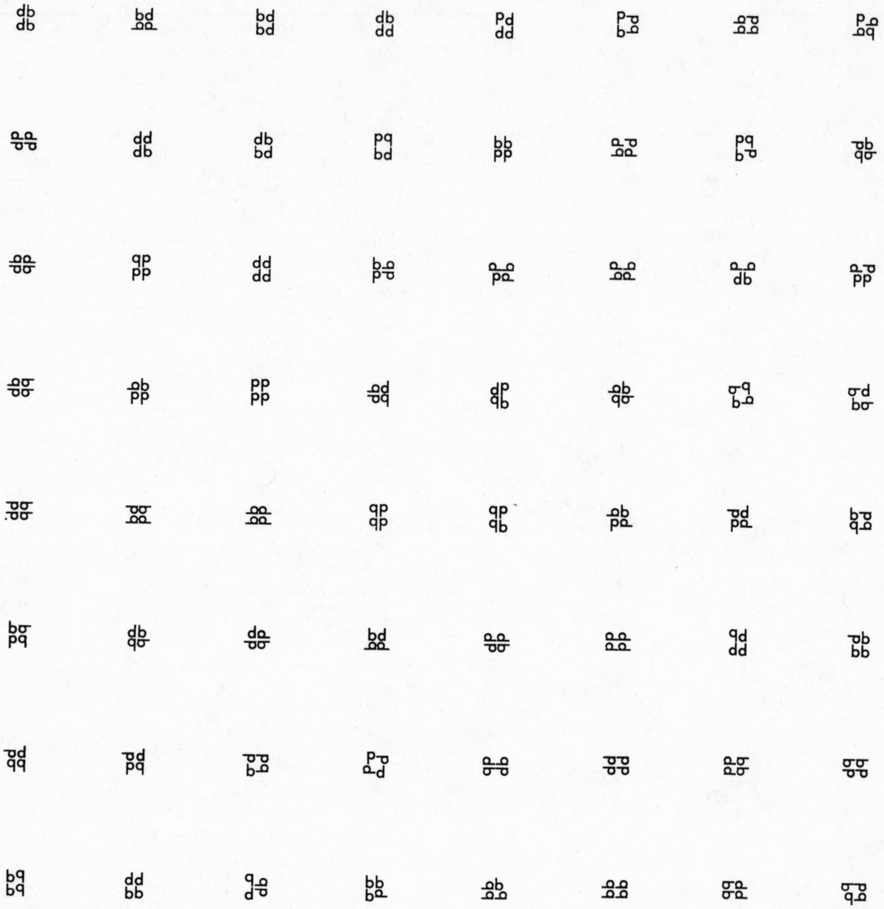

Diter Rot (1957)

"Some variations on 4^4." (D.R.)

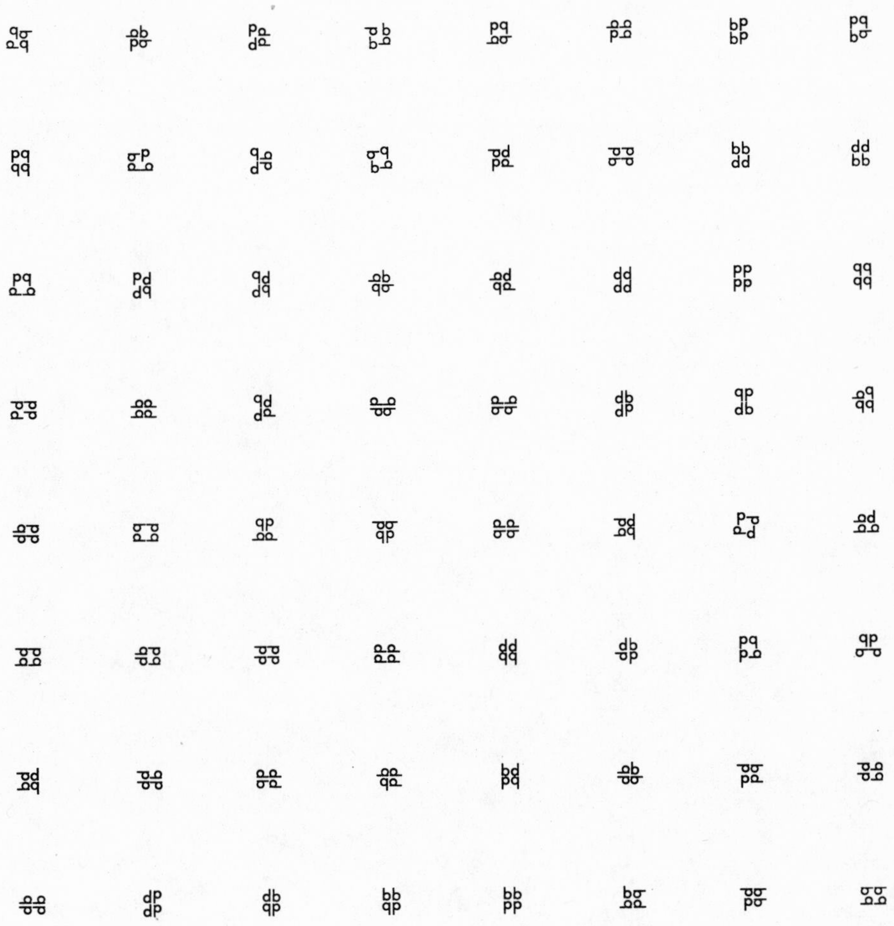

at

at at

em it it

em em it it

em em em it

it – – –

it it – –

it it it –

– . . .

– – . .

– – – .

.

. .

. . .

– – –

– –

–

– . . .

– – . .

– – – .

. om om om

. . om om

. . . om

om it it it

om om it it

om om om it

it am am am

it am am

it am

.
.
.
– – – .
– – . .
– . . .
to to to –
to to – –
to – – –
mi mi mi to
mi mi to to
mi to to to
tu tu tu mi
tu tu mi mi
tu mi mi mi
me me me tu
me me tu tu
me tu tu tu
ta ta ta me
ta ta me me
ta me me me
mu mu mu ta
mu mu ta ta
mu ta ta ta
te te te mu
te te mu mu
te mu mu mu
ma ma ma te
ma ma te te
ma te te

Diter Rot (1957)

"A piece for voice and silence." (D.R.)

Diter Rot (1958)

"Advertising my typewriter." (D.R.)

die nacht
und die tochter der nacht
und die tochter der tochter der nacht
und die tochter der tochter der tochter der nacht

der tag
und der sohn des tages
und der sohn des sohnes des tages
und der sohn des sohnes des sohnes des tages

der sohn
und
die tochter

und alle ihre verwandten alle verwandten

sie blicken auf das geschwisterpaar

sie blicken auf den sohn und die tochter
des sohnes und der tochter
des sohnes und der tochter

und es wird tag
und es wird nacht

Gerhard Rühm (1954)

the night / and the daughter of the night, etc.
the day / and the son of the day, etc.
and all their kindred all kindred
they look at the brother and sister, etc.
and day is breaking
and night is falling

blueinblueinblueinblue

manbymanbymanbyman

theblue

thebluemanbyman

blueman

Gerhard Rühm (1954)

Translated by the editor.

uuuuuuuuuuuuuuuuu
uuuuuuuuuuuuuuuuu
uuuuuuuuuuuuuuuuu
uuuuuuuuuuuuuuuuu
uuuuuuuuduuuuuuuu
uuuuuuuuuuuuuuuuu
uuuuuuuuuuuuuuuuu
uuuuuuuuuuuuuuuuu
uuuuuuuuuuuuuuuuu

Gerhard Rühm (1954)
The word imprisoned within itself.

sternsternsternsternst
stern   stern   stern
stern   stern
gestern
stern
geste

Gerhard Rühm (1954)

stern = star, fate, stern (of a boat)
ernst = seriousness, seriously, serious
gestern = yesterday
geste = gesture

leib leib leib leib
leib leib leib leib
leib leib leib leib
leib leib leib leib
leib leib leib leib
leib leib leib leib
leib leib leib leib
leib leib leib leib
leib leib leib leib
leib leib leib leib
leib leib leibleib

Gerhard Rühm (1955)

leib = body
bleib = to stay

For the German reader there are several associations:
jemandem vom Leibe bleiben (keep away from someone) and
bleib mir damit vom Leibe (don't bother me with that).

Gerhard Rühm (1958)

jetzt = now

jetzt

Jetzt

Jetzt

jetzt

Jetzt

Jetzt

jetzt

jetzt

jetzt

jetzt

jetzt

Jetzt

nedn nedn
a nedn nedn
un nedn nedn
aun nedn
un
un daggn daggn
o daggn daggn
ein daggn daggn
un nedn
un
un nedn daggn
nedn duggn
nedn daggn duggn
o deggn deggn
aun daggn daggn
un nedn
un
nedn daggn duggn

Gerhard Rühm (1959)

Rühm calls this a "poem in the Viennese dialect," but the reader should not strain to make sense out of the sound. In Rühm's reading of the poem, the accents, in the first five lines, fall on *a, un, aun* and *un*. The poem is read very rapidly.

[redacted]

Lehrsätze über das Weltall

mit Beweis in Form
eines offenen Briefes
an Professor Einstein

[redacted]

Gerhard Rühm, *Lehrsätze über das Weltall* (1965)

A poetic reworking of a refutation of Einstein's theories. The text reads: "Now if I could intercept the maximal distance between two stars with a single infinitely great star . . ."

[redacted]

Lehrsätze

1.
2.
3.
4.
5.
6.
7.

[redacted]

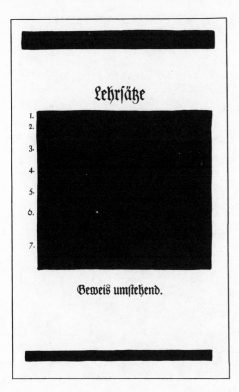

Beweis umstehend.

[redacted]

[redacted]

Herrn

Professor Einstein,

Berlin.

Betr. Weltall.

[redacted]

Wenn ich nun

[redacted]

Gerhard Rühm, *Lehrsätze über das Weltall* (continued from facing page)

[redacted]

dem größten Abstand

[redacted]

[redacted]

zwischen zwei Sternen

[redacted]

miteinander

einen einzigen unendlich großen Stern

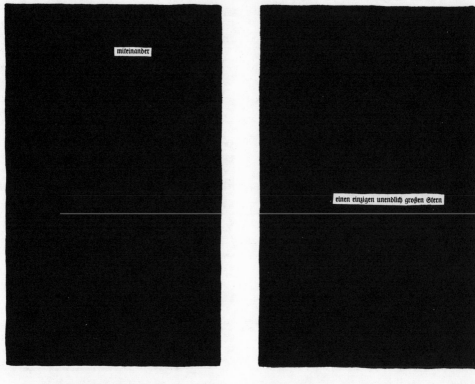

Gerhard Rühm, *Lehrsätze über das Weltall* (continued from previous page)

nach innen reißen

könnten,

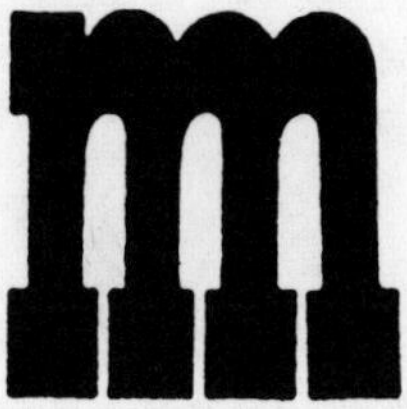

Aram Saroyan (1965–66)
A poster-poem.

```
.        .        .
ian hamilton finlay
```

Aram Saroyan (1965–66)

"I write on a typewriter, almost never in hand (I can hardly handwrite, I tend to draw words), and my machine—an obsolete red-top Royal Portable—is the biggest influence on my work. This red hood hold the mood, keeps my eye happy. The type-face is a standard pica; if it were another style I'd write (subtly) different poems. And when a ribbon gets dull my poems I'm sure change." (A.S.)

wwww
wwww
. . . .
waww
wakw
wake
. . . .
walw
walk

Aram Saroyan (1965–66)

eyeye

Aram Saroyan (1965–66)

W
O P E N
R   O B E
D

shoe dead

vake

toes wait

John J. Sharkey, Stills from OPENWORDROBE (1964)

"The first part of the film was designed to create a definite mood; from the opening single letters of the title, to the different blocks of variations of the three words within it (stills 1,2,3). Thereafter the changes became more rapid and fluid with different letter-types and sizes; incorporating permutated blocks (I Ching hexagrams); moving dot and O motif; random design elements with irregular shaped cards with colour words, tossed in front of the camera lens; free association of words in a literal transcription of object and colours that a full wardrobe might contain. In still no. 4, I changed the w of wake into vake to diminish this association and create some discord. The first movement of the film is repeated at the end with an elaborate construction of the title words; the base line increasing with each dropping letter until **OPENWORDROBE** is reached at the bottom of the final frames." (J.J.S.)

s c h o e n b e r g
s c h o e n b e r g
s c h o e n b e r g
s c h o e n b e r g
s c h o e n b e r g
s c h o e n b e r g
s c h o e n b e r g
s c h o e n b e r g
s c h o e n b e r g
s c h o e n b e r g

John J. Sharkey (1963)

"John Sharkey is a Schoenberg addict, and despite the preconceptions about his theories, finds the music simple and pure. In deciding to make a concrete poem out of Schoenberg's name alone, he was commenting on these qualities. It was initially designed in both upper and lower case with the transition from one to the other assuming the form of a diagonal with the top line in lower case and the bottom in capitals. Here a permutation was evolved employing five different type sizes of which the relationship would be analogous to Schoenberg's twelve-tone theory, and which would retain the original diagonal. Despite a satisfactory formula Sharkey found that the printed version lacked the symmetry and tightness of the original conception." (Jasia Reichardt, introduction to **concrete poetry britain canada united states**, in which the above version, interpreted typographically by Simon Lord, first appeared.)

John J. Sharkey (1963)

Sharkey's original conception of the poem opposite. The publisher of the other version, Hansjörg Mayer, could not go along with Sharkey's conception because Mayer does not use upper-case letters in his graphic production style.

s c h o e n b e r g

S c h o e n b e r g

S C h o e n b e r g

S C H o e n b e r g

S C H O e n b e r g

S C H O E n b e r g

S C H O E N b e r g

S C H O E N B e r g

S C H O E N B E r g

S C H O E N B E R g

S C H O E N B E R G

at

as

st as is

sta**t**u**e**

as

stet

you

Edward Lucie Smith (1966)

"Form determines meaning. Better still, form *is* meaning. The cart before the horse, or, rather, the cart becoming the horse. The poet, it seems to me, is a man who is listening to a voice holding a conversation with himself, and this continues whether he is actually writing or not. A concept is a kind of framework. It is a way of handling an object or a given piece of information. Objects singly. Facts singly. Nothing could be more mysterious. But put two objects or two facts together, or add an object to a fact, and already something starts to emerge. There are thousands, even millions, of possible concepts to choose from. Within each lies the possibility of organization, but each differs. To take a simple example. Pictorial logic is different from verbal logic. A sequence of images may be recognized as a sequence without narrative connections. It is essential to choose. It is also essential to explore what one has chosen to the full. One is driven on by the unknown element, the dark side of the planet. A new concept, properly filled, can reveal powers which the writer himself never knew he possessed." (E.L.S., notebooks)

Mary Ellen Solt (1966)

"The design of 'Forsythia' is made from the letters of the name of the flowering shrub and their equivalents in the Morse Code. The text is part of the design." (M.E.S.)

"Forsythia" and the next two poems by Mary Ellen Solt were typographically concretized by John Dearstyne. In the introduction to *Flowers in Concrete*, George Zadek writes: "Traditionally the typographer has given visual form and order to words, thus serving both the writer and the reader. His problem is mainly one of clarity of communication, literary meaning, and hopefully aesthetic contribution to the art of the printed page. When publishing concrete poetry, it is sometimes difficult to draw a line between the contributions, as well as final responsibilities, of the poet and the typographer. The literary and visual meaning of concrete poetry as conceived by the poet and interpreted by the typographer is somewhat analogous to a stage performance of a play."

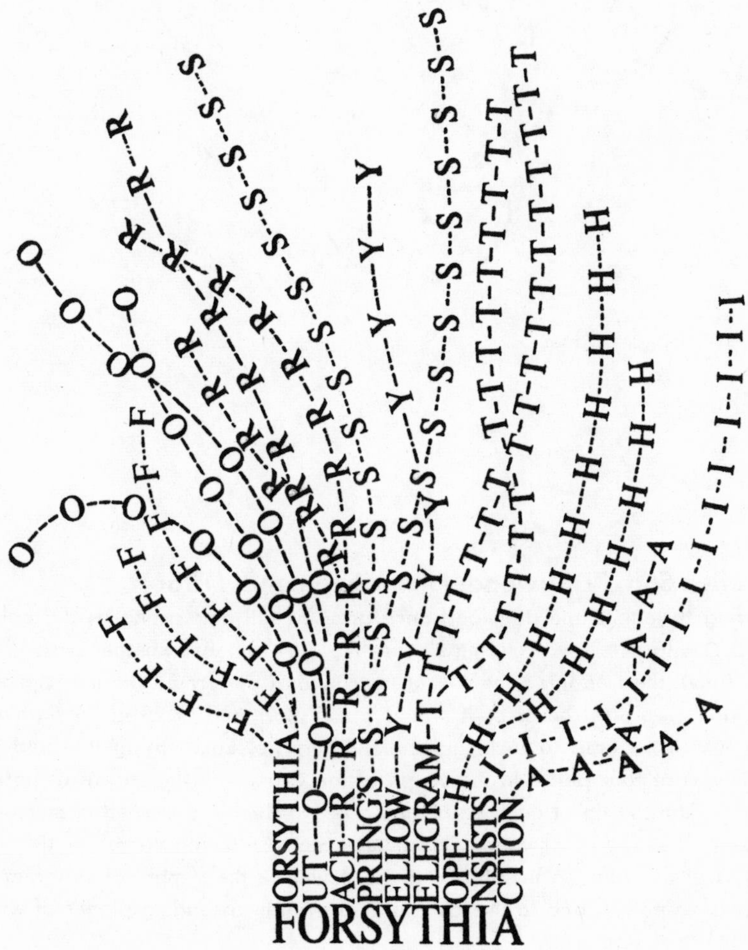
FORSYTHIA
UT
ACE
PRING'S
ELLOW
ELEGRAM
OPE
NSISTS
CTION
FORSYTHIA

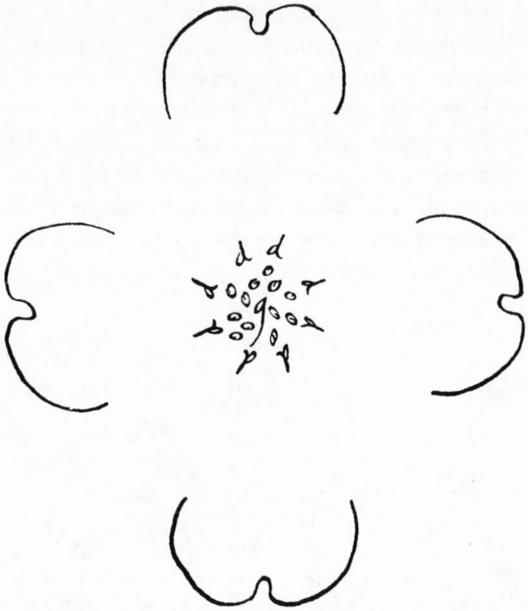

Mary Ellen Solt, "Dogwood: First Movement" (1966)

"According to legend the dogwood once grew as tall and strong as the oak. So to its great disgrace it was chosen as the tree most suitable for the Cross. Christ, though, pitied the tree in its shame and sorrow and performed the miracle of the dogwood. Henceforth, he said, it would grow short and crooked so that never again could it be used to such ignominious purpose. Each spring it would bear white flowers of four petals in the shape of the Cross with the crown of thorns at the center. And the tip of each petal would be notched and stained in memory of the nails and blood. 'Dogwood: Three Movements' attempts to relate the visual properties of the word to the shape of the flower as the symbol of suffering and its redemptive power, and to the laws of its growth in ascending planes of white." (M.E.S.)

Mary Ellen Solt, "Dogwood: Second Movement"

Mary Ellen Solt, "Dogwood: Third Movement"

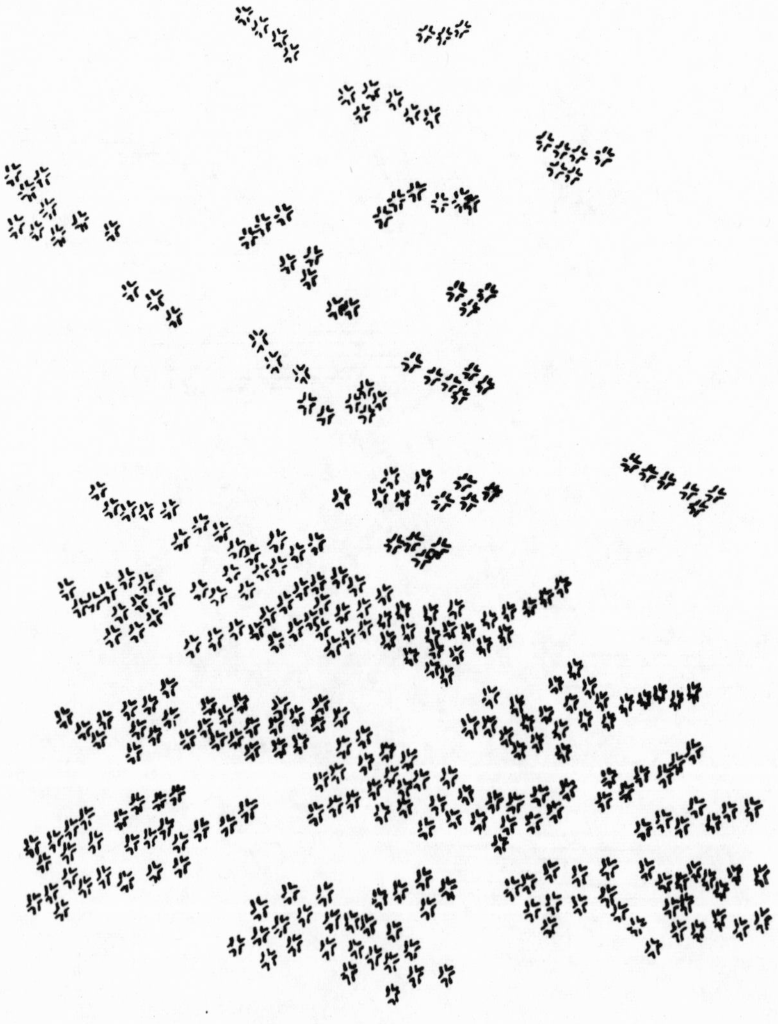

TIMES
GOD'S
SUMMER
MEASURES
SILENCE
EXIT
SUMMER
UMBELLAR
RESOUNDS
INTERPRETS
NO ONE
A CAPELLA
ANSWERS
RED
SEEN
EACH

Mary Ellen Solt (1966)

"A kinetic-visual poem. The text is made from the letters of the word 'geranium' and the final letters of the first series of words. The flower is made from the letters of the word 'geranium.' " (M.E.S.)

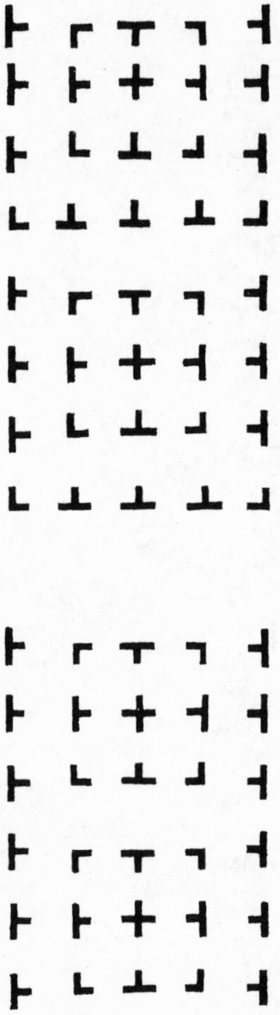

Mary Ellen Solt, "Moon Shot Sonnet"

"It has not been possible since the Renaissance to write a convincing sonnet on the moon. Looking at the moon photographs in The New York Times, it occurred to me that since the scientist's symbols for marking off areas on the moon's surface were presented five to a line and the lines could be added up to fourteen, a visual sonnet could be made of them. The poem is intended as a spoof of an outmoded form of poetry and as a statement of the problem of the concrete poet's search for valid new forms." (M.E.S.)

Designed by John Furnival, first printed in *Poor.Old.Tired.Horse.*

```
i n v i t a t i o n
  o             o
    n         i
      i     t
        s a
        t a
      i     t
    v         i
  n             o
i o n i s a t i o n
```

Adriano Spatola (1966)

Adriano Spatola, from *Zeroglifico* (1966)

The cut-up method applied to a single word.

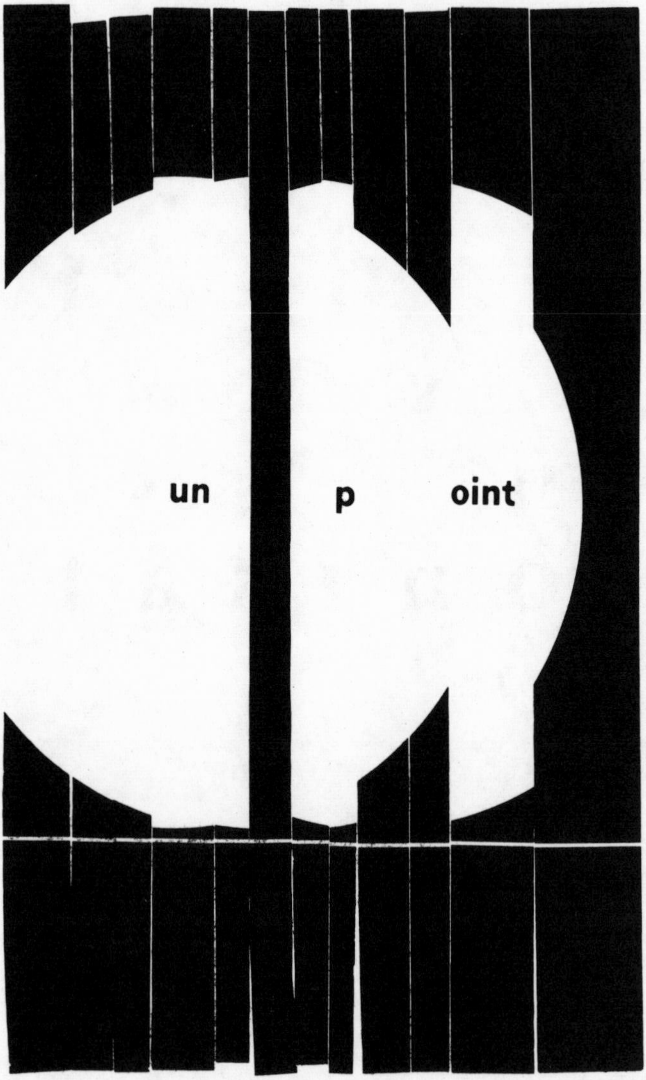
un
p
oint

das rezel kroitz wort
rezelt das wort kroiz
wort rezelt das kroiz

das kroiz wort rezel
kroizt das rezel wort
rezel kroizt das wort

Daniel Spoerri (1955)

das rezel = *das Rätsel* = puzzle, riddle, mystery
das kroiz = *das Kreuz* = cross
das wort = word
kroiz + *wort* = *kroizwort* = *Kreuzwort* = cross-word puzzle
rezelt = *rätselt* = guess a riddle (3rd person singular)
kroizt = *kreuzt* = crosses (3rd person singular)

"I wrote it in Berne in 1955. It was published in *Hortulus* about 1956 and then reprinted in a German anthology as an example of an aberration in poetry." (D.S.) The poem later appeared in *material 1*. *material* was a periodical edited by Spoerri in Darmstadt, Germany, and Paris from 1957 to 1959. *material 1*, ***kleine antologie konkreter dichtung***, was the first international anthology of concrete poetry.

Daniel Spoerri (1956)

imer = *immer* = always
maistens = *meistens* = usually
oft = often
manchmal = sometimes
selten = seldom
ni = *nie* = never

The strange spelling, without capitals, was part of a widespread battle (still raging) against traditional German orthography. Most of the early leaders of the revolt have returned to traditional spelling, but the fight against compulsory capitalization is gaining ground.

i m e r
i m e r
m a i s t e n s
i m e r
i m e r
m a i s t e n s
o f t
i m e r
i m e r
m a i s t e n s
i m e r
i m e r
m a i s t e n s
o f t
m a n c h m a l
i m e r
i m e r
m a i s t e n s
i m e r
i m e r
m a i s t e n s
o f t
i m e r
i m e r
m a i s t e n s
i m e r
i m e r
m a i s t e n s
o f t
m a n c h m a l
s e l t e n

n i

erst lezt das erste
lezt das erst lezte
das erst lezt lezte

lezt erst das lezte
erst das lezt erste
das lezt erst lezte

erst lezt das lezte
lezt das erst erste
das erst lezt lezte

lezt erst das erste
erst das lezt lezte
das lezt erst erste

erst erst das lezte
lezt das lezt erste
das erst erst lezte

lezt lezt das erste
erst das erst lezte
das lezt lezt erste

das erst erst erste

Daniel Spoerri (1956)
erst(e) = first
lezt(e) = *letzt(e)* = last

Vagn Steen (1965)

I
P
OI
OP
TOI
TOP
STOI
STOP
STOPI
STOPP

REGAL FORT SAGE ROTE MAT LOCH
ART LOT AN LIEGE SENSE MALE
WAS FUNK HAT MINDER LIST LAST
HOLE GRUBE TAG DOGMEN RING BORN
JE RATE HAUT AUGE BETE FANGE
SACHE EBENE TAGE ABREGE BUTTER BRUT
HOB SPIEL LAG LIEF WAND HELL
NUN GAB TOLL BALD AM STARK
LASS WAGE WO HEFT SAG KECK
BANG LUNGE GANG MUSS DING BELIEF
PASSE HIER REINE LACHE FASTE DORT
BRILLE PLAGE ARME BECHER GENE TOT
MESS KIND LOSE DURST WORT STERN
DIE TASTE BITTEN GLUT STILL GILT
LOG LINKS WERT FUND HART SUCH
TAT BLEND ALTER TRUNK NOT GUT
LASSE ALLER DONNER ELLE MAL BLINDE
BULLE MACHE FOLIE QUELLE BRIEF NEIGE
SIEGER SANG SONNE SEIN MANCHE VERSE
SOLANGE MONDE LESER GLAS BORNE NIE

André Thomkins (1955)

DOGMAT-MOT is a mobile composition of 120 words arranged on mobile discs which present the reader with ever-changing phrases. These 120 words are part of a larger body of words, taken from French-German and English-German dictionaries, all of which appear similar but have different meanings in two or three languages. This "game" for writing, speaking and reading several languages simultaneously—with all the attendant ambiguities—was published in 1965 by Galerie der Spiegel in Cologne.

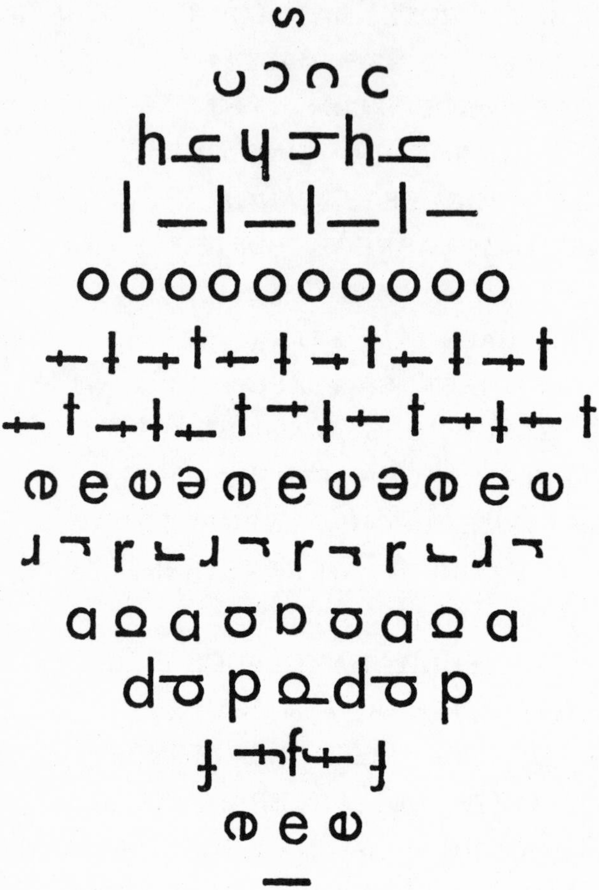

André Thomkins (1960)

"A *Schlotterapfel* (French *calville*) is an apple whose German name makes one think of it as wobbling and trembling, and the word, rendered literally, produces just such an apple in movement." (A.T.) It is also the apple from which calvados is made.

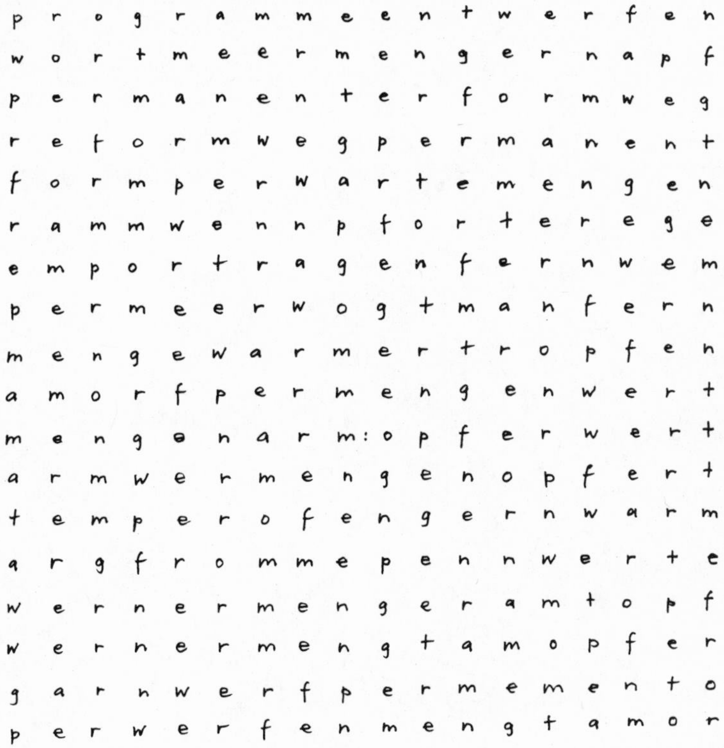
p r o g r a m m e e n t w e r f e n
w o r t m e e r m e n g e r n a p f
p e r m a n e n t e r f o r m w e g
r e f o r m w e g p e r m a n e n t
f o r m p e r w a r t e m e n g e n
r a m m w e n n p f o r t e r e g e
e m p o r t r a g e n f e r n w e m
p e r m e e r w o g t m a n f e r n
m e n g e w a r m e r t r o p f e n
a m o r f p e r m e n g e n w e r t
m e n g e n a r m : o p f e r w e r t
a r m w e r m e n g e n o p f e r t
t e m p e r o f e n g e r n w a r m
a r g f r o m m e p e n n w e r t e
w e r n e r m e n g e r a m t o p f
w e r n e r m e n g t a m o p f e r
g a r n w e r f p e r m e m e n t o
p e r w e r f e n m e n g t a m o r

André Thomkins (1964)

"*'Programme Entwerfen'* (Designing Programmes) is the title of a book by Karl Gerstner. I made a square of the title, constructed of as many anagrams as there are letters in the two words. Some of these anagrams fall within the perspective of Gerstner's ideas." (A.T.)

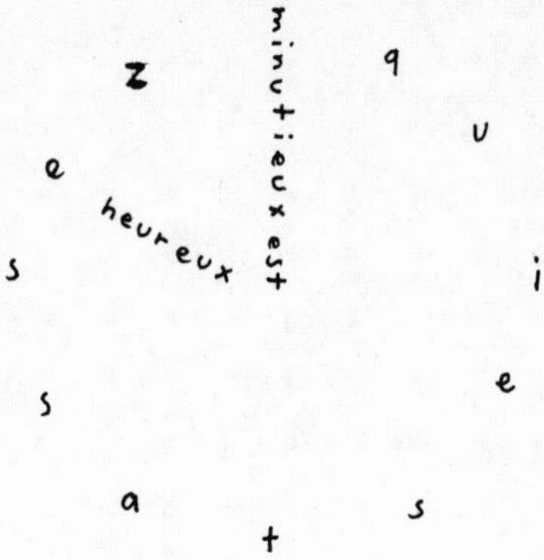
minutieux est
heureux
q
u
i
e
s
t
a
s
s
e
z

André Thomkins (1966)

"Qui est assez minutieux est heureux: c'est ce que prouve la montre et de manière minutieuse, heureusement!" (A.T.)

me urge la muerte
muerte
me urge la muerte
me urge la muerte
me urge nada
me urge la muerte
la muerte
la muerte
nada me urge
nada me urge
nada
me urge nada
me urge
nada me urge
me urge
me urge la muerte
me urge la muerte
nada
nada me urge
nada
nada
nada me urge
me urge
lamuertenadameurge

Enrique Uribe Valdivielso (1963)

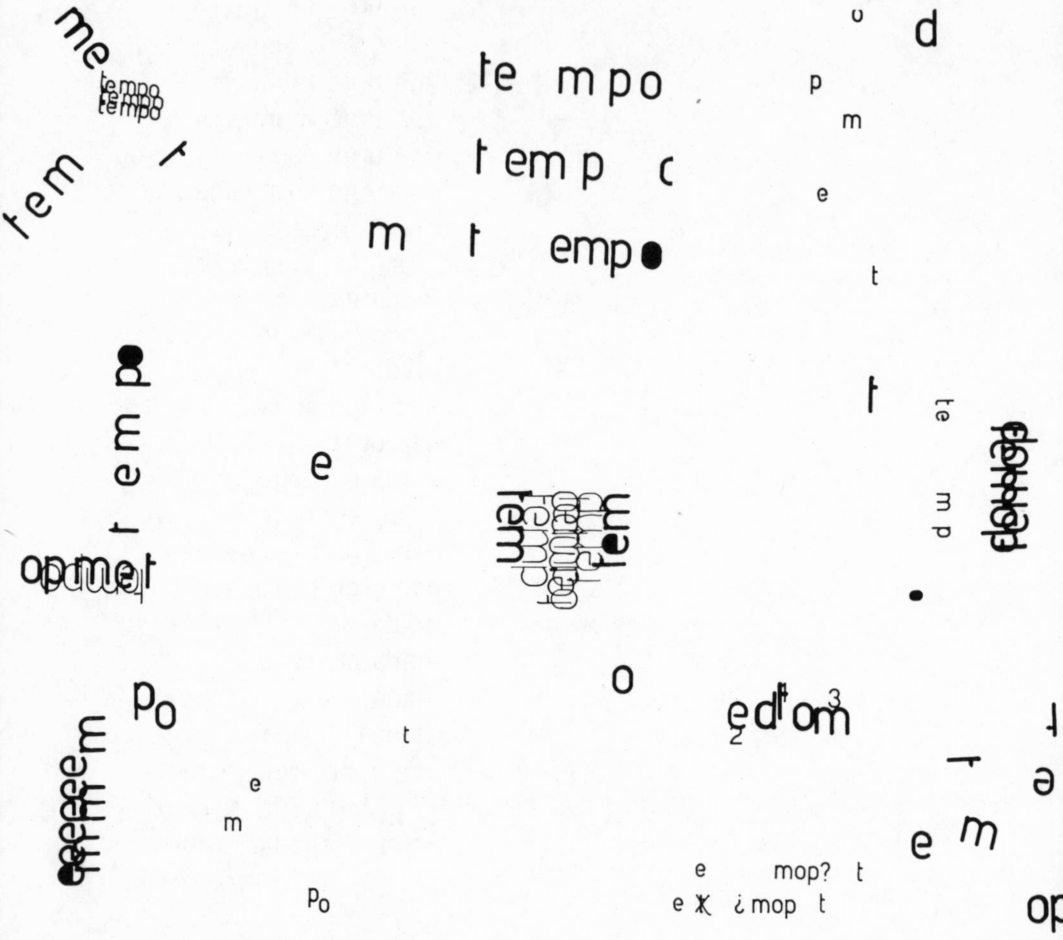
te mpo
t em p
m t emp
mop? t
¿mop t

Franco Verdi, from *tempo* (1966)

Verdi's rhythmical variations on a theme, with their often unutterable deviations from traditional orthography, invite comparison with the scores of those contemporary composers who have abandoned the "writing" of music in favor of the "drawing" of music. The 16 original variations are each 4½ x 6½ inches, drawn on numbered pages.

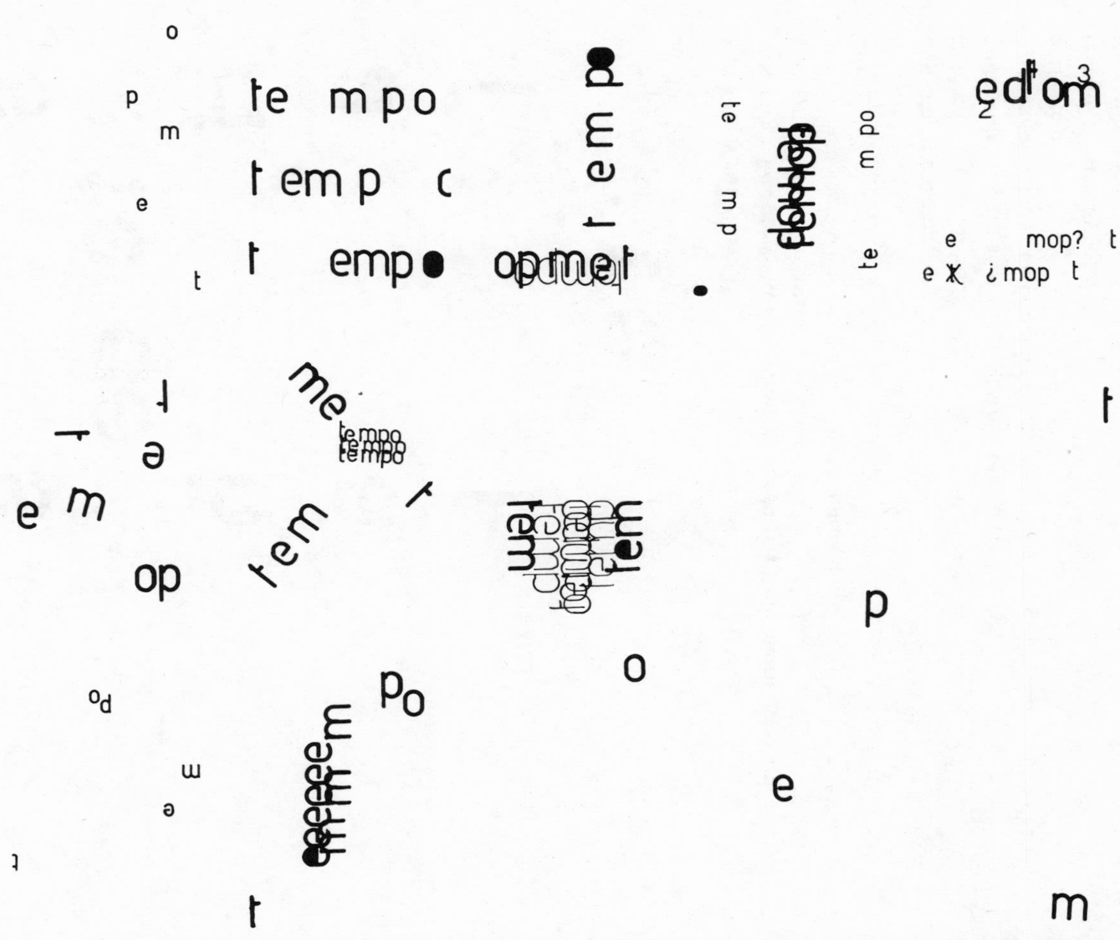
te mpo
temp
emp
opmet
temp
mop?
¿mop
tempo
tem
me
op
po

B i k i n i
u u
s s
te ge
H h
a a
l l
te

Paul de Vree (1963)

The author has provided the following key to this "intermetric topological poem":

B = symbol of the breasts

Bikini = the situation, the seduction, the temptation

B
H = (in Flemish) *buste houder* = brassiere

bushalte = bus stop

kus halte = stop for kissing

buste halte = come to a standstill when seeing the breasts

kùsgehalte = the more beautiful the breasts, the more desire is provoked, the more excitement

te-ge(n) = close(ly)

te = on the spot

een	**kleine**	**reus**	**viel**	**in**	**de**	**beek**	**verloren**
ee	**klein**	**reu**	**vie**	**i**	**d**	**bee**	**verlore**
e	**klei**	**re**	**vi**			**be**	**verlor**
	kle	**r**	**v**			**b**	**verl**
	kl						**ver**
	k						**ve**
							v
					d		
							v

Paul de Vree (1966)

The poet imitates the desperate gestures and sounds of a little giant who drowns in a brook.

Paul de Vree (1966)

"This kind of poem has a double use: it can be said as well as considered a graphic structure. It was composed with a kinetic intention: the question mark crosses the horizontal lines and causes a vibration (think of Soto). The question mark may also be taken as the staff of a bishop (= the church) with the implication of sacramental marriage. The suggestion: what to think about the rapport between man and woman. Are women happy? Are men honest?" (P. de V.)

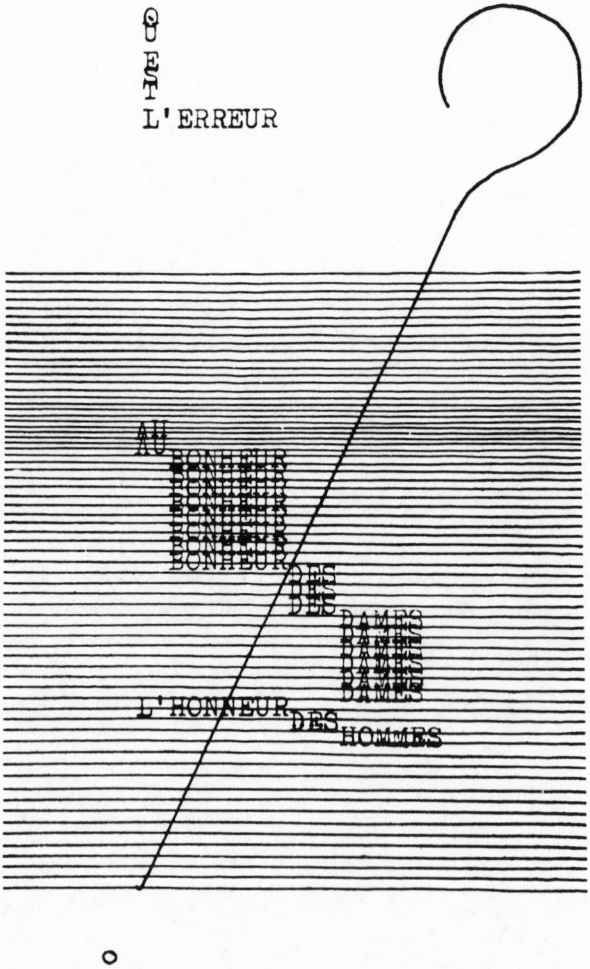

Q
U
E
S
T
L'ERREUR
AU
BONHEUR
DES
DAMES
L'HONNEUR
DES
HOMMES

O

TI VI

RAGE

CI MI

GA

Paul de Vree (1966)

In this "verbivocovisual" structure the author has made a "clock of modernity" out of six French words all of which contain *rage*, the tone-setting center-piece. They are *orage* (storm), by which he intends to evoke "the political clouds"; *cirage* (waxing, polishing), "all will be brushed up, clean"; *mirage*, "all men are fond of building castles in the air (cosmonautic dreams)"; *tirage* (press run, lottery drawing), "the daily press for millions, inquisitiveness, curiosity"; *virage* (sharp turn of a car), "the speed"; and garage, "the need of shelter."

Paul de Vree (1966)

De Vree calls this genre "mechanical poems." They are written with "psycho-physical impulsion." This particular one is intended to evoke April in Paris. The flying parentheses represent the wings of birds.

SENSE SOUND

SONSE SEUND

SOUSE SENND

SOUNE SENSD

SOUND SENSE

Emmett Williams (1954–55)

"From an unpublished novel, **The Clouds**. The text above was part of an eye-and-ear test administered by Aristophanes to the hero of the novel, a deceased button-hole puncher who knows more about linguistics than his earthly vocation would seem to have prepared him for. The letters of each word are swapped back and forth until sense is sound and sound sense." (E.W.)

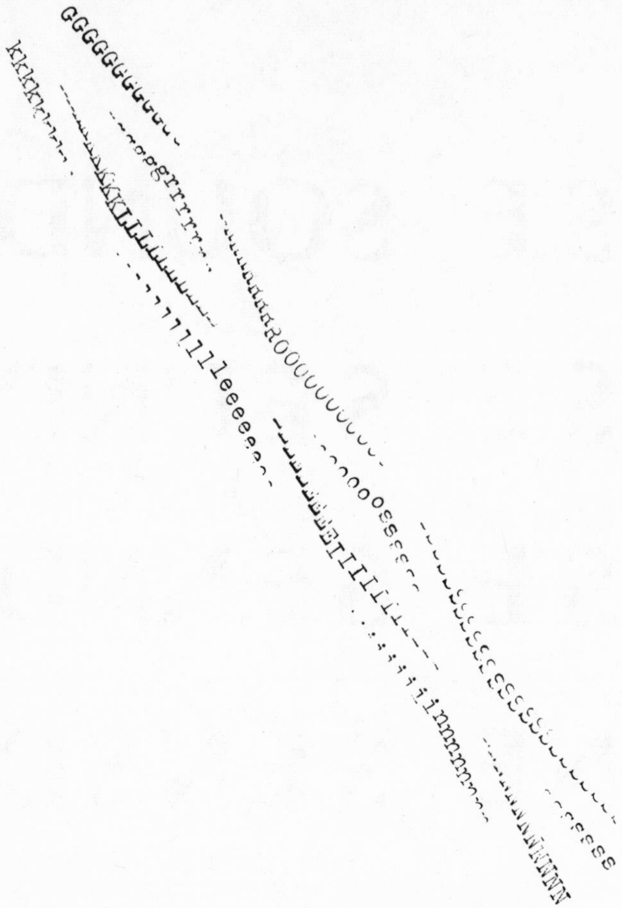

Emmett Williams (1958)

"Small (*klein*) and capital (*gross*) letters are on the same type bar. The expressive changeover from one to another is shown through the gradual engagement and disengagement of the shift key." (Claus Bremer and Daniel Spoerri, introduction to **konkretionen**.) Bremer and Spoerri also explain the odd position on the page of this and all the poems in **konkretionen**: "Since the concretions are systematic in themselves and related only to themselves, their position on the page has been left to chance."

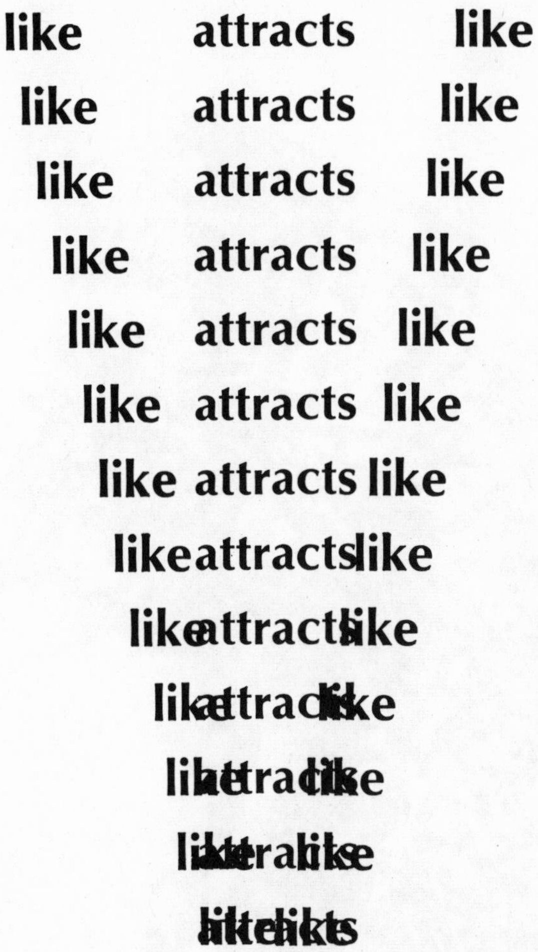
like attracts like
like attracts like
like attracts like
like attracts like
like attracts like
like attracts like
like attracts like
likeattractslike

Emmett Williams (1958)

"Ernst Jandl, in a note on his own work, observes: 'There must be an infinite number of methods of writing experimental poems, but I think the most successful methods are those which can only be used once, for then the result is a poem identical with the method by which it is made. The method used again would turn out exactly the same poem.' This particular poem says what it does, and does what it says, and I can't think of three other words that would work as well in this construction." (E.W.)

Emmett Williams (1958)

"A rubber-stamp poem, from a genre I called 'universal poems,' probably because I furnished spectators with rubber stamps and let them construct the poems. The first of these public works was made at the Maiudstellingen in Copenhagen in 1960; the largest covered an entire wall of Gallery One in London in 1962." (E.W.)

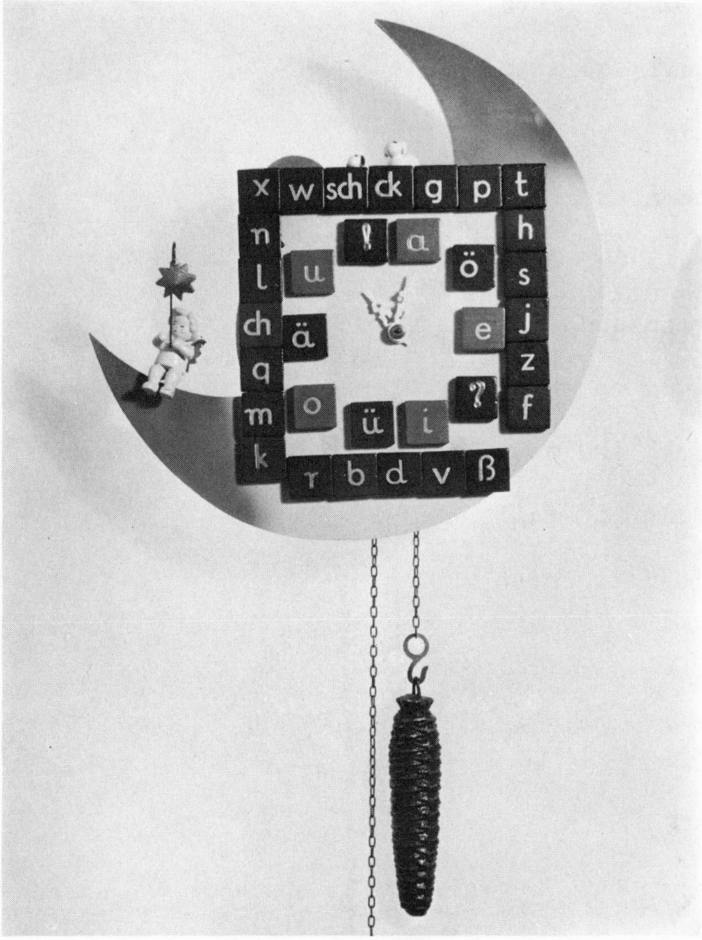
x w sch ck g p t
n l ch q m k
h s j z f
r b d v ß
a ö u ä e o ü i

Emmett Williams, "Poetry Clock" (1959)

"The 'Poetry Clock,' along with a poem constructed by alphabetized live carp, was conceived for an *Hommage pour Anton Müller* by Jean Tinguely, Daniel Spoerri and myself at the Galerie 59 in Aschaffenburg. The show was first postponed, then cancelled, and the clock wasn't exhibited publicly until the Salon de Mai in Copenhagen in 1962. I have a collection of poems made by clock-watchers at the exhibition." (E.W.)

the moon is green
and full tho miin
es graan und fell
thi meen as gruun
end foll the maan
us green ond fill
tha muun es groon
ind fell thu meen
os griin and fall
the moon is green

Emmett Williams (1958)

"The vowels of *der mond ist grün und voll* are displaced progressively until the sentence is achieved a second time." (Bremer and Spoerri, *loc. cit.*) Translated by the editor.

she loves me
she loves me not
she loves
she loves me
she
she loves

she

Emmett Williams (1965)

Extract from a letter answering questions posed by a critic: "Is it about chance? Well, yes, in the same sense that plucking petals off a daisy to the tune of 'she loves me, she loves me not' leaves the answer up to the number of petals on the particular daisy. Is 'she' likely to love herself? That *could* be a comment to the poem, a reflective post facto comment, because the poem was written while I was living with someone who did indeed love herself more than she loved me, and maybe the poem wouldn't have been written if things had been otherwise. But this information is hardly pertinent to poetic analysis, and my unluckiness in love has very little to do with the way the poem works out. I think it's important to say here that the poem has nine lines, the seventh and ninth of which are blank, but I haven't yet found a way to represent that fact in black and white on a flat sheet of paper. What did I start with, the visual idea or the words? Both: the poem is an attempt to render the daisy love divination ritual typographically and lyrically." (E.W.)

first voice: somewhere
second voice: bluebirds are flying
third voice: high in the sky.
fourth voice: in the cellar
fifth voice: even blackbirds are extinct.

somewhere bluebirds are flying high in the sky. in the cellar even blackbirds are extinct.
somewhere bluebirds are flying high in the sky. even blackbirds are extinct. in the cellar
somewhere bluebirds are flying in the cellar high in the sky. even blackbirds are extinct.
somewhere bluebirds are flying in the cellar even blackbirds are extinct. high in the sky.
somewhere bluebirds are flying even blackbirds are extinct. high in the sky. in the cellar
somewhere bluebirds are flying even blackbirds are extinct. in the cellar high in the sky.
somewhere high in the sky. bluebirds are flying in the cellar even blackbirds are extinct.
somewhere high in the sky. bluebirds are flying even blackbirds are extinct. in the cellar
somewhere high in the sky. in the cellar bluebirds are flying even blackbirds are extinct.
somewhere high in the sky. in the cellar even blackbirds are extinct. bluebirds are flying
somewhere high in the sky. even blackbirds are extinct. bluebirds are flying in the cellar
somewhere high in the sky. even blackbirds are extinct. in the cellar bluebirds are flying
somewhere in the cellar bluebirds are flying high in the sky. even blackbirds are extinct.
somewhere in the cellar bluebirds are flying even blackbirds are extinct. high in the sky.
somewhere in the cellar high in the sky. bluebirds are flying even blackbirds are extinct.
somewhere in the cellar high in the sky. even blackbirds are extinct. bluebirds are flying
somewhere in the cellar even blackbirds are extinct. bluebirds are flying high in the sky.
somewhere in the cellar even blackbirds are extinct. high in the sky. bluebirds are flying
somewhere even blackbirds are extinct. bluebirds are flying high in the sky. in the cellar
somewhere even blackbirds are extinct. bluebirds are flying in the cellar high in the sky.
somewhere even blackbirds are extinct. high in the sky. bluebirds are flying in the cellar
somewhere even blackbirds are extinct. high in the sky. in the cellar bluebirds are flying
somewhere even blackbirds are extinct. in the cellar bluebirds are flying high in the sky.
somewhere even blackbirds are extinct. in the cellar high in the sky. bluebirds are flying
bluebirds are flying somewhere high in the sky. in the cellar even blackbirds are extinct.
bluebirds are flying somewhere high in the sky. even blackbirds are extinct. in the cellar
bluebirds are flying somewhere in the cellar high in the sky. even blackbirds are extinct.
bluebirds are flying somewhere in the cellar even blackbirds are extinct. high in the sky.
bluebirds are flying somewhere even blackbirds are extinct. high in the sky. in the cellar
bluebirds are flying somewhere even blackbirds are extinct. in the cellar high in the sky.
bluebirds are flying high in the sky. somewhere in the cellar even blackbirds are extinct.
bluebirds are flying high in the sky. somewhere even blackbirds are extinct. in the cellar
bluebirds are flying high in the sky. in the cellar somewhere even blackbirds are extinct.
bluebirds are flying high in the sky. in the cellar even blackbirds are extinct. somewhere
bluebirds are flying high in the sky. even blackbirds are extinct. somewhere in the cellar
bluebirds are flying high in the sky. even blackbirds are extinct. in the cellar somewhere
bluebirds are flying in the cellar somewhere high in the sky. even blackbirds are extinct.
bluebirds are flying in the cellar somewhere even blackbirds are extinct. high in the sky.
bluebirds are flying in the cellar high in the sky. somewhere even blackbirds are extinct.
bluebirds are flying in the cellar high in the sky. even blackbirds are extinct. somewhere
bluebirds are flying in the cellar even blackbirds are extinct. somewhere high in the sky.
bluebirds are flying in the cellar even blackbirds are extinct. high in the sky. somewhere
bluebirds are flying even blackbirds are extinct. somewhere high in the sky. in the cellar
bluebirds are flying even blackbirds are extinct. somewhere in the cellar high in the sky.
bluebirds are flying even blackbirds are extinct. high in the sky. somewhere in the cellar
bluebirds are flying even blackbirds are extinct. high in the sky. in the cellar somewhere
bluebirds are flying even blackbirds are extinct. in the cellar somewhere high in the sky.
bluebirds are flying even blackbirds are extinct. in the cellar high in the sky. somewhere
high in the sky. somewhere bluebirds are flying in the cellar even blackbirds are extinct.
high in the sky. somewhere bluebirds are flying even blackbirds are extinct. in the cellar
high in the sky. somewhere in the cellar bluebirds are flying even blackbirds are extinct.
high in the sky. somewhere in the cellar even blackbirds are extinct. bluebirds are flying
high in the sky. somewhere even blackbirds are extinct. bluebirds are flying in the cellar
high in the sky. somewhere even blackbirds are extinct. in the cellar bluebirds are flying
high in the sky. bluebirds are flying somewhere in the cellar even blackbirds are extinct.
high in the sky. bluebirds are flying somewhere even blackbirds are extinct. in the cellar
high in the sky. bluebirds are flying in the cellar somewhere even blackbirds are extinct.
high in the sky. bluebirds are flying in the cellar even blackbirds are extinct. somewhere
high in the sky. bluebirds are flying even blackbirds are extinct. somewhere in the cellar
high in the sky. bluebirds are flying even blackbirds are extinct. in the cellar somewhere

Emmett Williams, "cellar song for five voices" (196?)

" 'cellar song for five voices' was written to celebrate the fifth or somethingth anniversary of an artists' club in the cellar of the castle at Darmstadt, Germany. It is a moral allegory—or so insists a friend in Texas concerning the 120 permutations of five phrases during which the blackbirds and the bluebirds change places. As his authority for this interpretation he cites St. Bernard: *suo nobis descensu suavem ac salubrem dedicavit ascensum* (by his descent he established for us a joyful and wholesome ascent). Is this any more far-fetched than the Freudian interpretation of all the birds that fly in and out of so many of my poems? Be that as it may, it was first performed at the now defunct Living Theatre in New York in 1962, and directed by Jackson Mac Low. I have been told that the performers got all mixed up

high in the sky. in the cellar somewhere bluebirds are flying even blackbirds are extinct.
high in the sky. in the cellar somewhere even blackbirds are extinct. bluebirds are flying
high in the sky. in the cellar bluebirds are flying somewhere even blackbirds are extinct.
high in the sky. in the cellar bluebirds are flying even blackbirds are extinct. somewhere
high in the sky. in the cellar even blackbirds are extinct. somewhere bluebirds are flying
high in the sky. in the cellar even blackbirds are extinct. bluebirds are flying somewhere
high in the sky. even blackbirds are extinct. somewhere bluebirds are flying in the cellar
high in the sky. even blackbirds are extinct. somewhere in the cellar bluebirds are flying
high in the sky. even blackbirds are extinct. bluebirds are flying somewhere in the cellar
high in the sky. even blackbirds are extinct. bluebirds are flying in the cellar somewhere
high in the sky. even blackbirds are extinct. in the cellar somewhere bluebirds are flying
high in the sky. even blackbirds are extinct. in the cellar bluebirds are flying somewhere
in the cellar somewhere bluebirds are flying high in the sky. even blackbirds are extinct.
in the cellar somewhere bluebirds are flying even blackbirds are extinct. high in the sky.
in the cellar somewhere high in the sky. bluebirds are flying even blackbirds are extinct.
in the cellar somewhere high in the sky. even blackbirds are extinct. bluebirds are flying
in the cellar somewhere even blackbirds are extinct. bluebirds are flying high in the sky.
in the cellar somewhere even blackbirds are extinct. high in the sky bluebirds are flying.
in the cellar bluebirds are flying somewhere high in the sky. even blackbirds are extinct.
in the cellar bluebirds are flying somewhere even blackbirds are extinct. high in the sky.
in the cellar bluebirds are flying high in the sky. somewhere even blackbirds are extinct.
in the cellar bluebirds are flying high in the sky. even blackbirds are extinct. somewhere
in the cellar bluebirds are flying even blackbirds are extinct. somewhere high in the sky.
in the cellar bluebirds are flying even blackbirds are extinct. high in the sky. somewhere
in the cellar high in the sky. somewhere bluebirds are flying even blackbirds are extinct.
in the cellar high in the sky. somewhere even blackbirds are extinct. bluebirds are flying
in the cellar high in the sky. bluebirds are flying somewhere even blackbirds are extinct.
in the cellar high in the sky. bluebirds are flying even blackbirds are extinct. somewhere
in the cellar high in the sky. even blackbirds are extinct. somewhere bluebirds are flying
in the cellar high in the sky. even blackbirds are extinct. bluebirds are flying somewhere
in the cellar even blackbirds are extinct. somewhere bluebirds are flying high in the sky.
in the cellar even blackbirds are extinct. somewhere high in the sky. bluebirds are flying
in the cellar even blackbirds are extinct. bluebirds are flying somewhere high in the sky.
in the cellar even blackbirds are extinct. bluebirds are flying high in the sky. somewhere
in the cellar even blackbirds are extinct. high in the sky. somewhere bluebirds are flying
in the cellar even blackbirds are extinct. high in the sky. bluebirds are flying somewhere
even blackbirds are extinct. somewhere bluebirds are flying high in the sky. in the cellar
even blackbirds are extinct. somewhere bluebirds are flying in the cellar high in the sky.
even blackbirds are extinct. somewhere high in the sky. bluebirds are flying in the cellar
even blackbirds are extinct. somewhere high in the sky. in the cellar bluebirds are flying
even blackbirds are extinct. somewhere in the cellar bluebirds are flying high in the sky.
even blackbirds are extinct. somewhere in the cellar high in the sky. bluebirds are flying
even blackbirds are extinct. bluebirds are flying somewhere high in the sky. in the cellar
even blackbirds are extinct. bluebirds are flying somewhere in the cellar high in the sky.
even blackbirds are extinct. bluebirds are flying high in the sky. somewhere in the cellar
even blackbirds are extinct. bluebirds are flying high in the sky. in the cellar somewhere
even blackbirds are extinct. bluebirds are flying in the cellar somewhere high in the sky.
even blackbirds are extinct. bluebirds are flying in the cellar high in the sky. somewhere
even blackbirds are extinct. high in the sky. somewhere bluebirds are flying in the cellar
even blackbirds are extinct. high in the sky. somewhere in the cellar bluebirds are flying
even blackbirds are extinct. high in the sky. bluebirds are flying somewhere in the cellar
even blackbirds are extinct. high in the sky. bluebirds are flying in the cellar somewhere
even blackbirds are extinct. high in the sky. in the cellar somewhere bluebirds are flying
even blackbirds are extinct. high in the sky. in the cellar bluebirds are flying somewhere
even blackbirds are extinct. in the cellar somewhere bluebirds are flying high in the sky.
even blackbirds are extinct. in the cellar somewhere high in the sky. bluebirds are flying
even blackbirds are extinct. in the cellar bluebirds are flying somewhere high in the sky.
even blackbirds are extinct. in the cellar bluebirds are flying high in the sky. somewhere
even blackbirds are extinct. in the cellar high in the sky. somewhere bluebirds are flying
even blackbirds are extinct. in the cellar high in the sky. bluebirds are flying somewhere

half way along and started giggling, and that Jackson had to pull down the curtain (metaphorically at least) and start them off all over again." (E.W., program notes to Copenhagen performance.)

Emmett Williams (1966)

"The first of two number games. The second one, an obscenity aimed at Southern law-enforcement officers, was rejected by the Berlin publisher." (E.W.)

6Y

3o

5e

2l

1i u8

9!

7o

4v

```
m                   m
mi                 im
mis               sim
miss             ssim
missi           issim
missis         sissim
mississ       ssissim
mississi     ississim
mississip   pississim
mississipp ppississim
mississippippississim
 i                 i
 is               si
 iss             ssi
 issi           issi
 issis         sissi
 ississ       ssissi
 ississi     ississi
 ississip   pississi
 ississipp ppississi
 ississippippississi
  s               s
  ss             ss
  ssi           iss
  ssis         siss
  ssiss       ssiss
  ssissi     ississ
  ssissip   pississ
  ssissipp ppississ
  ssissippippississ
   s             s
   si           is
   sis         sis
   siss       ssis
   sissi     issis
   sissip   pissis
   sissipp ppissis
   sissippippissis
    i           i
    is         si
    iss       ssi
    issi     issi
    issip   pissi
    issipp ppissi
    issippippissi
     s         s
     ss       ss
     ssi     iss
     ssip   piss
     ssipp ppiss
     ssippippiss
      s       s
      si     is
      sip   pis
      sipp ppis
      sippippis
       i     i
       ip   pi
       ipp ppi
       ippippi
        p   p
        pp pp
        ppipp
         p p
         pip
          i
```

Emmett Williams (1966)

"'A festive marching song in the shape of 10 dixie cups' was written for *WIN*, a publication of the New York Workshop in Nonviolence. Printed with it was a note, lifted from a letter to Jackson Mac Low, that 'i think it would sound lovely hissed aloud by masses of folks.'" (E.W.)

do you remember

when i loved soft pink nights
and you hated hard blue valleys
and i kissed mellow red potatoes
and you loved livid green seagulls
and i hated soft yellow dewdrops
and you kissed hard pink oysters
and i loved mellow blue nights
and you hated livid red valleys
and i kissed soft green potatoes
and you loved hard yellow seagulls
and i hated mellow pink dewdrops
and you kissed livid blue oysters
and i loved soft red nights
and you hated hard green valleys
and i kissed mellow yellow potatoes
and you loved livid pink seagulls
and i hated soft blue dewdrops
and you kissed hard red oysters
and i loved mellow green nights
and you hated livid yellow valleys
and i kissed soft pink potatoes
and you loved hard blue seagulls
and i hated mellow red dewdrops
and you kissed livid green oysters
and i loved soft yellow nights
and you hated hard pink valleys
and i kissed mellow blue potatoes
and you loved livid red seagulls
and i hated soft green dewdrops
and you kissed hard yellow oysters
and i loved mellow pink nights
and you hated livid blue valleys
and i kissed soft red potatoes
and you loved hard green seagulls
and i hated mellow yellow dewdrops
and you kissed livid pink oysters
and i loved soft blue nights
and you hated hard red valleys
and i kissed mellow green potatoes
and you loved livid yellow seagulls
and i hated soft pink dewdrops
and you kissed hard blue oysters
and i loved mellow red nights
and you hated livid green valleys
and i kissed soft yellow potatoes
and you loved hard pink seagulls
and i hated mellow blue dewdrops
and you kissed livid red oysters
and i loved soft green nights
and you hated hard yellow valleys
and i kissed mellow pink potatoes
and you loved livid blue seagulls
and i hated soft red dewdrops
and you kissed hard green oysters
and i loved mellow yellow nights
and you hated livid pink valleys
and i kissed soft blue potatoes
and you loved hard red seagulls
and i hated mellow green dewdrops
and you kissed livid yellow oysters
and i loved soft pink nights?

Emmett Williams, "do you remember" (1966)

This poem, which first appeared in *Underground*, was 'translated' into a six-color, 24-foot-long graphic work silk-screened and collaged by Alison Knowles, to whom it was dedicated. It is structured by six vertical progressions:

and	i	love	soft	pink	nights
	you	hated	hard	blue	valleys
		kissed	mellow	red	potatoes
			livid	green	seagulls
				yellow	dewdrops
					oysters

nly black only black only black
nly white only white only white
nly black only black only black
nly white only white only white
nly black only black only black
nly white only white only white
nly black only black only black
nly white only white only white
nly black only black only black
nly white only white only white
nly black only black only black
nly white only white only white
nly black only black only black
nly white only white only white
nly black only black only black
nly white only white only white
nly black only black only black
nly white only white only white
nly black only black only black
nly white only white only white
nly black only black only black
nly white only white only white
nly black only black only black
nly white only white only white
nly black only black only black

Jonathan Williams

"A Mnemonic Wallpaper Pattern for Southern Two-Seaters" is from Williams' forthcoming **Blues & Roots/Rue & Bluets**, rustic applications of concrete. There are 100 poems, and 100 photographs by Nicholas Dean, with a prose introduction by Williams telling of the "perils and delights of hiking 1,500 miles on the Appalachian Trail, etc."

OXEYE
DAISY
CHRYS
ANTHE
MUMLE
UCANT
HEMUM

Jonathan Williams
"A Blazon, Built
Of the Commonest of All Common Eurasian Weeds
Of the Fields and the Wayside"

u wahuhu wahuhu wahuhu wahuhu wahuhu wahuhu wahuhu wahuhu w

ku uguku uguku uguku uguku uguku uguku uguku uguku uguku

huhu huhu huhu huhu huhu huhu huhu huhu huhu huhu huhu huhu huh

lalu lalu lalu lalu lalu lalu lalu lalu lalu lalu lalu lalu lalu lalu lal

u talatu talatu talatu talatu talatu talatu talatu talatu talatu talatu t

tsikilili tsikilili tsikilili tsikilili tsikilili tsikilili tsikilili tsikilili

ki tsikiki tsikiki tsikiki tsikiki tsikiki tsikiki tsikiki tsikiki tsikiki

kagu kagu kagu kagu kagu kagu kagu kagu kagu kagu kagu kag

waya waya waya waya waya waya waya waya waya waya waya way

h yeah yeah yeah yeah yeah yeah yeah yeah yeah yeah yeah yeah y

guna guna guna guna guna guna guna guna guna guna guna guna gun

sa sasa sasa sasa sasa sasa sasa sasa sasa sasa sasa sasa sasa

u kununu kununu kununu kununu kununu kununu kununu kununu kunu

dustu dustu dustu dustu dustu dustu dustu dustu dustu dustu dustu

Jonathan Williams,
"A Chorale* of Cherokee Night Music
As Heard Through an Open Window in Summer Long ago"

*screech owl, hoot owl, yellow-breasted chat, jar-fly, cricket, carolina chickadee, katydid, crow, wolf, beetle, turkey, goose, bullfrog, spring frog

cheio
vazio
cheio

cheio
vazio
cheio

cheio

cheio

Pedro Xisto (1960)
cheio = full
vazio = void

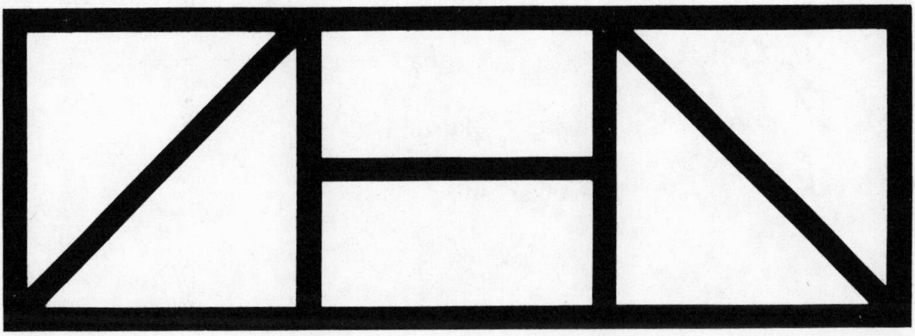

Pedro Xisto (1966)
a logogram: ZEN

ふラいぱん	fu**ra**ipan
ト	**to**
カん	**ka**n
ト	hi**to**
ひト	hi**to**
ト	**to**
うチわ	u**chi**wa
アーり	**a**ri
ト	**to**
オば	**o**ba
クるみ	**ku**rumi
かなしイ	kanashi**i**

Yasuo Fujitomi, "Pan"

The exalted title, "Pan," is contained in the first line, fuRAipan, which turns out to be the humble fRYing-pan. The emphasized syllables, accented more for rhyme than for reason, one might say, give the poem a sound-sense (or non-sense) unrelated to the words in which these syllables occur. Exact equivalents for this word-play are impossible in English. TO, for example, might be rendered "with" or "and," but to the Japanese ear it also carries the weight of "door," "party," "shutter," etc. An English adaptation, substituting notes of the scale for the accented syllables, might go something like "frying PAN / DOugh / TIn can / DOe / FAmily / . . . LAment." This is, of course, a very rough approximation.

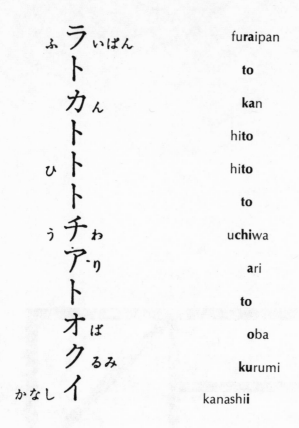

Biographies

Biographies

Friedrich ACHLEITNER: Born 1930 in Schalchen, Upper Austria. Studied at the Academy of Fine Arts in Vienna (1950–53). Graduate of the Clemens Holzmeister School of Architecture (1953). Has taught history of architecture at the Academy of Fine Arts since 1963. A co-producer, with H. C. Artmann, Konrad Bayer, Gerhard Rühm and Oswald Wiener, of the *"literarisches cabaret"* in Vienna (1958–59). His literary publications include **hosn rosn baa** (Wilhelm Frick Verlag, Vienna 1959), a volume of dialect poetry including works by Artmann and Rühm; **fleckerlteppich**, an Austro-Bavarian dialect book; **schwer schwarz** (Eugen Gomringer Press, Frauenfeld 1960), number 10 in the *poesia concreta* series; and the play **super rekors extra 100** (Kapfenberg 1961), a collaboration with Gerhard Rühm.

Alain ARIAS-MISSON: Born in Brussels of an English mother and a Belgian father. Emigrated to the United States as a refugee at the age of 2. Raised in New York City and New England. Harvard graduate in Greek studies. Extensive travels in North Africa. Has worked for the United Nations and U.S. Department of State in information and cultural fields. He and his wife, the Asturian painter Nela Arias, live in Madrid. Arias-Misson has published extensively in French and Spanish reviews. He has given readings of his experiments in phonetic poetry in the United States, South America and Europe. His latest poem-objects are complex constructions in plastic.

H. C. (Hans Carl Bronislavius) ARTMANN: Born 1921 in Vienna. A founder of the *"Wiener Gruppe"* that dominated Viennese avant-garde activities from 1952 to 1959. His publications include **med ana schwoazzn dintn** (Otto Mueller Verlag, Salzburg 1958), Austrian dialect poems; **Von denen Husaren und anderen Seil-Tänzern** (Piper Verlag, Munich 1958); **Der Schlüssel des heiligen Patrick** (Otto Mueller Verlag, Munich 1959); **hosn rosn baa** (Wilhelm Frick Verlag, Vienna 1959), a volume of dialect poetry including works by Friedrich Achleitner and Gerhard Rühm; and many plays for the theater and television. He lives in Malmö, Sweden.

Ronaldo AZEREDO: Born 1937 in Rio de Janeiro. Since he joined the Noigandres Group in 1956 his concrete poems have appeared regularly in *Noigandres* anthologies and *Invenção*. According to Décio Pignatari, "Ronaldo Azeredo never wrote verses in his life: directly to concrete poetry. Owns an extraordinary form intuition. Now pursuing a sort of 'graphic prose'." He works in advertising.

Stephen BANN: Born 1942 in Manchester, England. Has lived in Cambridge since 1960, with frequent excursions to France, Germany and Austria. Met Ian Hamilton Finlay in August 1964, and helped to organize Mike Weaver's Cambridge exhibitions of concrete and kinetic poetry the end of the same year. Bann is co-author of **Four Essays on Kinetic Art** (Motion Books) and editor of an anthology of concrete poetry published by Alan Ross in London. He edited the concrete poetry number of the *Beloit Poetry Journal* in Fall 1966, co-edits the quarterly magazine *Form*, and has contributed to various anthologies.

Carlo BELLOLI: Born 1922 in Milan. Eldest son of the 14th Count of Seriate. Doctor of letters and philosophy, and professor of aesthetics. Poet, art historian and critic. An early innovator in the new poetry that during the 1950s came to be called concrete. His books and portfolios of poems include **testi poemi murali**, Edizioni Erre, Milan 1944; **tavole visuali**, Edizioni Gala, Rome 1948; **corpi de poesia**, Mediterranean Publishing Company, Rome & New York 1951; **tavole visuali** (second series), Edizioni Meps, Milan 1956; **textes audiovisuels**, Édition Matérial, Paris 1959; **stenogrammi della geometria elementare**, Scheiwiller, Milan 1960; **texte poème poème texte**, Eugen Gomringer Press, Frauenfeld 1961; **sole solo**, Edition Hansjörg Mayer, Stuttgart 1967. His books on aesthetics, art history and criticism include **La**

Vita nell'Era Feudale (1946), **Il Senso del Colore nella Letteratura** (1950); **Arte Mediterranea** (1951), **Filologia Cibernetica e Linguaggio dell'Estetica** (1953), **Elementi Mediterranei nell'Architettura Brasiliana** (1956), **Cinema d'Avanguardia** and **Storia delle Tecniche e Critica delle Estetiche** (1957); **Brasilien Baut Brasilia / Brasil Constroi Brasilia** (1958), **Manifesto del Neomediterranismo** and **Arti Plastiche** (1959), **Lo Spettacolo Futurista** and **Teatro, Cinema, Radio, Danza** (1962), **La Integrazione delle Arti nell'Estetica Neomediterranea** (1962), **Nuove Direzioni della Cinevisualitá Plastica Totale** (1962), **Tensioni Lineari di Paul Mansouroff** (1963) and **Il Contributo Russo alle Avanguardie Plastiche** (1964).

Max BENSE: Born 1910 in Strasbourg. Studied mathematics, physics and philosophy at the universities of Bonn, Cologne and Basel. Worked as a physicist in private industry until World War II, when he was interned by the Nazis. Later, lecturer and professor at the University of Jena. Since 1950, professor of philosophy and science at the Technische Hochschule in Stuttgart. He has been guest-lecturer at the University of Hamburg, the Hochschule für Gestaltung in Ulm, and in Brazil. Interest in his theory of text, and in his own experimental writing, has spread far beyond Germany; a **Bense Reader**, to be published by the Something Else Press early in 1968, will help the non-German-speaking reader assess Bense's contribution to modern aesthetics. His non-theoretical publications include **Grignan**, *rot 1*, Verlag der Augenblick, Stuttgart 1961; **Bestandteile des Vorüber**, Kiepenheuer & Witsch, Cologne 1961; **Entwurf einer Rheinlandschaft**, Kiepenheuer & Witsch 1962; **Vielleicht zunächst wirklich nur**, *rot 2*, Stuttgart 1963; **Präzise Vergnügen**, Limes Verlag, Wiesbaden 1964; **tallose berge**, Edition Hansjörg Mayer, Stuttgart 1965, and **Zerstörung des Durstes durch Wasser**, Kiepenheuer & Witsch, Cologne 1967.

Edgard BRAGA: Born 1898 in Alagoas, Brazil. Physician. Augusto de Campos writes: "After a long experience with modernist (post-symbolist) poetry, he came to concrete poetry, in 1959, with his book **Suburbio Branco** (White Suburb) followed soon after by **Extralunario** (Extralunarian), 1960. **Soma** (Sum), his next book of poetry, 1963, radicalizes the spatial structures of the earlier collections, and gives us his purest concretes, where some hints of medieval Portuguese lyrics may be found. In his recent book—his 'tactilograms' and his 'tatoo poems'—Dr. Braga develops a sort of ideographic handwriting where letters and drawings interrelate in a gestation of form which has something to do with his professional activities as a surgeon: some 15,000 babies born in his hands."

Claus BREMER: Born 1924 in Hamburg. Studied philosophy, literature and art history at the University of Freiburg. In Freiburg, where he also trained as an actor and director, Bremer began his close friendship and collaboration with the late Rainer M. Gerhardt, poet, editor and publisher of the review *Fragmente*, created to help close the "culture gap" imposed on Germany by the Nazis. In 1952 he began eight years of collaboration with Gustav Rudolf Sellner at the Landestheater in Darmstadt, earning a Europe-wide reputation for his research in experimental theater. In Darmstadt he also edited *Das Neue Forum*, a clearing house for writings on avant-garde theater, and was closely associated with Daniel Spoerri and Emmett Williams in the "*Darmstädter Kreis*" of concrete poets, kinetic art, dynamic theater, etc. In 1960 he became *Chefdramaturg* of the municipal theater in Bern, Switzerland, and in 1962 was appointed to a similar post in Ulm. From 1962 to 1965 he taught at the Ulmer Hochschule für Gestaltung. He now lives at Siedlung Halen, near Bern, where he works as free-lance writer, translator, and guest director. His publications include **poesie** (Karlsruhe 1954); **tabellen und variationen** (1960) and **ideogramme** (1964), both published by the Eugen Gomringer Press in Frauenfeld; **Theater ohne Vorhang** (St. Gallen 1962) and **Das aktuelle Theater** (1966), collections of his writings on the theater; and **engagierende texte**, Edition Hansjörg Mayer, Stuttgart 1966. Bremer has translated plays by Sophocles, Aristophanes, Shakespeare, Beaumont and Fletcher, Tzara, Ionesco, Audiberti, Prévert, Gatti and Spoerri.

Henri CHOPIN: Born 1922 in Paris. In 1943, deported as a forced laborer, later interned in camps in Czechoslovakia and Germany. 1945, Soviet Union. Returned to France to find his family had been exterminated. Joined the military, served in Indochina, returned to Paris sick and "*surtout antitout*." Chopin's earliest preserved writings are poems of the resistance written during his internment in Czechoslovakia. His collections of poems include **Signes**, Édition Caractères 1957; **Chant de Nuit**, Édition Tour de Feu 1957; **Présence**, Édition poésie Nouvelle 1957; **l'Arriviste**, Édition Caractères 1958, and **La Peur**, Édition Cinquième Saison 1959. Many of his audiopoems, including **Vibrespace, La Fusée Interplanétaire, Indicatif 1, l'Energie du Sommeil** and **Sol Air**, have been released in the *OU* series of Cinquième Saison, of which Chopin is editor. **Sol Air** and **Vibrespace** served as the nuclei of experimental ballets performed in Paris, and the film version of **l'Energie du Sommeil**, made with Béguier and Bertini, was awarded the Prix Antonin Artaud in 1966. Part of a novel, **Le Dernier Roman du Monde**, was published in *OU 26/27* in 1966. Chopin's review *OU* is a major forum of concrete and audio-visual poetry. He has arranged more than 30 exhibitions of objective and visual poetry, and his critical writings have been widely published.

Carlfriedrich CLAUS: Born 1930. Lives in Annaberg-Buchholz, German Democratic Republic. Early influences: the philosopher Ernst Bloch and the Lurian cabbala. The most comprehensive guide to the work of Claus (labeled "the most radically fantastic and elegant of the new poet-artists" by a writer in the London Times Literary Supplement) is **Notizen zwischen der experimentellen Arbeit—zu ihr**, published by Typos Verlag in Frankfurt-am-Main as a catalogue to the 1964 retrospective exhibition of his work in Baden-Baden. Claus' work can be roughly divided into his Klang-Gebilden (1952–59); the *Sprechexercitien* experiments on magnetic tape (1959); *Phasen* and other typewritten texts (1958–); the *Geschichts-Kombinat*, dialectically interrelated texts printed on transparent paper (1959–64), and the *Reflektierende Reflexionen*, script montages on glass and mirrors (since 1961).

Bob COBBING: Born 1920 in Enfield, Middlesex, England. Lives in London. Co-editor and publisher of Writers Forum Poets. Cobbing has made monotypes using typewriter and/or duplicator since 1942. His first sound poems date from 1954. His publications include **Massacre of the Innocents** (1963), with John Rowan; **26 Sound Poems** (1965) and **Extra Verse No. 17** (1966). In 1966 he made a record of sound poems with the Austrian poet Ernst Jandl. His tapes include **Sound Poems**, made in collaboration with the BBC Radiophonic Workshop and broadcast in January 1966; **Chamber Music, Are your children safe in the sea** (broadcast in July 1966), **Worm** and **Kurrirrurriri**, produced independently.

Augusto De CAMPOS: Born 1931 in São Paulo, Brazil. Co-founder, with his brother Haroldo and Décio Pignatari, of the Noigandres Group in 1952, and co-author of the "pilot plan for concrete poetry" (1958). His first concrete poems were published in the anthology **Noigrandres 2** (1955), the same year the colored poems in his **poetamenos** series were presented at the Teatro de Arena of São Paulo projected on a screen and read by four voices. His publications, apart from the large body of his work in *Noigandres* anthologies and **Invenção**, include **O Rei Menos o Reino** (1951); a translation of Ezra Pound's **Cantos** (1960), in collaboration with his brother and Pignatari; **e. e. cummings—10 poemas** (1960) and **Panaroma do Finnegans Wake de James Joyce** (1962), translations (with his brother) of eleven fragments, with notes and critical texts, and **Teoria da Poesia Concreta** (1965), with his brother and Pignatari. "It was chiefly through exchanging letters and books with Augusto de Campos—who sent them the 'pilot plan'," writes Pignatari, "—that Ian Hamilton Finlay, Scotland, and Dom Sylvester Houédard, OSB, came enthusiastically to concrete poetry."

Haroldo De CAMPOS: Born 1929 in São Paulo, Brazil. Co-founder, with his brother Augusto and Décio Pignatari, of the Noigandres Group, and co-author of the "pilot plan for concrete poetry." A profound student of global literature, he has translated or collaborated on translations from Chinese, English, French, German, Italian, Japanese, Russian, Spanish, etc. In 1957, after the launching of the international movement for concrete poetry, de Campos wrote to Kitasono Katue in Tokyo, introducing him to the problems of concrete poetry—and the result was the first Japanese concrete poem, by Katue. In similar fashion, through travels and correspondence, he has proselytized for the new poetry throughout the world. In addition to the large body of his work in *Noigandres* anthologies and *Invenção*, he has published **Auto do Possesso** (1949), **Servidão de Passagem** (1962), **Panaroma do Finnegans Wake de James Joyce** (1962), translations (with his brother) of eleven fragments, with notes and critical texts; **Alea I—Semantic Variations** (1964), and **Versuchsbuch Galaxien** (1966).

Paul De VREE: Born 1909 in Antwerp. Teacher, novelist, poet, painter, film-maker, critic. President of the Belgian National Center of Modern Art, and secretary of the review *De Tafelronde*. His publications include **Egelronde** (poems), 1957; **Throw In** (criticism), 1959; **Grondbeelding** (poems), 1960; **Close-Up der Vlaamse Dichtkunst van nu** (a four-volume study of recent Flemish poetry), 1961–63; **pl. acid. amore** (poems), 1963; **h. eros. hima** (poems), 1965; **Vlaamse Avant-garde** (an anthology), 1966; **explositieven** (visual poems), 1966; and **zimprovisaties** (a collection of his concrete and audio-visual work), in preparation.

Reinhard DÖHL: Born 1934 in Wattenscheid, Germany. Lives in Stuttgart. His publications include **11 texte** (1960), **missa profana** (1959–61), **so etwas wie eine geschichte von etwas** (1962), **fingerübungen** (1962), **porträt einwände** (1962), **prosa zum beispiel** (1965), **4 texte** (1965) and es **anna** (1966). In 1963 he edited **zwischen räume.**

Torsten EKBOM: Born 1938 in Stockholm. Lives in Uppsala. Ekbom has published five novels, the last two incorporating many of the procedures of concrete poetry. **Signalspelet** (The Signal Game) is written by a fictive computer as the "prose machine" using material from an old Biggles book of W. E. Johns. His latest, **Spelmatriser för Operation Albatross** (Game Matrices for Operation Albatross), is based on the theory of games: fifteen matrices are elaborated by computers for two opposing powers, the Reds and the Blues, a model of the Cold War. Communications via spy satellites, teleprinters, TV, etc., form a global intrigue, and the international cast is manipulated by tables of random numbers. The author, who likens the method to Dr. Strangelove interpreted by Marshall McLuhan, calls the result a "strategic puppet theatre." His work in progress is a pseudo-political novel with flow diagrams and other concepts borrowed from cybernetics. Ekbom was editor of the review *Rondo* (1961–64) and currently edits *Gorilla*, which has recently published manifestos on art and technology, cybernetic comic strips, Timothy Leary, Buckminster Fuller, Marshall McLuhan, Murray the K and Susan Sontag. Ekbom translated John Cage's **Silence** and Samuel Beckett's **Watt**. He writes critical articles for the Stockholm newspaper *Dagans Nyheter*, and recently published a monograph on painter-poet Öyvind Fahlström.

Öyvind FAHLSTRÖM: Born 1928 in São Paulo, Brazil, of Swedish and Norwegian parents. Family returned to Sweden in 1939. Studied history of art and archaeology. In 1950 he started writing poems and plays, and critical articles for Stockholm papers. In 1953, the year after the first one-man show of his paintings and drawings, he published **Manifesto for concrete poetry**. Since he came to New York on a scholarship in 1961, and settled there, he has had one-man shows of his paintings in Paris, Stockholm, New York and other cities, and represented Sweden at the XXXIII Biennale in Venice in 1966. Much of Fahlström's pictorial work shows the influence of his early interest in concrete poetry: The variable diptych "The Planetarium" (1963), for example, utilizes magnetized costumes that can be placed on "characters" who change sex and identity as the "conversation" proceeds; on a smaller picture by the big one, every figure is represented by words from the conversation, and these words change depending on the clothes put on the figures. Verbs correspond to skirts or pants, pronouns to blouses and shirts, nouns to coats, etc. There has been renewed interest in Fahlström's poetry with the republication of his early concrete work in **Bord Dikter 1952–1955**, Bonniers, Stockholm 1966.

Carl FERNBACH-FLARSHEIM: "As for the 'bio-bibliographical' notes you request: I was born at 8 pm (I was told) September 8 (Virgo), 1921, and acquired gray hair sooner than some. I was born in Gleiwitz, Germany, or Gliwice, Poland, in the province of Upper Silesia. As for the rest . . . why do they want to know? You might ask them . . . the readers (aficionados)."

Ian Hamilton FINLAY: Born 1925. Lives in northern Scotland. Poet, toy-maker, typographer. His first collection of poems, **The Dancers Inherit the Party** (1959), attracted the attention of a number of established poets in the United States; his next book, **Glasgow Beasts, An a Burd—Haw, An Inseks, An, Aw, a Fush** (1960), which eschewed literary Scots in favor of the industrial dialect, attracted the attention of Edinburgh authorities, who were forced to ban demonstrations against it. The same year he founded the Wild Hawthorn Press, and there followed a succession of works, typographically rendered by Finlay, that established him as the major concrete poet in the British Isles, whose work has influenced many of the younger poets there and in North America. These works include **Concertina** (1961); **Rapel, 10 fauve and suprematist poems** (1963); **Canal Stripe series 2, Canal Stripe series 3,** and **Telegrams from my Windmill** (1964); **Ocean Stripe series 2, Ocean Stripe series 3,** and **Cythera** (1965); **6 Small Pears for Eugen Gomringer, 6 Small Songs in 3's, Autumn Poem** and **Tea Leaves and Fishes** (1966). Two collections, **The Blue and the Brown Poems** and **Honey by the Water**, are scheduled for publication in 1967. In addition, Finlay has made a series of standing poems; **Earthship**, a paper-sculpture poem, and large poem-constructions in glass and concrete. A collection of short stories, **The Sea-Bed and Other Stories**, was published in 1958, and Universal Editions in Vienna released a German translation of his early **Walking Through Seaweed and Other Plays** in 1965.

Larry FREIFELD: Born 1941 in New York City. Poet, graphic artist, composer and performer. Freifeld writes of himself: "Studied music under scholarship at Henry Street Music School. Appeared on the cover of *Dance Magazine* in 1952. . . . He never went to class because he had a date and when he was 16 he wrote 'I am a fool I am a fool for twenty years I went to school Now everytime I pass I pee on New York University.' First published in *Wagner Literary Magazine* 1965 under the name Jacob Yuder. Other publications in *Kauri, WIN, Hika*. Demonstration and reading Jan. 25th, 67, St. Marks. Shares his home with actress Lois Unger and their 18 month old daughter Jennifer Rose two of the most beautiful women in the world . . . Blah."

John FURNIVAL: Born 1933 in London. Lecturer at the School of Graphic Design and Audio-visual Communications, Bath Academy of Art. Studied at Wimbledon School of Art and the Royal College of Art. Co-editor, with Dom Sylvester Houédard and Edward Wright, of *Openings*. Furnival has done typographical renderings of the work of many poets, including Mary Ellen Solt and Ronald Johnson. His constructions have been widely exhibited in Great Britain, the United States and Europe, and his poems have appeared in many periodicals and anthologies.

Heinz GAPPMAYR: Born 1925 in Innsbruck, Austria. Lives in Innsbruck. Designer. His publications include **zeichen**, Pinguin Verlag, Innsbruck 1962; **zeichen II**, Innsbruck 1964; **Zur Theorie der Konkreten Poesie** and **Antonio Calderara**, lecture-essays published by Studio UNd, Munich, in 1965, and *"La poesia del concreto"* in the review *modulo*, Genoa 1966. Gappmayr has had one-man shows of his visual poems at Studio UNd in Munich and at the Studio di Informazione Estetica in Turin. His work has been widely anthologized.

Ilse GARNIER: Born 1927 in Kaiserslautern, Germany. Studied at the universities of Mainz and Paris. Lives in Amiens. Her publications include **L'Expressionisme allemande** (in collaboration with Pierre Garnier, q.v.), Editions A. Silvaire, Paris 1962; **Poèmes mécaniques** and **Prototypes—textes pour une architecture**, both with Pierre Garnier; and numerous critical articles in European reviews. Her Spatialist short story **Jeanne d'Arc** will appear in 1967.

Pierre GARNIER: Born 1928 in Amiens. Studied at the universities of Paris and Mainz. Professor of German at the Lycée d'Amiens. Since 1963 Garnier has edited *Les Lettres*, the Spatialist review, an invaluable source of international experimental writing. His pre-concrete collections of poems include **Les Armes de la Terre**, Editions A. Silvaire, Paris 1954; **La nuit est prisonnière des étoiles**, Silvaire 1958; **Seconde Géographie**, Gallimard, Paris 1959, and **Les Synthèses**, Silvaire 1961. His **Collected Poems 1952–61** were translated into Greek and published by Difros Press in Athens, as was his novel **Et par amour voulaient mourir.** He has published a collection of essays on Nietzsche, Heine, Novalis and Goethe (Seghers) and a study of Gottfried Benn (Silvaire). His concrete publications, all of which have appeared in the Spatialist collection of Editions Silvaire, include **Poèmes mécaniques** and **Prototypes—textes pour une architecture**, both with Ilse Garnier; **Poèmes franco-japonais**, with Seiichi Niikuni, and **Poèmes spatiaux picards. Othon III**, a Spatialist novel, will appear in 1967.

Mathias GOERITZ: Born 1915 in Danzig. The architect-painter-sculptor has lived in Mexico since 1949, directs the visual education workshops of the Mexican National School of Architecture, and is a professor at the Ibero-American University. From 1941 to 1949 he lived in Morocco and Spain. His early sound-poems and graphic constellations, written during this period, were published under the name Werner Brünner. Since he built his *"poema plástico,"* a sculptured poem in iron, for the experimental museum El Eco (which he designed) in Mexico City, his poetic energy has taken a monumental turn. From ground-plans that resemble one-letter and one-word constellations have risen such poems in concrete as the five towers of Ciudad Satélite (between 135 and 190 feet high) outside Mexico City, the 150-foot-high Automex Towers, symbol of the new Mexican automobile industry, and the 90-foot-long VAM road-marker on the Mexico City—Toluca highway. Goeritz' most recent concrete publication is **mensajes del oro**, which dates from 1960, published by Edition Hansjörg Mayer, Stuttgart 1965. In 1966 he arranged an international exhibition of concrete poetry at the University of Mexico, the nation's first.

Eugen GOMRINGER: Born 1924 in Cachuela Esperanza, Bolivia. Educated in Switzerland, studied art history in Berne and Rome, and served as Max Bill's secretary at the Hochschule für Gestaltung at Ulm, Germany, from 1954 to 1958. He founded the Eugen Gomringer Press in Frauenfeld, Switzerland, in 1959, which through the years has made available the basic texts of concrete poetry. Since 1959 he has worked as an art director in Swiss industry. His publications include **konstellationen**, Spiral Press, Berne 1953; the manifesto *"vom vers zur konstellation"* in *Augenblick* No. 2, Agis Verlag, Baden-Baden 1954; *"max bill und die konkrete dichtung"* in **max bill**, a volume of tributes to the artist, Arthur Niggli Verlag, Teufen 1958; **33 konstellationen**, Tschudy Verlag, St. Gallen 1960; **5 mal 1 konstellation**, Eugen Gomringer Press, Frauenfeld 1960; **die konstellationen** (his collected constellations), Frauenfeld 1963; **das stundenbuch**, Max Huber Verlag, Munich 1965, and **manifeste und dartstellungen der konkreten poesie 1954–1966**, Galerie Press, St. Gallen 1966.

Ludwig GOSEWITZ: Born 1936 in Naumburg, Germany. Lives in Berlin. Composer, poet, jazz musician. Studied Germanistics at the University of Marburg. His publications include **typogramme**, Eugen Gomringer Press, Frauenfeld 1962; *"dazwischentext,"* in *dé-coll/age* 5, Cologne 1966; **12 partituren für vokale äusserungen**, Edition Et, Berlin 1966; and poems and texts in various reviews and anthologies. His **würfeltext** was manufactured in a limited edition of 20 by Edition Et, Berlin 1966. Gosewitz's visual poems and poem-

objects have been exhibited in Amsterdam, Berlin, Darmstadt and other European cities.

Bohumila GRÖGEROVA: Born 1921. Lives in Prague. Her published writings include a montage diary, a play for the absurd theater, many children's books, translations of St. John Perse, Eugène Ionesco, Peter Weiss and others, and parts of a work in progress, **Philosophical Schemata**. For her collaboration with Josef Hirsal on **job boj** see note to "*manifesto*" on page 138.

Josef HIRŠAL: Born 1920. Lives in Prague. Teacher, journalist, editor and publisher. His works include five volumes of poetry, a series of children's books, translations of Christian Morgenstern, Edgar Allan Poe, North American folk poems, Heinrich Heine, Hans Magnus Enzensberger, Helmut Heissenbüttel, Raymond Queneau, and Renaissance poetry from Dubrovnik. He is preparing an international anthology of experimental writing. For his collaboration with Bohumila Grögerova on **job boj**, see note to "*manifesto*" on page 138.

José Lino GRÜNEWALD: Born 1931 in Rio de Janeiro. Lawyer and journalist. A well-known film and movie critic, Grünewald also writes a weekly political column for the Correio da Manha, the most important opposition newspaper in Brazil. His book **Um e Dois** appeared in 1958, the year he joined the Noigandres Group. Since then his work has appeared regularly in *Invenção* and *Noigandres* anthologies. Grünewald has published translations of Eisenstein, S. I. Hayakawa, Garcia Lorca and William Carlos Williams.

Brion GYSIN: Born 1916 in England of a Swiss father and a Canadian mother. Lives in Tangier. An American citizen, Gysin has spent most of his life abroad, chiefly in Paris and North Africa. His publications include **Minutes to Go** (with William Burroughs, Sinclair Beiles and Gregory Corso), Two Cities Editions, Paris 1960; and **The Exterminator** (with William Burroughs), The Auerhahn Press, San Francisco 1960. Both volumes have examples of the cut-up method and permutated poems; **The Exterminator** contains five of Gysin's calligraphic poems. Gysin, a founder of the Domaine Poetique in Paris, gives frequent performances of his work, and his poems have been broadcast in France and England. He is the inventor of the "Dream Machine," a rotating psychedelic "visual aid" which functions only when the eyes are closed. His first novel will be published in 1967.

Al HANSEN: Born 1927 in New York City. Worked in commercial art and graphic design until 1958 when he founded, with Dick Higgins, the New York Audio-Visual Group, and launched his first Happenings and multiscreen projections. In 1962 Hansen opened the Third Rail Gallery of Current Art. A one-man show at the Judson Gallery in the winter of 1964 and a second at the New York Six (which first featured his Hershey Bar wrapper collages) established his reputation as a Pop artist. His work hangs in several museums and many private collections. His publications include **A Primer of Happenings & Time/Space Art** (Something Else Press, New York 1965) and **Incomplete Requiem for W. C. Fields** (Great Bear Pamphlets, New York 1966). He is currently at work on a new book, **New Trends in Art Today.**

Vaclav HAVEL: Born 1936 in Prague. Dramaturgist at the Theater on the Balustrade in Prague. He has written two plays, **The Garden Party** and **The Memorandum**, both performed in Prague and other European cities, and soon to be published by Grove Press in English. His collection of typographical poems, **The Anticodes**, was recently published in Prague together with his plays and two essays in **The Minutes**. He is presently finishing his third play.

Helmut HEISSENBÜTTEL: Born 1921 in Wilhelmshaven, Germany. Studied Germanistics and art history at the University of Hamburg. Since 1957, an editorial director of the South German Radio Network in Stuttgart. One of the most original contemporary German poets, he has received the Lessing Prize and other literary awards. His works include **Kombinationen** (1954) and **Topographien** (1956), both published by Bechtel Verlag, Esslingen; **ohne weiteres bekannt**, Eremiten Press, Stierstadt 1958; **Texte ohne Komma**, Eugen Gomringer Press, Frauenfeld 1960; and **Textbuch 1** (1960), **Textbuch 2** (1961), **Textbuch 3** (1962), **Textbuch 4** (1964) and **Textbuch 5** (1965), all published by Walter Verlag, Olten and Freiburg. Walter Verlag has also issued a volume of his essays, **Uber Literatur** (1966).

Åke HODELL: Born 1919 in Stockholm. Director of the avant-garde publishing house Kerberos, and an editor of the review *Gorilla*, published by Bonnier in Stockholm. Hodell's books, which apply the techniques of concrete, visual and sound poetry to longer literary forms, include **flyende pilot** (1953); **igevär** (1963), **sssvvviiissscchhh** (an anthology, 1964), **General Bussig** (1964), **Bruksanvisning för symaskinen Singer Victoria** (1965), **Orderbuch** (1965), **Laagsniff** (with phonograph record, 1966), **C A 36715 (J)** (1966), and **Verner von Heidenstam, Nya dikter** (1967). **verbal hjärntvätt** (1965) is a phonograph record with selections from **General Bussig** and **igevär**. In addition, Hodell has written and produced experimental plays and Happenings at the Moderna Museet and the Pistol Theater in Stockholm, and his graphic work is represented in the collection of the Swedish National Museum. Hodell's most recent experiments with sound poetry were presented at the Moderna Museet in April 1967, and broadcast by the Swedish Radio.

Dom Sylvester HOUÉDARD: Born 1924 on the island of Guernsey. Studied at Elisabeth College (St. Peter Port), Jesus College (Oxford) and St. Anselmo College in Rome. Joined Prinknash Abbey, Gloucester, in 1949. Leading theorist of concrete, visual, phonetic and kinetic poetry in the British Isles. Houédard has been interested in typewriter arabesques ("that led direct to typestracts") since 1945. His work has been published extensively in European and North American reviews and anthologies.

Ernst JANDL: Born 1925 in Vienna. Studied Germanistics and English at the University of Vienna. Since 1949 Dr. Jandl has taught at grammar schools in Vienna. He began his experiments in language in the mid-fifties, as an act of protest against the traditionalism prevalent in poetry. "Later," he writes, "when manipulating linguistic material became an absorbing end in itself, aggressiveness was no longer a major concern. Disregard of the conventions of language was rewarded by the discovery of new ways of making grotesque poems, many of which were meant to be spoken rather than read quietly. Moreover, the experimental poem was willing to accomplish what its more conventional relative was only ready to describe." His publications include **Andere Augen** (poems), Bergland Verlag, Vienna 1956; **lange gedichte, Rot-Text** No. 16, Stuttgart 1964; **klare gerührt** (visual poems), Eugen Gomringer Press, Frauenfeld 1964; **mai hart lieb zapfen eibe hold**, Writers Forum Poets No. 11, London 1965; **sprechgedichte**, Writers Forum Record No. 1, London 1965; **szenen aus dem wirklichen leben**, *Manuskripte No. 17*, Graz 1966 (first performed at Theater an der Wien, Vienna, June 18, 1965), and **Laut und Luise** (poems), Walter Verlag, Olten 1966. Jandl's translation of Robert Creeley's **The Island** was published by Insel Verlag, Frankfurt, in 1965.

Bengt Emil JOHNSON: Born 1936 in Saxdalen, Dalecarlia, northern Sweden, where he lived until 1965, working as a village shopkeeper. In 1965 he moved to Stockholm, where he works in the music department of the Swedish radio. A pianist and composer, he studied music from the age of 6. He wrote his first poems when he was 5. His publications include **Hyllningarna** (The Ovations), 1963; **Essaer om Bror Barsk och andra dikter** (picture poems), 1964; **Gubbdrunkning** (a record with textbook), 1965; **Släpkoppel med vida världen**, 1966; and **Semikolon** (sound-poetry, with record, done in collaboration with Lars-Gunnar Bodin), 1966. Since 1962 Johnson has written and performed radio-poetry, stage-poems and sound-poems for groups of readers, and several compositions for piano and chamber ensemble, performed in Stockholm and other cities. He has published essays on music and literature in newspapers and reviews, and a book on the Swedish sculptor Elis Eriksson. His most recent work, a four-channel poem for many voices and concrete and electronic sounds, lies "somewhere between 'poetry' and 'music'." Johnson has made an English version of **Semikolon**, which will be released in 1967.

Ronald JOHNSON: Born 1935 in Ashland, Kansas. "Education—Columbia / Cedar Bar, Class of '60. Boar's Head Prize for Poetry, Columbia, 1960. Inez Boulton Prize from Poetry (Chicago), 1966. My early poems celebrated pre-television Dodge City and were, according to Mina Loy: 'gracious to buffalo.' My poems have always been obstinately optical, composed only on the typewriter for the size of a typewritten page. Concrete poetry offers, to me, not the 'purity' of Mondrian, etc., but the added possibility of transcending the linearity of type. How to make a poem flat as a prairie? How to plant trees between the letters or to balance a real moon on the word 'moon'? These continually ask for answers. Gustav Mahler said 'to write a symphony, means to me, to construct a whole world, using all the available techniques. The ever new and changing content determines its own form.' I want a concrete poetry, not of exclusion, but of inclusion. A wholer world."

Hiro KAMIMURA: Born 1930 in Tokyo. Teaches German language and literature at Kansai University in Osaka. In 1966–67 he did research work at the University of Marburg and Stuttgart. He has written on German Expressionist writers, and has translated Ernst Stadler and Georg Heym into Japanese. The selection of his work in this anthology is reprinted from **5 vokaltexte**, Edition Hansjörg Mayer, Stuttgart 1967.

Kitasono KATUE: Born 1902 in Mie-ken, educated at Chuo University. Lives in Tokyo. Founder and editor of the avant-garde magazine *Vou*. The Japanese interest in concrete poetry can be traced directly to Katue, one of the most important contemporary poets in Japan. "In 1957," recalls Haroldo de Campos, "after the launching of the international movement for concrete poetry, I wrote to Kitasono Katue, introducing him to the problems of a concrete poetry and trying to establish some connection with his theory of ideoplasty (as expounded by e.p., **Guide to Kulchur**, pp. 137–40). He answered me very positively: doing a concrete poem—*'tanchona kukan'* (monotony of void space), published in *Vou* No. 58, Nov. 1957. I translated it into Portuguese, and he reprinted my translation in *Vou* No. 63, Sept. 58. This was the first concrete Japoem and the bridge for the movement in that country." He has published poetry, criticism and translations from the French. Selections of his work have appeared in English in **New Directions**, the *Quarterly Review of Literature*, **A Little Treasury of World Poetry** (Scribners) and **New World Writing** (6th Mentor Selection).

Jiří KOLÁŘ: Born 1914 in Protivin, Czechoslovakia. Lives in Prague. From 1941 to 1957 he published seven collections of poetry. In 1959 Kolár wrote his **Tribute to Kasimir Malevich**, followed by Y 61, a collection of constellations, fragments of conversations, newspaper clippings, linguistic concretions, etc., and **Signboard for Gersaint** (1962) which introduced his "evident poetry." Kolár has collaborated on translations of Carl Sandburg, Walt Whitman, T. S. Eliot, St. John Perse, Samuel Beckett and other writers, and his collages have been exhibited in one-man shows in Prague, London, Miami, Lisbon, Vienna, Genoa and other cities.

Ferdinand KRIWET: Born 1942 in Dusseldorf. Self-taught. Lives in Dusseldorf. His publications include **Rotor** (1961); **10 Sehtexte** (1962); **Sehtexte 2** (1964); **Leserattenfänge** (1965), commentaries on his visual texts, all published by M. DuMont Schauberg, Cologne; and **Durch die Runse auf den Redder**, Wolfang Fietkau Verlag, Berlin 1965. His works for the theater include **Offen**, performed in Ulm in 1962; **Aspektakel**, a play for mobile theatre, commissioned by the municipal theater in Gelsenkirchen; **Texttheater** (1963) and **Lecture** (1965). His acoustical texts for radio include **Hörtext 1** (1963) and **Jaja** (1965). Since 1963 he has had one-man shows in Dusseldorf, Gelsenkirchen, Stuttgart, Ulm, Zeist (the Netherlands), Berlin, Paris and New York.

Arrigo LORA-TOTINO: Born 1928 in Turin. Founder (1960) and director of *antipiugiu*, a review devoted to experimental writing, and director of the review *modulo*, the first number of which was an international anthology of concrete poetry. With Enore Zaffiri and Sandro de Alexandris, Lora-Totino founded the Studio di Informazione Estetica in Turin, which has explored the interaction of diverse artistic forms. His paintings have been widely exhibited since his first one-man show at the Galleria Il Prismo, Milan, in 1959. With Carlo Belloli, he helped establish the Museum of Contemporary Poetry at Turin.

Jackson MAC LOW: Born 1922 in Chicago. Studied music there from the age of 4, began composing music and poetry at 15, and did work in philosophy and comparative literature at the University of Chicago from 1939 to 1943. After moving to New York, he continued his musical studies, worked at various jobs, co-edited an anarchist newspaper, and obtained a B.A. in Greek at Brooklyn College in 1958. In 1954, with his **5 biblical poems**, Mac Low invented a kind of verse in which the unit is the "event" rather than the foot, syllable, stress or cadence. His play **The Marrying Maiden** (1958) is constructed with a vocabulary of words and phrases from the Chinese **Book of Changes** (**I Ching**), chosen by objective systematic chance operations. Similar operations supplied the characters, speeches, divisions of scenes, gradations of loud and soft and fast and slow, and a set of adverbs and adverbial phrases serving as "regulations of manner" for the actors. The play was produced in New York in 1960 by the Living Theatre, directed by Judith Malina, with a score by John Cage the use of which was determined by dice throws. Mac Low's **Stanzas for Iris Lezak** (his wife), which the Something Else Press will publish in 1968, is a book of stanzaic-acrostic chance poems written in 1960. The separated stanzas, with words and phrases drawn from such widely different sources as newspapers and scientific treatises, have been copied on more than 700 cards and used as texts for simultaneous performances comprising musical sounds and noises. **The Twin Plays**, two plays with identical structures but written in different English languages, was published in 1966 as a *Great Bear* pamphlet. Mac Low has also done paintings, collages and constructions, and remains active in the peace, civil rights, and anarchist movements.

Hansjörg MAYER: Born 1943 in Stuttgart. Typoet, printer, and editor. He has been described by Haroldo de Campos, who coined the word "typoet" in a tribute to Mayer, as "a man who eats reality with types and reinvents reality through types, reality being for him texts." Mayer studied with Max Bense at the Technische Hochschule in Stuttgart, and at the Engineering School for Industrial Graphics. He is a frequent lecturer at the Bath Academy of Art in England. One of the most original of the younger designers and typographers, he has made available through his press (Edition Hansjörg Mayer, Stuttgart) the works of the major experimental writers of Europe, England and North America. These publications include the *futura* series of large folded broadsheets, the *Rot Texte* series (edited by Elizabeth Walter and Max Bense) and a succession of de luxe portfolios. His own publications include **19 typographien** (1962); **alphabet** (1963), **alphabetenquadratbuch 1** (1965) and **typoactions** (1967). He has contributed to many magazines and anthologies, and his work is represented in the collections of the Museum of Modern Art in New York, the Walker Art Center in Minneapolis, the Stedelijk in Amsterdam, the Gemeentemuseum in The Hague, and the Museo de Arte Moderna in Rio de Janeiro.

Cavan McCARTHY: Born 1943 in Bristol, England. Studied Russian at Leeds. Works as a librarian in the College of Technology and Design, Blackburn. Founded and edits the magazine *Tlaloc,* devoted to concrete poetry. European editor for *Directory of Little Magazines* and *Small Press Review.* His work has been published in several magazines and anthologies, and he had a one-man show of his work at the Bristol Arts Centre in 1967. He has read selections of his poems on the BBC Third Programme.

Franz MON: Born 1926 in Frankfurt-am-Main. Studied Germanistics, history and philosophy. Founded Typos Verlag in 1963, today one of West Germany's leading avant-garde publishers. His publications include **artikulationen**, Neske Verlag, Pfullingen 1959; **protokoll an der kette** (14 poems with lithographs and drawings by Bernard Schultze), Galerie der Spiegel, Cologne 1960–61; **verläufe** (with lithographs by Karl Otto Götz), Galerie Müller, Stuttgart 1962; **spiel hölle** (a radio play), in *Akzente* 1/1962; **sehgänge**, Fietkau Verlag, Berlin 1962; **rückblick auf isaac newton**, (with a Lichtgraphik by Hajo Bleckert), Hake Verlag, Cologne 1965. Editor (with Walter Höllerer and Manfred de la Motte) of **movens: Dokumente und Analysen zur Dichtung, bildenden Kunst, Musik, Architektur**, Limes Verlag, Wiesbaden 1960. Mon has published poems and essays in many periodicals and anthologies, and lectures frequently on language and literature.

Edwin MORGAN: Born 1920 in Glasgow. Senior lecturer in English at Glasgow University. His publications include **Beowulf: A Verse Translation into Modern English** (1952); **The Cape of Good Hope** (1955), a long poem; three books of concrete poetry, **Starryveldt** (Eugen Gomringer Press, Frauenfeld 1965), **Scotch Mist** (Renegade Press, Cleveland 1965) and **Sealwear** (Gold Seal Press, Glasgow 1966). Soon to be published are **The Second Life** (concrete and non-concrete poems), Edinburgh University Press; translations of Quasimodo and Attila Jozsef for Northern House Pamphlets; and a volume of poems in the Review Pamphlets series. Morgan edited the **Albatross Book of Longer Poems** (Collins 1963), and is represented in the **Oxford Book of Scottish Verse** (1966), **Modern Scottish Poetry** (Faber 1966) and other anthologies.

Maurizio NANNUCCI: Born 1939 in Florence. Studied painting in Italy and Berlin. Since 1960 his works have been exhibited in Venice, Florence, Rome, Milan, Paris and Barcelona. Started experiments in concrete poetry in 1961. He works at the Studio Fonologico Musicale in Florence.

bp NICHOL: "born in vancouver in 1944. lived in various western canadian cities. presently and probably far into the future in toronto. poetry to me is a specific use of language and any use of language involves communication or should. concrete an attempt to use communication tools in a new way and thus promote new understandings of the multi-levels of language. if present tendencies carry thru will undoubtedly retire from hassle of current poetical scene and push off quietly on my own into multi-communication areas now opening up for me." Nichol's publications include **Cycles, Etc.**, Seven Flowers Press, Cleveland 1965; **Scraptures: 2nd sequence** (1965), **Scraptures: 3rd sequence** (1966), both published by Ganglia, Toronto; **Scraptures: 4th sequence**, Today Press, Niagara Falls 1966; **Calendar**, Openings Press, Gloucester (England) 1966; the "Tonto or" series, privately printed in 1966 by the author at the Coach House Press, Toronto: **Fodder Folder, Portrait of David, A Little Poem For Your Fingertips, Langwedge, Alephbit, Stan's Ikon** and **The Birth of O; Journeying & the returns, Letters Home** and the record **Borders**, all published by Coach House Press in 1967 and issued in one package; and **Konfessions of an Elizabethan Fan Dancer**, Writer's Forum, London 1967. Nichol has co-edited three poetry magazines: *Ganglia, Synapsis* and *Gronk*.

Hans-Jorgen NIELSEN: Denmark.

Seiichi NIIKUNI: Born 1925. Lives in Tokyo. Of all the Japanese concrete poets, Niikuni is the purest. His book **Zero.On**, published in 1963, a collection of visual and phonetic poems, is based on "a cosmic philosophy," in the words of Pierre Garnier. Garnier and Niikuni collaborated on a supranational collection of poems published in the Spatialism series, **Poèmes franco-japonais**.

Ladislav NOVÁK: Born 1925 in Turnov, Czechoslovakia. Poet, painter and "unorthodox Surrealist." Studied at Charles University in Prague 1945–50. Lives and teaches in Trebic. Novák's "alchemical collages" have been widely exhibited in Central and Western Europe. A representative selection of his experimental writings from 1959 to 1964 has been published as **Pocta Jacksonu Pollockovi** (Homage to Jackson Pollock), Mlada Fronta, Prague 1966. His recent activities include performance pieces and events, some of which have been published in European periodicals.

Yüksel PAZARKAYA: Born 1940 in Izmir, Turkey. Completed his studies in chemistry at the Technische Hochschule in Stuttgart; now studying Germanistics, philosophy and political science. He has written plays for the stage and radio, fiction, and poetry (now and then concrete). His concrete work has appeared in **konkrete poesie international** and **16/4/66**, both published by Edition Hansjörg Mayer, Stuttgart.

Décio PIGNATARI: Born 1927 in São Paulo, Brazil. Poet ("language designer"), graphic artist, professor of information theory (language and text) at Brasilia University and the School of Industrial Design in Rio de Janeiro. Co-founder, with Augusto and Haroldo de Campos, of the Noigandres Group in 1952, and co-author of the "pilot plan for concrete poetry" in 1958. Director of the review *Invenção*, since its founding in 1962 one of the most influential sources of international avant-garde writing and thinking. In 1954 Pignatari visited Eugen Gomringer in Switzerland, a meeting that helped launch "concrete poetry" (the name suggested for the new poetry by the Brazilians) as an international movement. His concrete poetry and essays have appeared in all numbers of *Noigandres* and *Invenção*. He is co-author, with Augusto and Haroldo de Campos, of **Teoria da Poesia Concreta** (1965), and has published translations of Ezra Pound's **Cantos** (with the de Campos brothers).

Vlademir Dias PINO: Born 1927 in Rio de Janeiro. Typographer, engraver, painter and poet. His books of poems include **Os Corcundas** (The Hunchbacks), 1954; **A Maquina ou a Coisa em Si** (The Machine or the Thing Itself), 1955; **a ave** (the bird), 1956, his first volume of concrete poems; **poema espacional** (1957); **solida** (1962), a poem without words, consisting of a series of three-dimensional pasteboards, in which lines and geometrical patterns are substituted for the letters in **poema espacional**.

Luiz Angelo PINTO: Born 1941 in São Paulo, Brazil. Student of engineering and social sciences at the University of São Paulo. Launched with Décio Pignatari, in 1964, a branch of concrete poetry called "semiotic poetry" (code poems). His poems have appeared in *Invenção* 4 and 5, the *London Times Literary Supplement* (Sept. 3, 1964) and in several foreign magazines. He co-authored, with Décio Pignatari, the essay "Criticism, Creation and Information."

Carl Fredrik REUTERSWÄRD: Born 1934. Lives in Stockholm. Writer, painter, teacher, Happener. Studied painting in Paris (with Fernand Léger) and Stockholm. He has had one-man shows in Stockholm, London, Paris, Milan, Brussels and Lausanne, and participated in the São Paulo Biennale (1959), the International Surrealist Exhibition in New York (1960) and the Venice Biennale (1964). In 1966 the Louisiana Museum in Denmark arranged the first retrospective exhibition of his work. He is represented in the collections of the Moderna Museet in Stockholm, the New York Museum of Modern Art, and the Guggenheim Museum. Reuterswärd has been active in concrete poetry, action poetry and Happenings since 1954. His publications include **Abra Makabra** (1955), **I Lagens Namm** (1957), **Angaaende Disciplinen Ombord** (1958), **Prix Nobel** (1960), **Paa Samma Gang** (1961), **VIP** (1963) and **Andouille** (1964).

Diter ROT: Born 1930 in Hannover, Germany. At the age of 17 he was apprenticed to an advertising designer in Bern, Switzerland. In 1952 he rejected this field and supported himself as a carpenter, ditchdigger and waiter, while studying art. In 1954 he was awarded a foundation grant after a group show in Bern, and two years later was invited to join the Copenhagen textile firm Unica-Vaev as a fabric designer. (His fabrics won a gold star medal at an international competition in San Francisco.) In 1957 he married and moved to Reykjavik, where he produced a series of books now famous in the world of Op art and concrete poetry. His paintings, sculpture, constructions, films, engravings and commercial designs have been widely exhibited in the United States and Europe. A prolific writer, Rot's more important publications include **bok 56-59** (Reykjavik 1959), the basic collection of his ideograms; a series of albums with loose sheets of paper (black and white, or red and blue, or red and green) perforated with slots of different widths hand-cut by the artist (1958–61); the **copley book** (London 1965), a random collection of printed materials published for the William and Noma Copley Foundation; **scheisse** (Providence 1966), 100 "classical" poems; **die blaue flut** (Stuttgart 1967), the artist's American diary. An English-language edition of his selected writings will appear in 1967.

Gerhard RÜHM: Born 1930 in Vienna. Lives in Berlin. Composer, poet, playwright, essayist. One of the most adventurous of the "*Wiener Gruppe*" during the 1950s. His publications include **hosn rosn baa** (dialect poems, with Friedrich Achleitner and H. C. Artmann), Frick Verlag, Vienna 1959; *der fliegende holländer* (a play, with Konrad Bayer), in **movens**, Limes Verlag, Wiesbaden 1960; **konstellationen**, Eugen Gomringer Press, Frauenfeld; **farbengedicht, betrachtung des horizonts, Lehrsätze über das Weltall, rhythmus r** and **DU, eine Buchstabengeschichte für Kinder**, all published by Magdalinski Verlag, Berlin; and **Der Selbstmörderkranz**, Rainer Verlag, Berlin. Rühm edited **Die Pegnitzschäfer** (a baroque anthology) for Gerhardt Verlag, Berlin, and **der 6. sinn** (texts of Konrad Bayer) for Rowohlt Verlag, Hamburg. His forthcoming books include two anthologies of the *Wiener Gruppe*. Rühm reads his own sound poems on several records, and he has had one-man shows of his visual poems in Vienna, Berlin, Darmstadt and other European cities.

Aram SAROYAN: Born 1943 in New York City. Attended Trinity School in Manhattan, University of Chicago, New York University and Columbia, without achieving freshman credit, and has wandered extensively in the United States and Europe. His poems have appeared in *Poetry*, *Art and Literature*, *The Paris Review*, *The Nation*, *C*, *Lines* (which he edited and published in New York) and various anthologies. Twenty-four of his poems have been collected in **Works**, New York 1966.

John J. SHARKEY: Born 1936 in Dublin. Lives in London, where he manages the gallery of the Institute of Contemporary Arts. His poems have appeared in the *London Times Literary Supplement*, *OU*, *Link*, *Tlaloc*, *Poetry Ireland*, *LISN* (the poster-poem magazine he publishes with Sonia Sharkey) and several anthologies. After finishing the film-poem **OPENWORDROBE** in 1964 he made his first wall poems, one of which, the 20-foot-long "Magic Poem," was exhibited at the Oxford kinetic and concrete exhibition in 1964. He has also written a number of plays for the stage and radio.

Edward Lucie SMITH: Born 1933 in Kingston, Jamaica, where he lived until he was 17. Read history at Oxford, and has since worked as an art critic, literary journalist and broadcaster. He writes a regular series of articles on art for *The London Times*, and is a frequent contributor to *The Sunday Times*, *The Listener*, *The New Statesman* and *Encounter*. In addition to **Cloud Sun Fountain Statue** (*Futura* 10, Edition Hansjörg Mayer, Stuttgart 1966), from which the selection in this anthology is taken, he has written two volumes of non-concrete poems, **Tropical Childhood** and **Confessions and Histories**, both published by Oxford University Press. He edited **The Penguin Book of Elizabethan Verse** and **A Group Anthology** (with Philip Hobsbaum). He has several books in preparation, including **What Is Painting?**, one on 18th century English painting, and one on all the arts since 1945.

Mary Ellen SOLT: Born 1920 in Gilmore City, Iowa: "I became interested in concrete poetry when I visited Ian Hamilton Finlay in Edinburgh in August 1962. He showed me the Brazilian anthology **Poesia Concreta**, which I sent for when I returned to the United States and which I received from Augusto de Campos in December. I studied the poems with great interest and excitement for several weeks with the aid of a Portuguese dictionary. That spring I began to write flower poems using visual forms. These poems were not like the Brazilian poems. Eventually they became the poems of **Flowers in Concrete**. I was unable fully to comprehend the esthetic arguments in the Brazilian 'pilot plan for concrete poetry' as I had at that time had practically no experience of concrete art of any kind, but they interested me greatly. The flower poems are probably more the result of several years' study of the objectivist method of William Carlos Williams and Louis Zukofsky except that until I saw the concrete poetry of Brazil I had been unable to find for myself a satisfactory way to go on from what had been done by Williams and Zukofsky. I have also been greatly influenced by the work of Ian Hamilton Finlay, particularly the fauve and suprematist poems, and by the introduction to them in *Typographica 8* by Dom Sylvester Houédard." **Flowers in Concrete** was published in 1966 by the Fine Arts Department of the University of Indiana.

Adriano SPATOLA: Born 1941 in Sapjane, Yugoslavia. Lives in Italy. His publications include **L'Obló** (a novel), Feltrinelli, Milano 1964; **Poesia da montare** (a "puzzle" poem), Sampietro, Bologna 1965; **L'Ebreo Negro** (poems), Scheiwiller, Milan 1966; and **Zeroglifico** (cut-up poems), Sampietro, Bologna 1966. He has had one-man shows in Reggio Emilia and Modena, and has participated in group shows in Rome, Florence, Milan, Rotterdam, Madrid and other European cities.

Daniel SPOERRI: Born 1930 in Galati, Romania. After his father was killed by the Nazis in 1941, the family fled to Switzerland. Spoerri studied classical dance with Preobrajenska and mime with Decroux in Paris, later was first dancer with the Bern Opera. In 1957 he became an assistant to Gustav-Rudolf Sellner at the Landestheater in Darmstadt, Germany, published a series of articles on experimental theater with Claus Bremer, and founded the periodical *material*, whose initial number was the first international anthology of concrete poetry. In 1959 he started Edition Mat, a series of mass-produced art objects by Hans Arp, Marcel Duchamp, Soto, Tinguely, etc., and in 1961 with Billy Klüver organized the exhibition of art in motion ("*Bewogen Beweging*") in Amsterdam and Stockholm. Spoerri's *tableaux-pièges* or snare pictures have been exhibited in one-man shows in Milan, Copenhagen, Paris, New York, Cologne, Frankfurt and Zurich. His publications include **Topographie Anecdotée du Hasard** (Paris 1962), expanded by Spoerri and translated and reanecdoted by Emmett Williams as **An Anecdoted Topography of Chance** (Something Else Press, New York 1966); the play **Ja Mama, das machen wir** (performed in Ulm in 1963), and **l'Optique Moderne** (with François Dufrêne), Fluxus Editions, Wiesbaden 1963. Spoerri lives in Greece, where he edits the review *Petit Colosse de Simi*.

Vagn STEEN: Denmark.

André THOMKINS: Born 1930 in Lucerne. Studied at the École des Arts et Métiers in Lucerne, with study-trips to Holland and France. He has lived in Germany (Essen) since 1951. Thomkins describes his pursuits as "*spéculation picturale et poetique*." His works, either "*picturale*" or "*poetique*," have appeared in the catalogue to the painter-poets exhibition in St. Gall, 1957; *Das Neue Forum*, Darmstadt 1958–59; **movens**, Limes Verlag, Wiesbaden 1960; *nota* no. 4, Munich 1960; **oh! cet echo** (palindromes), Essen 1963; **DOGMAT-MOT**, Galerie der Spiegel, Cologne 1966; **shadowbuttonegg**, Schleiden 1966; *edition et 1*, Berlin 1966, and the catalogue to *Labyrinthe*, Berlin 1966. Thomkins collaborated with Eckhard Schulze-Fielitz on an architecture based on the "mecanohedron," and a demonstration of his "laque-dynamorphose" was presented at the Institute of Contemporary Arts, London, in 1960. Thomkins has been a serious student of palindromes and anagrams for many years; in his latest works, these traditional linguistic games have become the vehicle for an expressive, and challenging, poetry.

Enrique Uribe VALDIVIELSO: Born 1940 in Bilbao, Spain. After completing studies for his baccalaureate in Bilbao, he studied management techniques at San Sebastián and philosophy and letters at Pamploná. Lives in Jaén, where he manages a hotel and bus station. Uribe Valdivielso was the first Spanish member of the international Spatialist movement, and he organized, with the Argentine poet Julio Campal, the first Spatialist exhibition in Spain (at Bilbao). His works have appeared in the *London Times Literary Supplement*, *Les Lettres*, and other European publications.

Franz Van Der LINDE: Born 1940. Lives in Rotterdam. Editor of the review *Kentering*. His poems have appeared in *Kontakt*, *Ontmoeting*, *Les Lettres* and other European publications, and in several collections of concrete and visual poems. He has translated French, German and Czech authors.

Franco VERDI: Born 1934. Lives in Verona. In addition to one-man shows of his own visual and audio-visual work in Verona, Bologna and Ferrara, Verdi has arranged exhibitions of international experimental poetry in several Italian cities. His publications include **Aperti in Squarci** (visual poem 1962–64), **tempo** (1966) and philosophical essays in various Italian reviews.

Emmett WILLIAMS: Born 1925 in Greenville, South Carolina. Lived in Europe from 1949 to 1966. Studied poetry with John Crowe Ransom at Kenyon College, took courses in anthropology at the University of Paris, was an assistant to ethnologist Paul Radin in Lugano. Sometime journalist, travel and ghost writer. Collaborated with Claus Bremer and Daniel Spoerri in the Darmstadt circle of concrete poets, dynamic theater, etc., from 1957 to 1959. Former European coordinator of Fluxus. A founding member of the Domaine Poetique in Paris. Close friendship and collaboration with Robert Filliou, resulting in many co-productions and co-inventions. His publications include **konkretionen**, Krefeld 1958; **ja, es war noch da**, an opera, in *nota*, Munich 1960; **poésie et cetera américaine** (an anthology of action poetry), Paris 1963; **13 variations on 6 words of gertrude stein** (1958), Galerie der Spiegel, Cologne 1965; **rotapoems** (variations on a poem from Diter Rot's lyrical collection **Scheisse**), Edition Hansjörg Mayer, Stuttgart 1966; and **sweethearts**, a long erotic concrete poem cycle, Stuttgart 1967. Theater essays on Albee, Artaud, Beckett, Eliot, Gelber, Henry James, Pound, Wallace Stevens, Gertrude Stein, etc., in *Das Neue Forum*, *Berner Blätter*, *Ulmer Theater*. He translated and reanecdoted Daniel Spoerri's **Topographie Anecdotée du Hasard** (**An Anecdoted Topography of Chance**, Something Else Press, New York 1966), and edited Claes Oldenburg's **Store Days**, Something Else Press, 1967. His latest work, **a boy and a bird**, is a long cycle of shifting linguistic relationships.

Jonathan WILLIAMS: Born 1929 in Asheville, North Carolina. "St. Albans School, Princeton, Institute of Design, Hayter, Karl Knaths, Black Mountain College. Publisher and designer of Jargon Books since 1951. Poet, essayist, curator of iconography, and hiker. Guggenheim 1957 and not a damn dime since from any form of Establishment, until appointment 1967 as scholar-in-residence, Aspen Institute for Humanistic Studies in Colorado. American home in Highlands, North Carolina, until it joins the Grated Society and I opt out for Wharfedale in Yorkshire. Musical Director, Macon County North Carolina Meshugga Sound Society; Vice President, Cast Iron Lawn Deer Owners of America. Edward Dahlberg once wrote that I was 'the most lyrical of the young poets—and you can throw in most of the older, decayed ones too. The most cultivated of the whole brood.' Mr. Dahlberg now regrets the remark, particularly in the light of an affection I have for the devices and inventions of Concrete Poetry. It is my persistent observation that the three most saving and useful Americans are Thomas Jefferson, William Bartram, and Charles Ives."

Pedro XISTO: Born 1901 in Pernambuco, Brazil. Lawyer, critic, professor of literature. Former cultural attaché of Brazil in Bolivia, Canada and the United States. His book **haikais e concretos** (haiku and concrete poems) was published in 1962. His essays and poems have appeared in *Invenção* and several foreign reviews.

Fujitomi YASUO: Born 1928. Lives in Tokyo. Member of the Japanese Sento group, the Association of Modern Poets, and editor of the review *Sette*. Graduate of the Institute of Foreign Languages, and English teacher. Yasuo is an influential leader of the Japanese avant-garde not only through his own four collections of poems, but also his translations of e. e. cummings and other Western writers.

To Be Continued